The Sweetness *of Life*

An Exploration of Life, Death, and Self-Discovery

Jamie Zunick

BALBOA
PRESS
A DIVISION OF HAY HOUSE

Blessings,
Jamie Zunick

Balboa Press books may be ordered through booksellers or by contacting:

Balboa Press
A Division of Hay House
1663 Liberty Drive
Bloomington, IN 47403
www.balboapress.com
1 (877) 407-4847

Because of the dynamic nature of the Internet, any web addresses or links contained in this book may have changed since publication and may no longer be valid. The views expressed in this work are solely those of the author and do not necessarily reflect the views of the publisher, and the publisher hereby disclaims any responsibility for them.

The author of this book does not dispense medical advice or prescribe the use of any technique as a form of treatment for physical, emotional, or medical problems without the advice of a physician, either directly or indirectly. The intent of the author is only to offer information of a general nature to help you in your quest for emotional and spiritual well-being. In the event you use any of the information in this book for yourself, which is your constitutional right, the author and the publisher assume no responsibility for your actions.

Any people depicted in stock imagery provided by Thinkstock are models, and such images are being used for illustrative purposes only. Certain stock imagery © Thinkstock.

Printed in the United States of America.

ISBN: 978-1-4525-9187-2 (sc)
ISBN: 978-1-4525-9188-9 (hc)
ISBN: 978-1-4525-9189-6 (e)

Library of Congress Control Number: 2014902203

Balboa Press rev. date: 3/12/2014

With love
To my sisters, Theresa and Carol, and my brother, Anthony.
This is your story, too

To my nieces, Jennifer, Jessica, and Diana
And my nephews, Andy, David, and Logan
So proud of all of you

And to my Aunt Nancy Jenkins
Colon cancer survivor
You go, Girl!

Part One

GROUNDWORK

Chapter 1

"*J*amie, Jamie, wake up!"

I turned over from my place on the couch as Mom shook my shoulders and continued calling my name. "Get up," she demanded. "We have to go. We missed Kentucky!"

"What?" I stammered leaning up on my elbows to look at my mother's excited face.

"I was just looking back over the map, retracing our route," she explained, leaning down over me. "I don't know how we did it but we missed Kentucky. We have to go now…come on."

"Are you serious?" I demanded. "What time is it?"

"Four-thirty," she answered. "Come on. We can be on the road by five. C'mon. It's getting late." She gave my shoulder one final jarring shake before turning away and walking briskly back across the living room.

Late? I stumbled up slowly as Mom walked into the kitchen to start the coffee. It was true; it was getting late. According to my mother, four-thirty in the morning was sleeping in. She was always up early. It had become a habit after forty years as a wife and stay-at-home mother to four children. There were always meals to make, a husband to get off to work, children to drive to school, laundry, and housework. Mom had kept up her early morning routine even after the children had left home and her husband had passed away in 1999. Every day, Mom was finished with the dusting and vacuuming before the newspaper arrived around six in the morning. Only then would she relax with a cup of coffee and a single cigarette. Sleeping for Mom would merely be a necessity every now and then, never a chance to just relax and rejuvenate.

Through either habit or heredity, I, too, am not a good sleeper. I usually function on just four to five hours of sleep a night. I'm always afraid that I'll miss something when I go to sleep. I have always been painfully aware that life continues even when I am not consciously around to witness it. I usually have to sleep with the television on and the phone next to me. Anything can happen while I sleep; I want to be prepared. I constantly fight falling asleep and always have to be up early in the morning. *But four-thirty?*

Now, I smiled and pulled myself up in a daze, swinging my legs over the edge of the couch. I was exhausted and yet a strange exhilaration began to pulsate through me. Shaking my head, I stretched slowly and laughed for a moment. Oh, man, we just got home last night about six pm and here we were again, rushing out to my 2002 Toyota Tacoma, lovingly nicknamed Dog, to take off on another journey. The thought suddenly woke me up completely. Memories erupted in my mind, bringing me to full awareness.

Most of my life has been spent on the road driving aimlessly to unknown destinations. I never make any plans when I travel. I don't worry about time or space. I keep no schedule; I have no strategy. I don't worry about hotel reservations or notifying anyone where I am during the day. I always travel without any care or apprehension. I don't even worry about packing anymore. I have grown very comfortable just throwing clean underwear into a backpack and heading out the door. I am ready for any adventure or experience. I am a born roamer. I get that from my mother, who passed her restless nature onto me.

However, her own adventurous spirit would wither and fade when my mother, Leslee Jean Burgess, married my father, Joseph John Zunick, Jr., on Memorial Day in 1959. My mother would soon mourn her own broken spirit, which grew heavier with grief and sorrow every year until, over time, she would become angry and bitter toward the man for whom she had sacrificed forty years of her life. There would be no honeymoon, no date nights, no time away together, and very little traveling.

Traveling and family time were both done with great reluctance and irritation by my father. He didn't find any joy in either and only grudgingly went on family summer vacations at my mother's insistent urging. Otherwise, Mom would remain at home with her dreams to travel locked within her. Her world began to grow smaller, limited only to the little, three-bedroom house that she worked hard to keep neat and orderly for her family.

Mom wasn't always quiet and complacent, though. She would continually take out her frustration on the furnishings. Every couple of days, Mom would move the furniture around, banging it roughly against the walls and doorways in order to relieve her aggravation. She finally confessed to me one day that she moved the furniture around just to have a sense of change. She liked to rearrange the furniture and pretend that she had just moved into a new house. She also told me with a sly smile that she liked the way it confused my father. She would move the furniture from room to room so when Dad came home from work, he would be disoriented for a while, walking into wrong rooms and banging into displaced cabinets. Yes, he would swear and rage, but Mom would inwardly smile proving her dominance somewhere in the dysfunctional entanglement of their lives.

It took twenty-three years for Mom to convince Dad to let her move the furniture to a different house. Her meager possessions would only travel across State Avenue to another neighborhood just three miles away. It seemed to be the best compromise they could make. Mom wasn't happy in the new house. The circumstances of her life had remained the same; only the location had changed. For the next twenty years, she continued sadly shuffling furniture around until her children grew up and her husband passed away. Only then did her spirit return and she was ready again to wander.

My unrelenting wanderlust comes directly from my mom. It eases my mind that this is something that we share. I have always had concerns about my heritage for valid reasons. In my immediate family, I'm the only one who has never been married. I'm the only one without children. I'm the only one who has moved away from the family home state of Kansas. I'm the only one who has traveled abroad. I'm the only one who has driven cross-country countless times. I'm the only one who has graduated from a university. I keep asking my mom if I'm adopted and she assures me that I am not. She tells me that we are too much alike. However, while she can calm my fears about my family connections, she has always doubted her own.

Mom had always wondered herself if she had been adopted. She always believed that she did not belong in her family. Nobody ever acknowledged or commented on her fears. No one ever eased her mind about where she belonged. It just wasn't something that was discussed while she was growing up in the late '30s and '40s. Though it was never addressed by her family, Mom had always suspected that she was not the daughter of Ralph Leroy Burgess and Edith Marie McCurdy. No, thanks to family whispers and sly glances, Mom began to believe that she was actually the daughter of her Aunt Lil, Edith's sister.

Ah, Aunt Lil, who was rumored to look just like Rita Hayworth, was an absolute beauty with long auburn hair and almond-shaped, hazel eyes that gleamed golden green when she was happy. Honestly, her eyes would shine a brilliant green ringed with a glowing yellow. Aunt Lil was well-known for the way her fiery red hair matched her feisty, determined personality. Mom looked more like Aunt Lil than anyone else in the family. She had the unusually colored "cat" eyes and a petite body with tiny, delicate features. As a child, Mom had been enchanted by Aunt Lil whenever she came to visit. My mother always felt special with Aunt Lil. Besides the good looks, Aunt Lil gave Mom the attention she craved. It was the only notice Mom felt she could get from anyone in her family. It was just too bad Aunt Lil wasn't always around on a regular basis. Mom would never feel that she ever received the love and consideration she deserved.

So, that's something else Mom and I have always had in common. A feeling that we have never found our place in this world, that we don't know where we belong. So we both continue to search and explore and try to discover who we really are. We are constantly running somewhere, some place new to be...or some place old to forget.

Maybe that's why I constantly have this same recurring dream. I have it at least once a month and I still don't completely know what it means. I dream I'm being chased. Beginning from the house where I spent my childhood, I spend all night running nonstop through the neighborhood where I grew up. I don't know who is chasing me or why, but I continue to run for hours...and I am always on foot. In fact, once I even dreamt that I was driving my car and being followed. So I pulled over to the side of the road, parked the car, got out, and started to run. Why didn't I just take the car? I wake up completely exhausted and, for a moment, confused about where I actually am. I don't really know what it means, but I do know—dream or real life, running or driving—I have to move.

When I am not running in my dreams, I am still on the road. On nights when I can't sleep, my head spinning with dreams of flight, I continually picture miles of highway in my head. I focus on some far off vantage point and tell myself that by the time I reach that spot, I will be asleep. So, in my mind, I begin to follow the stream of highway. I make up the passing scenery of pastures, cows, trees, and rolling hills as I continue down my imaginary path until I finally drift off to sleep.

I think my fascination with being on the road started when I was a child. Children of my generation literally lived in the car.

Roaming was something that we always did when I was a kid. I grew up in an era when families would take long, meandering drives on lazy weekend afternoons as a form of entertainment. On Sundays, Mom would make a huge lunch of roast and potatoes that she would serve after we returned from church. Then off we would go, eight people piled on top of each other in a vintage station wagon, known as Betsy, heading across Interstate 70 between Kansas and Missouri. My parents, two sisters, brother, both grandmothers, and I would crowd into the car and, for several hours, Dad would drive us around Northern Kansas City, stopping only at the local Dairy Queen for ice cream on the way home. There was nowhere else to go. Nothing else to do. In the days of the late '60s and early '70s, most businesses were closed on Sundays, so many families spent those afternoons driving with no clear destination.

At that time, too, cars did not have CD players or connections for iPods or MP3 players. There were no video games or DVD players. Most radios in the vehicles only broadcasted AM stations that were mainly talk with scattered moments of music. Without pocket video games or cell phones, there was only one form of entertainment on these long drives. My family would sing in order to pass the time. Mom normally would start us off and then switch to a pure harmony while the rest of us tried to carry the melody. We mostly sang church hymns. With church every day but Saturday, hymns were the music we knew best. Everyone would take a part and, for a moment, Mom would get a brief reprieve from the bickering and complaints of four young children trapped together in a very small bit of space. There we were on Sunday afternoons, rumbling down the highway, sitting on each others' laps, hanging out the windows, feeling the wind blowing back our hair, singing at the top of our lungs, or arguing and pushing for more space while Dad continually threatened to turn the car around at any moment.

Long drives were also taken after violent storms. Kansas has always been well-known for brutal thunderstorms and fervent tornadoes.

There would normally be at least two or three heavy storms every spring into summer. As the wind would begin to moan, and thunder and lightning rolled across the sky, we would huddle in the basement around a few candles, waiting for the storm to end. Again, Mom would attempt to get all of us to sing and we would try, but usually ended up screaming and crying as the wind would threaten to beat down the walls and the rain would drum against the windows. Prayers would be said and sobs from the younger children could be heard above the thunder and rain.

However, after the skies finally cleared, the wind relaxed, and the rain wound down to a simple drizzle, all the local families would jump into their cars and drive around the neighborhood to view the damage the obstinate twister had created. The patriarchs of the families would drive by and call to each other from out of their car windows.

"Hey, Joe," Mr. Barnes would yell out to my dad, "did you see the oak tree down on 82nd street?"

"Not yet," Dad would answer. "But we saw the roofs torn off the houses on 86th."

With a nod and a wave, they would speed off in opposite directions to further assess any additional damage to the neighborhood.

Dad would always do the driving. Mom didn't get her driver's license until she was in her early thirties. In Mom's generation, it just wasn't considered necessary for married women to have licenses. Whenever Mom had to run errands, my widowed maternal grandmother would pick us up in her old white Oldsmobile, named Oldsie, and take us wherever we needed to go.

My grandmother always drove me to kindergarten, too, except for one particular day when Kansas had received a record feet of snowfall for that year. Grandma refused to drive in the heavy snow, so Mom dressed me up in bright red tights, a short little plaid dress, a small, thin coat, and knitted mittens. She packed up my little brother in a snowsuit, and walked us up to school. I literally did walk to school with the snow up around my hips. I have a vivid memory of Mom holding me by the hand and struggling to keep a solid grip on my two-year-old brother, Anthony, who wiggled and cried to be released into the clean white powder.

I was not so enthusiastic about the experience. In fact, I absolutely hated it. I remember trying to lift a small foot up above the level of the snow and then plunging down to my hips into the cold endless sea of flakes. The tears froze on my face as I slid and stumbled. No matter how much I protested, Mom was adamant that I was going to school that day. She dragged, pushed, and pulled me through the cold until we finally reached the doors of Stony Point North Elementary. I don't know how Mom survived that walk of four miles holding on to a squirming, screaming baby and gripping the hand of a whining, crying five-year-old, but she got us to the school. She left me at the front door, then walked back home and changed the baby, just in time to turn right around and walk back up to the school to get me when class was over at three-thirty. I have no memory how we got back home, but I do know this: I have hated snow ever since. I cannot stand being cold and the first snowfall does not make me feel all seasonal and jolly inside. Cold slides under my skin and into my tissues like an old soul. As soon as I had the opportunity to move out of state, I headed for a warmer climate.

Mom may have been thinking along that same vein. Maybe she was considering her own need to escape. After our snowy trek on that long ago, but much remembered, day, Mom finally decided it was time she got her driver's license. She took her driver's test when she was thirty-four years old. I didn't know at the time what was happening. I just remember sitting with my grandma on wobbly green plastic chairs in a small, tiled, and concrete lobby in a drab brown building while we waited for Mom to complete her test. Finally, Mom walked out of the testing area with tears streaming down her face. She hadn't passed her exam and would have to come back again. It was heartbreaking for Mom as she watched her chance for independence slipping away.

Failing the test was probably a big disappointment for my mother. Being able to drive could have been her chance to break away. My father seemed to be living a separate life, anyway. Though he never wanted to move or travel, Dad did spend many nights away from home, leaving Mom on her own with four small children. I was always happy when my father was away. No anger, no rages, no hitting, screaming, yelling. We would get a break from the abuse and anger for a while.

On those nights, Mom would make popcorn and we would stay up until midnight, watching the late night TV movies starring Jerry Lewis, Doris Day, and Elvis Presley. Mom would sit on the couch with the phone in her lap, ready to call out in case some emergency should happen. She would finally nap fitfully on the sofa after her children had gone to bed. She would not go into her bedroom on those nights, but stayed in the living room by the front door ready to protect her children from any would-be intruders.

In all the years I have lived on my own in single one-bedroom apartments, I have probably slept in the bedroom approximately ten times, maybe. That's usually when I had company who worried they were being rude to put me out of my own bedroom. To get a good night's sleep, I have to be in the front room, on the couch, television on, and phone within reach. For me, it may just be habit; for Mom, it was survival.

Mom had become desperate. Driving would be one thing she could do to begin taking care of her children on her own, if necessary. It may have even meant her very survival. When she received her license after her second attempt, Mom would drive everywhere. When my father would get into a rage, Mom would grab her keys, pile her children into the car and drive…just drive for most of the night. We would watch the moonlight reflect off the water of Wyandotte County Lake as we traveled over the winding side roads on hot summer nights. On some evenings, we would drive around the richer neighborhoods picking out houses we daydreamed about owning someday or looking at all

11

the beautiful, sparkly lights of decorated homes and businesses over the holiday season. It didn't really matter where we went just as long as we were able to get out of the house for a while.

I remember Mom sitting forward in her seat to reach the pedals, the wheel gripped tightly in her small hands as she slid effortlessly through traffic. Mom loved highway driving. Heavy traffic didn't scare her. There were times she was almost fearless when she drove. She refused to let me drive at all the first time we traveled together to New Mexico in 1995, and it was something we argued about for hundreds of miles. She just wanted to prove that she could do it, that she could drive all the way from Kansas to New Mexico and back again. And she did it! Even receiving a speeding ticket on the way home. It's true. We were traveling through Oklahoma. I was dozing in the passenger seat when I suddenly heard Mom exclaim, "Oh, there's a cop car behind me!" I was immediately fully awake as Mom pulled over to the side of the road. My sixty-two-year-old mother had been driving twenty miles over the speed limit. She had just lost track of her speed as she sailed down the highway, reveling in the purest sense of joyful self-determination.

Years later, I would know how she felt. I failed my written driver's test the first time and, like Mom, had to repeat it. Once we got our licenses, however, we never left the road.

Mom actually tried first to teach me how to drive. She began training me in the cemetery by our church when I was around twenty years old. I drove around the headstones for several hours with Mom in the passenger seat giving me loud, and sometimes annoying, instructions.

Mom thought that Chapel Hill Memorial Gardens was the best place for me to learn to drive because of a lack of heavy traffic and the low speed limit (15 mph). She may have also thought that I wouldn't run over anybody there, and if I did...well, they were already gone. Funny that even with the serenity of the cemetery and the calm countryside atmosphere, Mom finally gave up on me after just a few lessons. She never did say exactly why and I often wondered. I mean, if someone even refuses to teach driving in a cemetery, there must be a serious problem somewhere.

I just remember my first time at the controls. I gripped the steering wheel tightly in both hands. As I pushed my foot cautiously against the gas pedal and began to slowly roll forward, I jerked the wheel back and forth even though the road was headed straight without a single dip or turn. Mom just watched me in shocked silence for a moment before asking, "What the heck are you doing? Why are you bouncing the wheel? Sit still, for gosh sakes! Why does everyone think they have to bounce the wheel?" Oh! Okay! I just assumed I had to keep the steering wheel in motion just to move the car forward.

Thankfully, my brother, Anthony, got me back on the road again when Mom gave up. Anthony's idea was to get me right out on the highway and straight into heavy traffic. Though terrifying at times for both of us (once, I turned a corner just a little too fast and almost threw the car into a ditch), it must have been the right method. Though I had to repeat the written exam, I got my license when I tested for the first time on the driving process. The license even surprised Anthony. "But, you weren't ready yet. How did you get your license? I told you it was too soon," he protested. I wasn't going to argue. I finally had my license.

Strange that I was actually the last of my brother and sisters to receive my license and yet have logged the most miles. Not that it is a contest, but driving was always very important in my family because it was our main mode of transportation. We never flew anywhere. Family vacations were always taken by car and always to one of the same two locations. Every summer, we would either head west to Colorado to stay with Mom's family or east to St. Louis where the construction company Dad worked for had offices and hotel rooms he could write off at a discounted price.

Colorado seemed to be our summer getaway home. My Aunt Nancy, Uncle Joe, and Cousin Jo Jenkins lived in Estes Park on Prospect

Mountain. Yes, on the side of a mountain, which we from the flatlands of Kansas thought was extremely exotic. Their house was beautiful with a woodsy outdoor feel. I remember looking out of the big sliding glass doors at the back of the house and being face-to-face with the upper half of the mountain. It was right there in their backyard. It was the same view I saw almost every summer for twelve years. Summer vacations had a routine, a feel to them that never ended.

Every road trip actually started with Mom giving all four of the kids a healthy dose of castor oil before going to bed the night before we left. I never understood why but it had been such a family vacation tradition for so long, I never thought to question it. I just assumed everybody did this before they traveled. Mom clarified this ritual for me many years later.

"Castor oil," she explained with a shy smile, "helps everything slide through. If I gave you kids castor oil before you went to bed, hopefully in the morning you would be able to use the bathroom at home before we left on the trip so we wouldn't have to stop so often along the way. Hopefully, we would use fewer public toilets that way."

I'm not really convinced that that method actually worked but Mom swore by it and it was a travel ritual in our family for as long as I could remember.

Having to use the bathroom on long drives wasn't always fun. My father may be hard to motivate to travel but once he was on the road, he didn't want to stop. One time, my father finally got tired of our cries and moans and pulled over at a gas station so we could quickly run in to use the bathroom. "You have two minutes only or I leave without you!" he threatened. My maternal grandmother insisted that she was fine and didn't need to "spend a penny." ("Spend a penny" was my grandmother's usual euphemism for peeing. She referred to toilet paper as "hockey tickets.") So, once all the kids had piled back into the car within ninety seconds (we had reason to believe Dad), we were back on the highway again.

A little while later, Grandma began to twitch and groan. "Uh,

14

Joe," she called up to my dad in the front seat, "I need to use the bathroom."

"We just stopped an hour ago, Edith," Dad insisted. "Why didn't you go then?"

"Didn't have to," Grandma responded like a five-year-old child.

Dad sighed, breathing heavily in order to gain control of his temper. "Well, let me find a place to stop…" And we drove for another hour. There was no place to stop. No gas stations for miles. Grandma was becoming more uncomfortable with each passing minute. She was not a small woman and her seated peepee dance was causing the car to career in several different directions as we continued down the highway. Finally, totally exacerbated, and seeing no other choice, Dad at last pulled over by the side of the road near a scrawny, brittle clump of trees. "This is the best I can do, Edith," he told her. "Just go over by those trees."

Grandma looked absolutely horrified at the thought. "Listen," Dad tried to convince her, "we haven't found another gas station. We haven't even passed another car for miles. This highway is empty right now. There is no one else around. It's getting dark. You'll be fine. Nobody is going to see anything."

Grandma reluctantly climbed out of the car and looked up and down the long, lonely highway. Okay, it looked safe enough. She moved over to the crumpling clump of trees, raised her skirt, lowered her underwear, and…

…Twenty-five, thirty cars suddenly materialized out of nowhere, zooming past my grandmother with her pants down on the side of the road, their headlights illuminating her bare white bottom. She yanked up her pants and ran back to jump into the car. Dad took off while Grandma yelled at him for the next five miles as if he had purposely sat up that particular incident to keep anyone from asking to stop to pee again for the rest of the trip.

The inability to find bathrooms while on the road can be discouraging. It can be even worse, though, when the only one available for hundreds of miles is absolutely filthy. After several years of road travel, I completely understand Mom's concern about stopping at public toilets. Maybe the castor oil tradition was a good and useful ritual after all.

Dad also had his habits and procedures for traveling, as well. He always preferred leaving extremely early in the morning to beat the heavy, rush hour traffic. We would leave our home around four in the morning. If we were headed towards St. Louis, we usually would arrive in town about ten o'clock. Then we would drive around the city for two hours until we could check into our hotel room at twelve. Dad refused to pay for an extra day. My family became very familiar with St. Louis due to this process and actually considered it home. In fact, no matter where I travel, I always feel a surge of excitement whenever I come upon the Gateway Arch, which sits besides the Mississippi River in St. Louis, Missouri. I love the Arch. I don't know why I find it so magical. I think I just love what it means. The six hundred thirty foot loop was created in 1947-48 as a monument to early pioneers who were bravely traveling into the mysterious western frontier. The Arch is a gateway to a new life and a promise of the implementation of dreams. Of course, it has deep meaning to my gypsy soul. Seeing the Arch rise up above the highway always feels to me like the entryway leading back towards Kansas. I am on familiar ground. I am almost home. I begin to breathe easier. I am safe.

My family was very fortunate that all of our travels have been safe. Maybe because when we traveled there wasn't as much traffic or people weren't in such a hurry or everyone watched out for each other. But, whatever the reason, in the many years we had traveled on the road when I was a child, we didn't have any car wrecks or major mishaps. That's not to say we didn't have our share of interesting accidents, though they were always very minor and certainly laughable.

For instance, one day, as we were driving along some mountain passes in Colorado, a year-old Anthony was sleeping on my mother's lap. Mom had pulled off his small pair of shorts to cool him down in the hot car with no air conditioning. She placed the shorts over his face to keep the sun off of him. As Dad drove around a curve, Anthony's shorts went flying out of the open passenger window. I remember Mom screaming out but it was too late. The shorts were gone down the canyon, never to be seen again. Anthony spent the rest of the day in just a diaper until Mom could unpack some clean clothes for him.

Alright, that's just a short, little, so-what story. But wait a minute, think about this...my mother was *actually holding* my brother on her lap in the front passenger seat as we careened around the mountain passes. In the late '60s and early '70s, seatbelts and child car seats were not required. For almost eight complete years, Mom always had a baby on her lap whenever and wherever we traveled. We also sat three across in the front seat. My siblings and I would fight, squabble, and wrestle over a chance to set up front. We argued over who was going to sit by the windows or over the "hump" on the floor in the back. We hung out the windows and put our bare feet up on the dashboard. We were never buckled in. Wherever we were going, short errands or long journeys, Mom and Dad would just throw us into the vehicle, tell us to hang on, and away we would fly, bouncing and rolling all over the car, without a worry or any sense of danger.

In fact, my first introduction to my brother, Anthony, was in the front seat of my Dad's old Chevrolet. Just two weeks past my third birthday, my sisters, Theresa and Carol, and I were sent to stay with my maternal grandmother, Edith. At this time, women would spend up to a week in the hospital after having a baby. It may have been better for my mom...but it was agony for me. I was a momma's girl. I missed her horribly for the week she was gone. Now, Grandma Edie was a sweet woman, but I wanted my mom and this situation did not set well with me. I cried every night for my mom and threw tantrums continually at my grandmother's home. I didn't understand why I couldn't be with my mother.

I was relieved when Dad finally appeared one day to pick us up.

He explained that Mom had had the baby. Baby, huh, what? What baby? I do not remember hearing any talk or explanation for my mother's absence until that very moment. I don't have any memory of my mother telling me I was going to have a little baby brother or sister. I don't remember even noticing the rounding of her belly. A baby, huh?

Quickly, Theresa, Carol, and I got into the car for the ride to the hospital to pick up my mom. I remember sitting huddled with my sisters in the back of the car as Dad ran into the hospital. I remember Mom climbing into the passenger seat with a bundle in her arms. I remember leaning over the front seat while Mom settled herself in the car, the tightly wrapped package she carried now resting on her lap. Slowly, she pulled back the blanket, opening the bundle, and there was my baby brother, Anthony. I heard my sisters cooing, "He's so cute...." so I said it too. But in my head, I remember thinking, "This is it?!? This is why my momma had to leave me?!?" It just didn't seem right, but Anthony had already made himself comfortable in the front seat on my mother's lap (where I used to be) and that's where he would travel for the majority of our journeys over the next few years.

We were always safe and secure there in my mother's arms. There was only one incident that occurred while Mom was holding one of her babies in the front seat. This was before my brother usurped my place. I was the infant nestled in my mother's arms.

When my parents were newly married, my father had purchased an old Chevy. The passenger front door didn't always latch and would fly open at unsuspecting moments. One afternoon, Dad went zooming around a corner, the door flew open, and Mom and I went sailing out of the car. By reflex, Mom stuck her foot out of the open doorway and by some odd occurrence suddenly found herself standing peacefully on the side of the pavement with her baby girl still asleep in her arms. Mom felt as if she had been supported or carried to the side of the highway, away from the passing cars. She thankfully had a death grip on me and did not let go, so I remained right where I was, wrapped in Mom's arms, and sleeping through the whole ordeal.

In fact, the transition from car to street had been so smooth, Dad didn't even realize his wife and infant daughter were gone until he was halfway home. Surprised when he suddenly turned to his right and found an empty seat and open door, he turned around and retraced his path, finally coming upon Mom and me on the side of the highway. Pushing open the passenger door for us to climb in, Dad was still stunned. "What the hell's wrong with yous…Where the hell did yous people go?" Mom just sadly shook her head and climbed back into the car sitting closer to my dad this time as he cursed and yelled at her all the way home.

So, yes, for years, Mom rode everywhere with a baby in her arms, even when the experience would be hot and sweaty like on our family vacation trips. At the time, speed limits were set at fifty-five miles per hour. It would take us a day and a half to travel from Eastern Kansas to central Colorado. While Dad navigated down Interstate 70, Mom was in the front seat holding baby Anthony. Grandma Edie, my two sisters, and I would squeeze into the back seat and the open compartment in the rear of the station wagon, which also held all of the luggage. Seven people pushed, pulled, and crumpled in a station wagon with no air conditioning and barely enough room to breathe! We usually traveled with all of the windows rolled down to get some relief from the oppressive heat as we sat crunched together in a steamy car rolling down the highway on hot summer afternoons.

Nights were actually the worst, though. We never stayed in a hotel when we traveled. It was just too expensive for all of us. At night, Dad would just pull over to the side of the road and we would stretch out on top of each other in the car and try to get some sleep. We would wrestle around for a while, kicking and pushing each other until my dad would holler out for us to settle down or he would take us out of the car one by one and whip us. His threat, for once, did not have a great effect. It just wasn't possible for seven people to comfortably sleep in a station wagon on a humid Kansas summer night.

We should have just been happy that all of us arrived at our destination safely and fully intact. Well, usually we did, until one particular trip when my sister, Carol, arrived at our relatives' Colorado home with a large wedge of her hair left somewhere back on the highway. She had been chewing on a piece of gum when the lulling back and forth of the car had rocked her to sleep. She woke up to find that the gum had fallen out of her open mouth while she was napping and was now tangled up in her long, coppery red hair.

At the first rest stop, Mom tried to brush the gum out but that only seemed to tangle it in Carol's hair even more. Dad took over then and tried to yank it out by wrapping her tresses around his fist and giving a good yank. He soon gave up though on his effort when my sister's screams caused his head to pound along with hers. Finally, Dad drove us down the street to the nearest gas station and dragged my poor sister inside. He asked for a pocketknife from the clerk, and, while my mom watched in horror from the front seat of the car, Dad whacked the gum out of Carol's hair with one sharp twist of his wrist. The gum was gone…but so was about six inches of Carol's hair on the left side. Dad just tossed the wad of gummy hair into the trash, returned the knife, and we were immediately back on the road again.

When Dad was traveling, he always kept a very tight schedule. We had to be so many miles farther at a particular time. We did not always get the opportunity to stop for meals or use the restroom until Dad had met his mileage objective.

One day, Dad ran out of gas while on Interstate 70 in route to Colorado. It was a Saturday evening and Dad got us limping along to a gas station that sat like a slug on a deserted, dusty side street. There were just two old crank pumps in front of a run down, peeling, white one room office. It was already closed when we got there and there was no such thing as "pay at the pump" at this time. Everything was done by a gas station attendant who would fill the tank, check the oil, clean the windows, and send travelers back on the road with a smile, a handful of free maps, and a point in the right direction. So, it looked like we would just have to wait until the next morning when the attendant came to work.

We spent the night sprawled out on top of each other in the car that was parked right at the pump in the gas station parking lot. Dad was determined to keep to his schedule. He was positive that we would just relax, settle down to sleep, and the next morning we would just gas up when the attendant arrived and be right back on the road again by eight am, eight-thirty at the latest.

By seven am, Dad was awake and alert and sitting behind the wheel waiting to take off as soon as the tank was filled. Much to Dad's chagrin, the owner didn't show up any too early that day. We stayed in the parking lot (actually, there was nowhere else to go) and played in the dirt until nine-thirty am when the owner finally pulled up in front of his station. He came rolling out of his rusty old pickup truck in overalls with a blue baseball cap turned backwards on his head. He was a large, heavy-set man with a loud laugh.

"It's Sunday morning, folks," he said. "Didn't think anyone would be here! Why aren't you alls in church?" He smiled, laughed, spit a wad of tobacco, and sauntered into the station to fire up the coffee percolator as my dad, his fist squeezed together as he struggled to control his temper, climbed out of the car. I don't know what actually upset Dad the most: the long wait for the attendant who casually drank his second cup of coffee before pumping the gas, the attendant's huge belly laugh at our expense, our religious ethics being questioned, or the fact that we were finally on the road two hours past Dad's original plan. Total silence filled the car for at least an hour as we traveled west on Interstate 70. Everyone was afraid to make any noise at all as my Dad sat hunched behind the wheel, fuming over the delay in his schedule.

At least that was better than the way my dad normally drove. Dad was a fast, aggressive driver. He even refused to slow down for speed bumps, jolting over them at full velocity. "Well, they aren't called 'slow down bumps'," Dad would respond whenever Mom complained. My dad drove and swore as if he were a seasoned truck driver. His language would be crude and forceful. "Blow it out your ass," was usually his favorite response whenever he heard a horn honk whether it was aimed at him or not. Dad would also respond with a strong blast of his own horn. This, of course, was very upsetting to my mother, who believed honking the horn was very rude.

I drive by my horn, which always upset Mom whenever she traveled with me. "Be nice" was her constant mantra to me, but that doesn't get people out of my way. Mom never honked because she didn't want to scare the other drivers. Excuse me! Someone suddenly is heading towards me at seventy miles an hour in my lane...and I don't want to scare *him*? No, I'm going to let him know I'm there! My mother and I are very much alike. But when it comes to driving, there is no question that I am Joseph John Zunick's daughter!

There was one trip, however, when Mom was upset enough to swear herself. We were on our way home from Colorado one summer when, traveling down Interstate 70, the car suddenly veered and swerved back and forth for a moment before Dad pulled off to the side of the road. Blow out! The right back tire was completely gone. After unloading all of the luggage onto the side of the highway, Dad popped open the bottom compartment in the back of the station wagon to pull out the jack and spare tire. That was when Mom found the cause of the blow out.

Several days before we began the drive back to Kansas, Dad had been admiring the landscaping in the front of our relatives' home. They had a large rock garden that contained a few big boulders scattered among small, delicate flowers and colorful stones. Dad talked about his desire to have the same thing at our home in Kansas and Uncle Joe suggested generously that Dad take several of the rocks. And now there they were....in the back of the car...the car with the blow out on the side of the highway. To my mother's shock, there was more

than just a pile of small rocks. There, in the bottom of the car...
were two big boulders! Grunting and groaning with the effort, Dad
pulled them from the car in order to get to the jack and spare. Once
the tire was fixed, Mom refused to allow the boulders back into the
vehicle. As traffic continued to speed down the highway, Mom and
Dad stood on the shoulder screaming and cussing at each other over
two boulders and a small pile of rocks. We couldn't actually hear what
they were saying. Grandma Edith made us roll up all of the windows.
My brother, sisters, Grandmother, and I sat perspiring heavily in the
hot car as we stared out through the steam-encrusted windows at
Mom and Dad gesturing wildly to each other as their faces glowed
an angry red. Finally, Dad stomped away from her, climbed into the
car, and started it up as Mom yanked the passenger door open. Dad
peeled away down the highway as Mom swung her small body inside
the car and slammed the door. Dad's desire for a rock garden, along
with a heap of hard stones, was abandoned on the side of the east
bound interstate 70.

It was lucky that Dad was very handy with changing tires and
we survived the trips without injury or severe accidents. We were in
the middle of nowhere without any possibility of calling for help. We
didn't have any cell phones or GPS systems. We were real pioneers, on
our own, with nothing but maps and fellow adventurers traveling the
highways. All we had to depend on were ourselves and the kindness
of family, friends, and traveling allies. We lived dangerously...and we
survived. We learned how to stand on our own two feet and find our
direction.

Years later, Mom and I continued to travel this same way as we
journeyed through America. Just a map and stopping when we got
tired, never quite sure where we were going to end up. Wherever we
stopped, that's where we stopped. Thinking about it now seems as
foreign as the wild-west journeys by covered wagon. But people used
to watch out for each other then and travelers could always rely on
friendly locals for free directions, bitter cups of coffee, and interesting

conversations about quaint hometowns. We may have found ourselves lost every now and then, but we always eventually made it back home.

I suddenly remembered the first time I got desperately lost. The situation absolutely terrified me. I was five-years-old and thought of myself as a big girl. Every day when I went to kindergarten, Grandma Edith always dropped me off right at the front door. My classroom was just right inside, first door on the left. However, over the last couple of weeks, I happened to notice that several of my classmates were coming into the classroom from the opposite direction. They were coming in through the backdoor. I thought that was really cool. So one day, I made up my mind that I did not want to go in to school through the "baby" front door and told my grandmother to drop me off at the back of the building. Grandma was very hesitant at first.

"Are you sure you know the way?" she must have asked me five times as we circled around to the back of the building. Of course... well, maybe...but what difference did it make...I was on the very first of many amazing journeys. Grandma stopped at the back of the building and...uh, oh, there were two doors about five feet apart.

"Are you sure you know which door to use?" Grandma started to worry again. "Let's go back up front."

But I couldn't back down now. I quickly kissed her check, jumped out of the car, and without any hesitation, I walked to one of the doors. I just picked one. I swung it open, stepped inside...and was suddenly completely, totally lost! I had no idea where I was! Did I turn around? No. Did I step back out and try the other door? No. I just started walking...and walking...as if I knew where I was going. But I had no idea where I was or where I was headed. I just tried to pretend like I belonged (which seems to be a running theme in my life). I just ran up and down the hallways for about half an hour. The more I ran, the more confused I became. I started to panic and felt warm tears beginning to wind their way down my cheeks. The hallways were empty but I passed rooms full of people. I was just so shy and didn't know who to ask or what to say. So I kept walking as if I had somewhere to go…and I did…I just had no clue how to get there.

Suddenly, I turned a corner and out of nowhere a young girl was standing before me. She must have been about ten-years-old and she was holding the hand of a very small child. I didn't know who she was or where she came from…or especially who was the three-year-old child she had tightly grasped by the hand. The young girl looked at me and said, "Are you looking for the kindergarten classes?" I couldn't speak a word. I just nodded my head. "Go that way," she said, pointing down the hallway behind her. "Just go to the end of the hallway."

I took off at a run, even too shy and upset to say "thank you." I ran down the hallway and there it was…my kindergarten classroom. I stopped running now. I wiped my tears and nose with the back of my hands and then casually strolled into the room, hung up my coat, and took my seat, shaking my head and acting as if I had meant to be fashionably late. The teacher, Mrs. Gilbertson, stared at me for just a moment, but when I refused to say anything or show any kind of reaction, she simply went on with the class. The next day, Grandma dropped me off at the front door of the school and I never complained again. My big girl adventure was over.

Oh, and then there was the time…

"Jamie, come on. Kentucky's waiting," Mom now called out to me again from the kitchen. I showered and dressed quickly, emptied the contents of my backpack into the hamper, and grabbed a wad of clean underwear. What else could I possibly need? So at five in the morning, after just four hours of sleep, I grabbed my backpack, a cup of coffee, and headed out the door with Mom for our next adventure. Though other forces in my life would shape me as a sensitive, a reluctant intuitive, from Mom I developed my wanderlust, my constant need to roam and search, a hunger to explore. Mom and I were always happiest on the road, especially when home wasn't always a safe place to be.

CHAPTER 2

As a small child, before I started using visions of open highways to lull myself to sleep, I had a prayer I would recite repeatedly on nights when I was scared and anxious.

> Now I lay me down to sleep
> I pray the Lord my soul to keep
> If I should die before I wake
> I pray the Lord my soul to take
> Now I lay me down to sleep…

Even though I didn't fully understand the significance of the words, I repeated them to myself until I finally drifted off to sleep. I was on a journey, a search for comfort. I was terrified of the dark. I was terrified of everything, actually. I thought of prayers as magical chants that had the power to chase away the monsters that lurked behind the shadows in my bedroom.

I had been told that prayers were request for blessings. I had been told I would be safe if I believed in Jesus. I had been told I would go to heaven if I was a good girl. I was never quite sure how all of this worked, though. As a result, I thought religion and God were just as terrifying and confusing as the dark shadows that only appeared in my room at night.

My parents believed they were answering my questions and addressing my confusion by enrolling me in a Catholic elementary school in Kansas City, Kansas. My first grade experiences, however, only succeeded in creating more confusion inside of me. The nuns and priests who were in charge of the school expected all the students to be well behaved and devout. Strict rules were applied to ensure these objectives were met.

School began every day with mass at seven in the morning. While Father Brink conducted the service, the nuns patrolled the pews, slapping or shaking the students who were falling asleep or simply slouching in their seats. It was important to pay close attention to the sermon. When we returned to the classroom, our first assignment was to write down every word of the homily we could remember. Anyone who arrived late or couldn't recall important details had to spend the afternoon recess memorizing and reciting bible verses.

Most of my classmates didn't consider this a punishment. They actually preferred it to our usual recess activity. At precisely two o'clock in the afternoon, we were marched downstairs to the old basement gymnasium/cafeteria. In this large, rectangular multi-purpose room, with its green tiled floors and concrete brown walls, the nuns encouraged physical activity. With their long, black habits and dangling rosary beads swaying in time to the music, they instructed us in the finer art of square dancing.

The fact that first and second graders have no interest in touching someone of the opposite sex did not stop the nuns from closely monitoring each couple on the dance floor. They continually checked where we placed our hands and measured the distances between our bodies. While Sister Frances Joseph (Ole Frankie Joe as she was commonly known) clapped her hands and yelled, "Swing your partner! Promenade!" we stumbled awkwardly over each other while trying to avoid direct physical contact.

The girls were strictly limited in their movements. The nuns told us not to spin too fast or jump too high. They were afraid that any sudden movement could cause the back of our skirts to fly up around our thighs in a sinful manner.

Modesty was not taught but enforced on female students. While the boys just had to adhere to a strict dress code, the girls were required to wear uniforms. All female students were dressed in identical green plaid, pleated skirts and plain, white blouses. The blouses had to be long sleeved and buttoned at the cuff because the nuns believed the boys could peek inside wide, short sleeves whenever the girls raised their hands in class. The girls were also required to wear a green vest or blazer so the boys could not see through our white cotton blouses.

On the first Monday of every month, the female students were forced to kneel on the floor of the cafeteria. Sister Celine was in charge of measuring our skirts to make sure our hems were never more than three inches above our knees. If someone's skirt was discovered to be too short, the student would be suspended until the problem was solved.

Sister Celine may have taken her uniform inspection responsibilities too seriously. The yardstick she used to measure our skirts grew to be a permanent part of her body. With the wooden stick in her right hand beating against the palm of her left, her tall, thin figure moved through the cafeteria during our lunch periods. Whack! The sound of the yardstick suddenly smacking against the top of a table meant we were talking too loudly and must finish our meal in silence. Whack! The second strike meant she still heard a few chattering voices. This was the signal for us to rise from our chairs and remain standing until we were dismissed.

Though I never saw her hit anyone with the stick, I heard rumors to that effect. I believed the stories because I witnessed many students being hit and humiliated throughout the course of the school day. I can still hear the whistling of Sister Frances Joseph's rosary whipping through the air before striking against the neck of an unsuspecting student. Sister Anne Regina's weapon of choice was a chalk eraser that she hurled across the room at any student who failed to correctly answer a math equation.

Father Brink used a different technique. Obnoxious students were called to the front of the classroom and instructed to place their noses in small chalk circles drawn on the blackboard. Throughout the class hour, whenever Father passed by the students, he'd hit them in the back of the head, crumpling their noses against the board. Powdery chalk dust covered their faces and remained there for the rest of the day, branding the students as sinners. Many priests and nuns employed corporal punishment not only as a form of discipline but as an effective teaching device as well. Forgotten homework, tardiness, misspelled words on a test, or any other minor infraction always resulted in some kind of physical penalty.

My crime was simply the inability to speak correctly. I had a debilitating speech impediment that consisted of a slight stutter and an awkward pronunciation of certain letters. My r's always sounded like w's. My s's slid into an annoying "th" sound. I also tended to speak in my own gibberish language that no one could decipher.

Sister Alvera, my first grade teacher, found this situation intolerable. She notified my mother that I was "severely retarded" and should be removed immediately from her class. Mom refused to take me out of school. I remained in Sister Alvera's classroom for the full academic year.

Mom may have won the battle, but I was losing the war. Sister Alvera was convinced there had to be some cause for my verbal disabilities. She believed I was lazy, which happens to be one of the Seven Deadly Sins. Sister Alvera decided my penance. Whenever I was called to answer in class, she would hit me for every word I mispronounced.

One afternoon, Sister Alvera asked me to read a paragraph from our primary reading book out loud in front of the class. I stood up reluctantly and held the book close to my face, trying to hide behind it. I tried to focus on the words but the sound of Sister's hard-soled shoes clapping against the tile floor as she walked towards me broke my concentration. My hands shook so hard the black printed words appeared to dance on the page of my book. My knees quivered so violently I was afraid I would lose my balance and fall defiantly forward. I opened my mouth slowly and forced the words out. "Once upon a time, a little boy and girl…"

The second "girl" escaped my lips as "giwl," I knew I was in trouble. Sister Alvera's thick, hard covered book came crashing down on top of my head. "Read it again," she demanded.

"Once upon a time, a little boy and giwl…"

"Wrong!" she yelled as her book punctuated the word by slamming against my head once more. "Again," she demanded and I promptly spoke "giwl" at her request.

"No! GIRL! G-I-R-L!" Sister spelled out the word, hitting me with her book with each letter and emphasizing the "r" in particular. "It is pronounced GIRL! Read it again."

The room was deathly silent except for the sound of Sister Alvera's labored breathing. Humiliated and terrified, my knees buckled and I leaned against the side of my desk for support.

"Stand up, you lazy girl," Sister screamed as she grabbed the collar of my blouse and yanked me back to my feet. Out of fright, my knees locked stiffly in place, but that was the only thing I was able to accomplish. "Girl" continued to come out of my mouth in a variety of forms.

"Giwl."

"Gwil."

"Gril."

"Gill."

After each one, Sister Alvera's book hit against my head as she screamed, "Again!" I never did get it right and Sister was finally forced to give up. She laid down her weapon and decided to turn the matter over to God. Placing her hands on my shoulders, she pushed me onto my knees while saying, "You stupid, lazy girl. You are a sinner. Pray for God's forgiveness."

While the other children were dismissed from the classroom for recess, I remained kneeling on the cold, concrete floor. I forced myself not to cry as I listened to the laughter, smirks, and hateful comments of my classmates as they filed passed me to the door. Once recess was over, Sister Alvera decided my situation was too much of a distraction to the other children. Her solution was to lock me in the supply closet away from the other students for the rest of the afternoon. I was ordered to pray during my exile, and I did. I continually asked God what was wrong with me. I received no answer. My situation and shame kept me locked away from my peers who continually teased and bullied me during my grade school years

I soon learned it was much safer not to talk. I would not utter a sound. I refused to say a single word to anyone at school and soon became known and bullied as the "mute/retard." I just seemed to make the circumstances worse for myself. My refusal to talk caused a lot of humiliating situations for me.

One morning, when my classmates and I had been instructed to work independently in our Language Arts books, I had the sudden urge to use the bathroom. For the past hour, I had watched my fellow classmates raise their hands, ask permission from Sister Alvera, and leave the room. I was so incredibly shy and afraid to talk, I couldn't bring myself to follow their example. I began to squirm and twist in my seat. Finally, from her desk at the front of the room, Sister Alvera noticed my fidgeting and yelled at me to sit still. In terror, I did what she requested…and promptly peed all over my skirt, the chair, and the floor. Sister Alvera stared at me in disbelief for a moment. Then she quickly got up from her desk and stomped down the aisle towards me. She reached down, grabbed my shoulders, and lifted me onto my feet.

"You stupid, dirty girl," she chanted several times, shaking me by my shoulders. "I'm not cleaning this up." She released me then, throwing me back into my seat. "You'll just have to sit in it." I remained in that chair, horribly soaked in pee, for the rest of the school day. I was continually proving Sister Alvera right. My accident confirmed to her that she was accurate about my mental capabilities. Now, I was known as the mute/retard who couldn't control her bladder.

The next morning, I couldn't stop crying. I woke up in tears and cried throughout my mother's efforts to get her children ready for the school day. "I don't want to go to school," I screamed at Mom with tears streaming down my face. "Please, Mommy, I don't want to go to school."

My mom stared down at me, trying to hide her impatience as she struggled to get me to sit still long enough to pull a soft bristled hairbrush through my tangled long blond hair. "Why, Jamie?" she sighed at me. "Why don't you want to go?"

I didn't answer her. I just continued to sob out my plea. "Please, don't make me go to school." I could feel by the rough tugs of the hairbrush against my scalp that Mom was trying to contain her annoyance. My thin hair always seemed to tangle into tight little knots. It was always painful for me to have it brushed. Now, I felt as if my hair was literally being yanked out by the roots. I continued to scream even louder.

"You can't stay home," Mom tried to reason with me through my sobs. "You can't stay home unless you can tell me why? Why don't you want to go to school, Jamie?"

I pulled away from my mother's hands, turned around, and looked up at her with huge tears running down my face...and said nothing. I just stood there in front of her, gulping and gasping. I just couldn't seem to find the words to tell her what was happening. I couldn't find the words to express the terror I felt every day walking into my classroom.

So, I went to school that day...and the next...and the next until I was one of the few students to obtain a perfect attendance award at the end of the school year. I felt little pride in the honor at that time.

During the summer of that traumatic first grade year, I began speech therapy classes every Friday morning for about three months. I would sit in a room with cheerful multi-colored walls and very bright overhead lights. There were numerous shelves all around the room filled with toys and books, but I was too shy and nervous to play. I was separated from Mom but found out later that she was watching me from the next room through a one-way mirror. I became fascinated with that mirror once I learned that Mom was just on the other side. I thought of myself as Alice in Wonderland or Snow White looking for answers beyond the glass. I began to feel comfortable at the clinic, especially since I was the only student receiving a lot of attention from the young, kind speech therapist. Wanting to please her, I diligently practiced my letters as she guided me through activities to improve my speech.

So I wouldn't be scared, Mom had explained the speech classes to me by saying that the clinic was a special place that only I could go without my brother and sisters. This really got my attention. I suddenly realized that I had my mom to myself for several hours every Friday morning as we traveled about 120 miles round trip to the sessions.

I got to sit in the front seat next to Mom. That was very unusual. Usually, there was always a battle over riding shotgun when my brother and sisters were in the car. On the way to the clinic, Mom would stop at a small convenience store to buy sodas and candy. She would warn me that it was our secret and not to tell my siblings. I never did. I liked sharing secrets with my mom.

One Friday morning, during the drive back home, Mom and I were quiet as usual, just listening to the radio. Suddenly, I reached forward, turned off the stereo, and stated, "Mom, I want to talk like you and Grandma do." Mom thought this was very funny and repeated my words to my grandmother as soon as we returned home. She may have found it amusing, but I was serious.

I was usually sitting in the back squished in between my brother and sisters. I would lean over the front seat and listen to my mother and grandmother's conversations. I wasn't actually eavesdropping. I never concentrated on the actual content of what they were saying. Instead, I was fascinated by the sound of their voices. Maybe it was because of my own struggles with speech, but I was awestruck by how their words just streamed effortlessly together and their spoken thoughts flowed without strain or effort. It seemed miraculous to me that people could talk this way and I wanted to be a part of it. Even though I was only six-years-old, I wanted to discuss philosophy and life issues. However, a lack of experience and a speech impediment were the realities of my situation. Once I made my declaration of needing conversation, Mom and I remained silent for the rest of the ride home. Though my dream of cruising down the highway with Mom discussing life events would happen years later, at that time, I didn't know what to say. After the year of abuse and bullying, I had locked everything inside of me.

I never did tell my mom or dad what was happening at school. I had believed that the situation was all my fault. It humiliated me to talk about my experiences, especially when my brother and sisters seemed to be doing fine. I began to believe there was something seriously wrong with me. I believed I needed to be punished for the way I was.

The relationship with my father just enhanced these feelings. His temper terrified me. He would always become angry and erupt into rages over the most minor things. He seemed particularly angry and upset with me. I could stumble on my own feet and be greeted with shouts of "Idiot" from my father. He consistently called me stupid or retard if he cared to call me anything at all. My greatest anxiety came from his threats to send me away. I never quite knew where he was planning for me to go, but his constant warning to have me locked up would cause me to lie awake for hours, crying in the dark. My father simply, and without question, agreed with Sister Alvera's diagnosis of me, believing that I was seriously retarded. I certainly could not tell him that I was being abused at school for the way I talked and behaved. That would certainly proof his point and give him validation to send me away.

My mother wouldn't use the word retarded. She preferred "special" and responded by being so overly protective of me, it would take me years to finally break away. I couldn't talk to Mom about my ordeal either, especially when she was lost in her own abusive situations. She was continually trying to keep her family together while dealing with my father's consistent rages.

Early one morning, my sisters and I were asleep in our bedroom when we were suddenly awakened by my dad's loud angry voice echoing down the hallway from the kitchen. We sat up, staring at each other without a word as we listened to the sounds of feet stomping, doors slamming, and glass shattering. My sisters and I stayed frozen in our beds until we heard the rickety garage door open and bang close again, signifying that Dad had left for work. All three of us jumped from our beds then and ventured down the hallway to the kitchen.

We found my mother squatting down on the old, stained, green kitchen linoleum with the shattered remains of the glass coffee pot lying all around her. Coffee dripped down the walls and formed puddles on the kitchen floor. My father had thrown the full hot coffee pot at my mom just because she had dared to pour herself a cup of coffee before serving his. Mom was on the floor, picking up shreds of glass and attempting to wipe up the puddles of coffee with a torn dishrag.

Though her eyes sparkled with tears, she looked up at us with a smile and stated, "Oh, I was just so clumsy. I slipped and dropped the coffee pot. What a mess Mommy made, huh? You girls go watch TV. I'll get this cleaned up now and then we'll have some breakfast."

My sisters and I stiffly stood at the border of the dining room and kitchen as if it was neutral territory. "Go on," Mom smiled at us again. "Everything is fine, really, go."

My sisters and I sat together in the living room, but I couldn't concentrate on the cartoons that were flickering across the television screen. My mind was filled with the image of my mother in tears crouched down on the kitchen floor.

Denial was just one of the coping methods that I learned from my mother. I learned to smile through my tears and to respond with "I'm fine" whenever asked about any situation in my life.

Like my mother, I also began to search for solitude. We both felt safer when we were alone. Though my mother would occasionally spend an afternoon speaking to the neighbors over the backyard fence, she had few close friends. I would be the same; rarely letting anyone get close to me. I never knew what Mom was doing on the many afternoons that she would lock herself in her bedroom, leaving her children to fend for themselves. I, however, would write poems, songs, and short stories when I locked myself in the bathroom when I needed to be alone. Only anxious pounding on the door would finally bring me out of my hiding place. Fearfully knocking on the closed door of my mother's bedroom would have little effect. She rarely responded when she locked herself away.

My mother and I were constantly looking for methods of escape from the abuse and subsequent depression. Mom would clean and move around furniture. I would daydream so much, I would further humiliate myself by walking into walls and falling off curbs. I lived in a blissful fog for the majority of my childhood.

But our main method of escape was the road. When situations at home became too overwhelming, we would drive, just drive with nowhere to go. We would drive around Wyandotte County Lake, Bonner Springs Park, and random neighborhoods until Mom felt it was safe to go back home.

I actually loved those drives with Mom. I wanted to be in the car, just headed nowhere. The road had become my safe place. Though it took a few years, over time, I began to trust the situation enough to talk. Though I would never use words frivolously, I began to feel so safe on the road, I slowly found myself beginning to tell Mom stories of my life and listen to her secrets as well. This was one of the first stories I told her.

One night when I was in first grade, I was lying in bed, crying deep wracking sobs. I don't remember exactly why I was crying. I only remember being hurt and afraid. Well, I must have eventually cried myself to sleep because the next thing I knew it was morning. The first thing I noticed when I opened my eyes was bright golden sunlight pouring in through the window across from my bed. I just watched the sunlight, fascinated by its glimmering rays that completely lit up the whole bedroom. I was lying on my back with my left hand resting palm up next to my head on the pillow. I suddenly became aware of a warm pressure in my hand. I turned my head and saw a smooth hand with long slender fingers resting in mine. My eyes followed the hand up the arm to the shoulder until I found myself staring into the face of an angel who was sitting by my bedside. The angel was dressed in long white robes, her wings rustling softly behind her, and her halo lighting up her face and golden hair. Her lips curved into a gentle smile before her hand slipped out of mine and she began to move away from me. She floated effortlessly across the room and through the shaft of light that drifted in through the window. The golden glow followed her out of the room and left behind just normal morning light.

I hadn't told anyone about this before mainly because it just seemed so natural to me. I had the feeling it wasn't the first time an angel had been with me. I never could have predicted my mom's reaction, though. I suddenly realized she had driven along the highway in total silence as I finished my story. Then she parked the car on the side of the road, and without acknowledging me, she put her head in her hands, and cried for half an hour.

CHAPTER 3

When I was just six years old, my mother enrolled my sisters and me in Mrs. Bird's dance class. Every Wednesday night, ten chubby, awkward little girls stumbled their way through basic tap and ballet movements in Mrs. Bird's basement. I completely ignored the washer and dryer that stood against the back wall. I overlooked the bikes and old wooden broken-down pool table that were pushed into one corner of the room. To me, the cold room with its beige, speckled linoleum, green walls, and full-length mirrors was Julliard.

Now, this was a school where I could thrive. I didn't have to talk. All I had to do was watch and repeat the graceful movements of the petite and elegant Mrs. Bird, who preferred to be completely oblivious to the lack of talent among her students. As long as I followed her movements and did as I was told, I didn't have to say anything at all. That became my motivation. My round little body easily, if not gracefully, followed Mrs. Bird's gentle guidance until I honestly believed I was a prima ballerina.

Everything about the dance classes made me happy. I loved holding onto the wooden bar that ran the length of the mirrored wall on one side of the room. With total self-assurance, I would watch myself reflected in the clear full-length glass as I practiced moving into first and second position with the rest of the girls. Standing at the bar with my toes pointed, I felt that I belonged somewhere. It didn't matter that I shied away from speaking to the other little girls. I felt connected to the other students just by holding on to the bar and feeling the energy that propelled our awkward movements. I didn't bond closely with anyone, but, at least, I wasn't considered stupid or laughed at if I made some silly mistake. All of us were making silly mistakes as we stumbled over our own feet while shuffling around the room. Under Mrs. Bird's command, I could blend in and be just the same as everyone else.

I loved the tutus, leotards, and sparkly costumes that made me feel tall, thin, mature, and beautiful. I have always been a big daydreamer. The sequined attire made me believe I was a ballet dancer, ice skater, circus performer, princess...anything I wanted to be other than what I was.

I especially loved the tap shoes, which were black patent leather with long silky ribbons that Mom tied into neat bows over the top of my long feet. A small flat piece of metal graced the bottom tip of the toe and clacked against the floor with every step I took. What an amazing discovery! I could make sound by just moving my feet! I may never have to talk again! I could just tap my way around any conversation.

I was always excited on recital nights. As shy as I was, I couldn't wait to get out on stage. I suddenly didn't mind people watching me. I craved attention whenever I danced. I was always calm and focused when my feet hit the stage. After the performance, I loved the feel of my face and body tingling with adrenaline and happily glowing to the sound of the applause. People were actually clapping enthusiastically for our three-minute performance! I never thought about the fact that the audience was mainly filled with parents dutifully praising their children's clumsy efforts. In my mind, we were giving a command performance for royalty.

I took the recitals seriously; so seriously, in fact, that I would become irritated with my sisters if they refused to practice. During one performance, I was so anxious that my sister, Carol, would forget when to turn, I actually reached behind another dancer and pushed Carol in the back as a reminder to spin. I was a stickler for following all of the movements we had learned in class step for step. I wanted every dance to be perfect.

That's probably why my first baton twirling class devastated me. I had been so thrilled when Mom bought the shiny, smooth, thin, 21-inch metal rods for my sisters and me. We usually didn't have the money for any additional treats, so I knew that the batons had to be very special. I could not wait to get my small hands on one of them. Mom wouldn't let us play with them though. I think she was concerned that we would injure each other or break something in the house. Mom hid the batons away in her closet and wouldn't let us touch them until two nights later when we attended the first class.

As soon as we arrived, I grabbed one of the batons from Mom and ran out to the middle of the room, anxiously waiting for Mrs. Bird to descend the narrow stairway that lead from the upper part of her house to the basement. After a few minutes of standing at attention and gripping the baton tightly in my hands, Mrs. Bird finally appeared. She stood before her students and began a short lecture on the history and purpose of the baton while ten little girls tapped the rods against the floor, swung them back and forth, and almost cracked each other over the head. Realizing that we were becoming increasingly restless, Mrs. Bird finally raised her own baton up to chest level. With her fingers sliding easily over each other, she started the rod spinning effortlessly in quick motion in front of her body and under her arm.

Eager to get started, I gripped my baton in the center and held it up in front of my chest just as Mrs. Bird had done. But that's where the comparison ended. I began to push the baton with my long, crooked fingers and then watched in horror as it fell to the floor in slow motion, bouncing two or three times on its white rubbery ends. I quickly bent down and snatched the baton back up. Mrs.

40

Bird didn't say anything. She just smiled gently and nodded her head to me in encouragement to try again. That is why I loved Mrs. Bird. She didn't call me stupid when I stumbled. She didn't hit me for missing a beat. Feeling optimistic, I spun the baton again and promptly dropped it back to the floor. My small hands just could not hold on to that silly rod. I covertly glanced to my right and left quickly and was devastated. Though most of the movements were jerky, my classmates spun the batons as if they had been born with the silver sticks attached to their hands. Not a single other student allowed the baton to slip through her fingers.

The fifth time I dropped the rod, Mrs. Bird stopped the class. "Just a moment, girls. Let's help Jamie with her baton," she announced as she walked over to me. Nine little girls circled around me. Even the mothers who sat on the brown worn couches in the waiting area on one side of the room stopped their chattering to watch.

I craved attention, but this was not the way I wanted to be noticed. As Mrs. Bird held my baton with one hand and tried to position my fingers in the middle of the bar, I began to shake and sweat. I was the only student doing something wrong in a classroom situation again. I was being stupid and lazy. Even with Mrs. Bird holding onto the baton, it continually threatened to slip from my fingers. Out of fear that I would drop the rod again, I yanked up just as Mrs. Bird let go. To my surprise, the hard cold metal stick met the right side of my face with a solid thwack!

Though Mrs. Bird tried to apologize for the accident, I was upset. I was being hit for being stupid in class again! I was completely surprised that it happened in dance class. I dropped the baton to the floor, broke through the circle of laughing amateur dancers, and ran to my mother. I threw myself into her arms, not even trying to hold back my tears. Holding me carelessly with one arm, Mom stood up quickly, made our apologies to Mrs. Bird, gathered up our things, and led my sisters and me from the basement.

Even though Mom kept trying to tell me it had been an accident,

I was inconsolable on that first night of baton practice. Yes, it hurt to get smacked in the face, but I had wanted so badly to impress Mrs. Bird. I wanted to be the star performer and now here I was reduced to tears over my clumsy baton movements. I was upset that my beloved dance class now seemed as violent and scary as Sister Alvera's first grade classroom.

Instead of shying away from the baton, though, I practiced endlessly throughout the week. I didn't want my love for performing to slip away from me as easily as the baton fell from my fingers. My main motivator, however, was to prove that I was not an idiot. This moment created a ferocious competitiveness within me that would further alienate me. I would become aggressive, intense, and passionate in all of my endeavors. I was determined to prove myself the best at everything I did.

In our next class the following week, I didn't do the moves perfectly. The baton continued to wobble as I spun it around, but I didn't drop it once. Not once! When Mrs. Bird dismissed the class an hour later, I ran into the waiting area to fling myself again into my mother's arms. Mom just sighed deeply and pushed me away. Her refusal to recognize my accomplishment left me stunned and anxious. Couldn't she understand what this meant to me? I suddenly realized that Mom didn't want me clinging to her in front of the other parents. My tantrum of the week before had embarrassed her. She was choosing now to distance herself from any more of my emotional outburst.

My inability to talk out my feelings had left me an emotional mess. I cried constantly, but as Mom began to push me away, I started to lock down hard on my emotions. I slowly grew stoic. I would very seldom even laugh or smile. I brushed aside my feelings of hurt and rejection and just concentrated harder on the physical techniques of the dance, which become my only release.

After four years of instruction, however, my sisters' interest had waned. Mom put up with their complaints of attending classes until one evening she became aggravated by their lack of attention and concentration. Driving home after class, Mom furiously asked, "Do you want to stop dancing? Is that what you want?" Her small hands beat against the steering wheel. Her irritation over her unappreciated efforts was growing. "I have to scrape money together for lessons every week. I still owe Mrs. Bird for the last two classes. I have two daughters who won't pay attention and one who throws constant tantrums. I don't need to be doing this. I don't need to sacrifice for ungrateful bratty daughters. What do you want to do?"

My sisters answered quickly and, it seemed to me, without much thought. They strongly announced that they wanted to quit dancing. I sat quietly in the middle of the back seat, listening to the justifications that were running over me from both sides. Their logic came fast and in a flurry as they repeatedly interrupted each other. They had a litany of reasons why they no longer wanted to dance.

After a few minutes, when they had finally exhausted themselves, Mom turned her attention to me and asked what I wanted to do. Now, I realized I was completely outnumbered by my outspoken sisters…and I couldn't speak, not a single word came from my mouth. I couldn't possibly find the words to express what dancing meant to me.

When Mom asked again what I wanted, she sounded even more exasperated. "Come on, Jamie. Say something! What do you want to do? Do you want to dance or do you want to quit, too?" She sighed deeply as she awaited my answer. It wasn't coming. I couldn't get my voice to work. In fear and confusion, all I could do was shake my head. Yes, I wanted to dance. Mom, glancing quickly at me in the rearview mirror, interpreted the movement differently.

"Alright, fine, you're all agreed then," Mom stated. "I'll call Mrs. Bird when we get home and let her know we won't be returning to the classes."

Wait a minute…I wanted to dance! But I still couldn't find my voice. We never went to dance classes again. Because of my inability to talk, I lost the one thing in my life I absolutely loved, the one thing that had given me confidence and hope. I screamed out my protest in my head, but no one heard. It was just the first of many disappointments I would face because I couldn't speak up for myself. My failure to find my voice left me a broken, easy target.

I wouldn't even scream when, at the age of thirteen, a male teacher would continually sexually assault me throughout the spring semester of my eighth grade year. I would remain silent, not knowing how to ask for help. I didn't know how to express what was happening to me. I had learned early on that sex was a subject that made my mother uncomfortable and nervous. We never did have a sex talk while I was going through puberty. I learned about sex by secretly listening to my sisters talking late at night. The three of us shared one bedroom for several years. I would pretend to be asleep as I listened to their voices talking low and reticently about periods, pregnancies, and boys they liked. I would just lie there in the dark, listening, and trying to stop the silent tears that ran down my face. Through my mother's refusal to talk and my sisters talking too much, I began to realize that the situation at school with my teacher was inappropriate. These feelings of being dirty and disgusting would stay with me for years, developing into deep calloused scars that hindered many of my relationships throughout my life.

Six years after the assaults, when I was nineteen, the hurting was so bad, I couldn't stop crying. I had continuing flashbacks to several severe incidents. Suicide scenarios spun through my head as I lay awake in my bed every night. During the day, I would lock myself in the bathroom for hours, fascinated with a small tray of razor blades that was tucked away in the medicine cabinet. I would pick one up between the thumb and index finger of my right hand and hold it up to the light. I was enthralled with the shimmer that reflected off the metal piece. I would then bring it down towards my body and run it across my left forearm, wrist, or palm. I would just barely graze the cold metal edge over my skin. I would not cut deep. I made no wound, left no scar. I felt like there was a concrete barrier between the blade and my skin that I just could not seem to penetrate. I never knew what it was, but there was something blocking the metal from biting into my arm. Except one time.

One afternoon, I finally cut deep enough to draw a few scattering drops of blood that fell like red teardrops against the clean white porcelain of the sink. The sudden sight of scattered blood globules created a turning point inside of me. My eyes were suddenly open. I knew I had hit an extremely low point. What was I doing?

With tears flowing down my face, I wiped the blood from my arm and the sink with tissue and then flushed it down the toilet. I suddenly realized I needed to break my silence. It was coming down to a drastic choice. I had to decide between talking and dying. I finally decided I needed to tell Mom about the situation.

I left the bathroom and walked into the kitchen where I found Mom sitting at the table, finally having a quiet moment to herself. I pulled one of the dining room chairs away from the table and sat down. Mom looked up from her book, saw my tear-stained face, and sighed heavily. She didn't say anything but I could imagine the words zooming around in her head. *What now?* She would get aggravated with me when I cried, apparently for no reason.

Between my tears and finding the right words, I struggled to speak. I only found the strength when I realized that Mom thought this was just another one of my drama moments. Forcing the words from my mouth, I finally began. "Mom, at school, there was a teacher…"

Mom sat up straighter in her chair. "What happened?" she asked which caused me to just cry harder. Mom knew then what I was going to say. Her next words convinced me that she understood but didn't want to hear. "You can't talk right now," she stated. "It's okay. We'll talk about it later when you are able to."

She was up from her chair and gone then, out of the kitchen, through the living room, down the hallway, and back behind her closed bedroom door. I was left alone, just sitting there, sobbing in stunned silence. I knew my near confession had hurt her horribly. I would never mention the situation to her again. It was too painful for her.

My struggle to communicate had locked me into a prison that I fought continually to escape. When I couldn't, I just learned how to fend for myself. I would become fiercely independent and self-contained. Other than school, I would rarely venture outside. I would spend the time alone writing poetry, songs, and short stories, pouring onto paper all the emotions I couldn't express in any other way.

As I got older, I would find my voice, but it would emerge from my throat as a scream. When I couldn't speak, I became an expert at rolling my eyes, slamming down phones, and banging doors. My temper grew enormous. All my fear and rage would come shooting out of me when I felt in anyway threatened. I was angry and impatient. I wouldn't listen or allow anyone to touch me.

I practiced endless self-discipline and control until OCD patterns began to develop. I would continually retrace my steps three, four times, checking that doors were locked and appliances were unplugged. For other people, accidents may just make them unfortunate victims. For me, robberies, rapes, or injuries would be proof that I was a retard who couldn't take care of herself and needed to be locked away.

Anxiety attacks would soon cause me to curl up on the floor for hours, shaking and crying uncontrollably over imagined threats and dangers. I would wake up, drenched in sweat from night terrors, and too scared to close my eyes again. I would only sleep two or three hours every night. I would experience random episodes of anorexia. I would refuse to eat when my self-esteem was so low, I didn't think I deserved food. I would take up to twenty laxatives and exercise for three hours every day in a futile attempt to make myself disappear. I was a physical wreck. My lack of sleep and food contributed to my emotional breakdown. I was constantly cranky, irritable, and obstinate.

I began to rebel. Besides a brief flirtation with smoking and drinking that lasted only a few months, I didn't self-medicate with drugs and alcohol. That seemed too much like the popular choice and I was always an outsider. Instead, my rebellion took a very different form. I began to educate myself, reading everything I could get my hands on. I loved the classics and faithfully read the amazing works of John Steinbeck, Victor Hugo, Jane Austin, and the Bronte sisters. Finally, I pulled the ultimate rebellion. I demanded to go to college.

Many people were shocked by my decision to pursue higher education, which they believed would be a waste of my time and money. It seemed rather ironic to my parents that the only one of their children to go to a university was the retard Dad had threatened to lock up. When they refused to help with tuition, I worked three jobs to support myself. Mom finally became supportive when she realized this might be an opportunity for me to meet someone and become safely married. Even though my mother's marriage was extremely abusive, that was the only thing she saw in my future. Deeply offended, I would rebel by never marrying. When I graduated four years later with a Bachelor's Degree, I pretended along with my family that it was no big deal and didn't even bother to attend the ceremony.

My mini rebellions continued much to my family's dismay. I demanded to learn to drive at the age of twenty. Receiving my license was equivalent to finding the key to my cage. I packed my bags, got in my car, and drove away. I literally ran away from home in my twenties. I had no idea where I was headed. I didn't know where I was going to end up. I just knew I had to be gone.

I wouldn't stop running for years. I would run endlessly around the world. I lived in England for a while, traveled through Europe, found myself suddenly in Thailand, and backpacked alone across Malaysia. Mom would stay in touch with me throughout my journeys. She had been so overprotective all my life, angrily arguing with me when I wanted to drive, move out, or go to college. "You're too special. You're too sensitive," she would say. "You can't take care of yourself." But I was now into a full-blown rebellion. The world had become my home. Mom, however, was not going to let me go that easily.

I wasn't surprised that once I left Kansas, no matter where I was, letters from Mom would always find me. She would write long newsy letters about family and Kansas. She always signed every letter the very same way. "Have fun, honey, and always enjoy the sweetness of life. Love, Mom." Have fun? The sweetness of life? The words would haunt and torment me. I was on a voyage of endless self-discovery. Fear drove me forward. I couldn't settle down. I couldn't relax. Mom's letters mocked me as if I was on some frivolous holiday. There were days when I was so angry, I would rip Mom's letters in half, especially being careful to shred the "sweetness of life" message that ridiculed me from the bottom of the page. I found the words hatefully taunting. I had only known abuse, frustration, confusion, and bitterness. I didn't want my mother's words of wisdom. I just wanted to be left alone and lost in the world. I wanted to be left alone to walk the streets of Paris and stand in the mists of London. I wanted to hike the mountains of Switzerland and slog through the rice fields of Malaysia.

On the road, lost somewhere in the world, I finally began to find my voice. I had to learn to communicate with people, or I would not have survived. I began to talk to complete strangers and not be afraid. Slowly, over time, I began to realize, I *was* in Switzerland and England. I *was* in Scotland, Germany, Belgium, and France. How did this happen? Somewhere, along my path, I began to appreciate where I was on God's big earth. I began to lose the anger and confusion I had carried with me for years and found the beauty of the world around me. Somewhere, along the way, I found I wasn't alone. God began to walk with me. In the beauty of my travels, I cried and let go and was filled with the glory and power of God. My anger was beginning to dissipate as I was introduced to a world much bigger than myself. Somewhere in the world, on my journey, I lost my baggage. I sat down my pain and frustration and found myself open to situations I never thought possible before. Once more, I began to see and talk to angels.

God and the angels had given me another gift. I could watch the people around me and suddenly know things about them that they had never told me. I knew things about people just by being near them. I slowly began to see chakras and aura fields around people and interpret the energy. My heart was suddenly open and all kinds of answers began to come to me.

I began to look forward to my mother's letters and treasure their messages. They were my only connection to my world back home. The sweetness of life? I was still learning to feel it, to be aware of it. But I did begin to smile and enjoy the process of just being still in God's universe.

When I returned to America, I was energized by all of my many discoveries. I immersed myself in spiritual healing techniques like Polarity and Reiki, which lead to the study of medical massage and esoteric therapies. After working in spas for a while, I opened a massage office and healing center which I owned and operated for six years. I had built a solid clientele who continually commented on my ability to find and ease their pain. They praised me and I continually thanked and honored God and the angels. I knew the angles guided my hands and told me what to do. I was given the gift of visualization. I could look at my clients' bodies and see the solid line of their bones and muscles and the inner glow of their souls. I knew where their suffering resided and how to help them.

I had done so many things that were completely unexpected of me. I graduated college. I owned and operated a business. I worked as a reporter for local newspapers. I became a teacher. I lived successfully on my own. I traveled around the world with an endless hunger for new adventures. I wasn't fully healed myself yet though. I still occasionally indulged in angry tears and bitter frustration. During those moments, I knew it was time to get back on the road and out in the world to renew my energy.

I knew Mom worried about me as I traveled around but I was too restless to settle down. I moved from Kansas to New Mexico to Tennessee to California. I needed to be on the road. It was where I felt free and comfortable enough to be myself. In 2002, I decided it was time for more of my emotional healing. I discussed it with Mom one day over lunch.

"Mom," I began hesitantly, "Well, I've been thinking…I've traveled to so many places in the world. But I really want to see more of America. Next month, I'm going to drive across the country. I may be gone for a while again, but I feel like it's something I really need to do."

"But where exactly are you going to go now?" Mom asked after a moment.

"I don't know," I told her honestly. "I'm just going to drive."

"You don't have any plan?" she asked hesitantly.

"I never do," I laughed for a moment. Then I said seriously, "I have a map. I just have a map…." Even I knew that sounded pathetic.

She was silent for a moment and I braced myself for what I thought was coming next. *What are you thinking? You have no plan? Well, that's how your whole life has been! This is why you struggle so much! You're too impulsive! You don't think things through. You're "special." Grow up now. Get a home. Get a husband. Get a dog, for gosh sakes. Settle down and just stop the craziness!*

Mom's response was not what I had expected. We stared at each other in silence for a moment. Then she squared her shoulders, looked directly into my eyes without blinking, and said, "I'm coming with you." Her words took me by surprise. I thought she would be overprotective and tell me not to go. We were both silent then.

Minutes ticked by before I finally asked, "Mom, are you sure you want to come? We'll by traveling for long hours in the car. I don't know where we're going to end up…"

"I'm coming with you," she repeated again. "You need someone with you. You can't do this by yourself. You need protection."

I kind of laughed to myself at her words. I had already traveled all over the world on my own. Mom was coming to protect me? Besides, she has always been so tiny, so delicate, not even five foot tall and barely ninety pounds and she wanted to protect me.

Suddenly, I heard her voice again. "Please," she whispered. That was all, once and again, "Please."

There was something in her voice, just that one simple word, that made me realize how important this was to her. She wanted this experience. She wanted to be a part of this venture. I couldn't ignore the glimmer of hope and longing in her voice, which bordered on desperate. It was as if she was trapped under rubble or lost at sea and she was screaming out for help. How could I say no?

How could I say yes?

Several years earlier, Mom and I, just the two of us, traveled from Kansas to Colorado by Amtrak. We were stuck together in a sleek, silver, metal tube. We didn't have compartments and had to sleep upright in our seats. Mom spent most of the trip telling stories about our travels when I was just a kid. Some stories I didn't really want to hear because they made me feel as if I was still a ridiculous child.

After three days in Colorado, Mom and I arrived back at the Amtrak station for the journey back to Kansas. We were supposed to leave at seven o'clock that night. We didn't get on-board until after eleven pm. The train was late due to ice and snow on the tracks around the mountain passes. All the passengers waiting to board spent four hours camped out on the platform. Most of them were wrapped in blankets; some slept soundly; others chattered incessantly; some snacked endlessly; and others played music loudly.

When the train finally arrived and we climbed aboard, Mom and I were so relieved...at first. It was not a good trip back. The train had only two bathrooms, and the one closest to our seats clogged and stopped up within the first two hours of travel. Raw sewage began to ooze into the passenger car. The smell was disgusting and complaints to the conductor did not get us quick results. We were finally allowed to move to the dining car about two hours later. This was actually little comfort. Now, we were forced to sit up all night on hard dining room chairs. I was irritable from the lack of sleep. I was too exhausted...and too immature...at the time to see the humor in our situation. I spent the two-day trip back in a horribly grumpy mood, frustrated and disagreeable. For hundreds of miles, Mom's attempts at conversation were meet with frosty glances and big, hateful sighs from her ungrateful daughter.

After that experience, I'm surprised Mom wanted to travel alone with me again. Over the years, there were times when my mood didn't seem to improve much since that Amtrak experience. Mom and I were in turn each other's best friends and most stubborn jailers. We would in turn cling to each other and fight to get away. Mom would alternately be overprotective until she tired of taking care of a grown daughter and pushed me away. I wanted my mother's love and attention and yet fought against the protective hold she had on me. I would continually demand my independence and yet run to Mom first whenever my heart was broken. This would be a continuing theme in our relationship, a constant push and pull, of holding on and letting go. I was trying to run away again and here I was bringing my cage along with me.

One day, when I was about five years old, Mom treated all of her kids to ice cream cones at Baskin Robbins. I remember feeling overjoyed with the simple treat and happily licked at the sliding, melting vanilla ice cream as we walked out of the shop. I took one big lick...and knocked the ice cream right out of the cone and onto the dirty, cracked sidewalk. The very moment the ice cream slurped onto the ground, I burst into a flood of tears. Mom just scooped up the ice cream with her bare hands and stuck it right back on my cone. I was happy again as I skipped down the sidewalk, licking joyfully at the dirt encrusted ice cream.

Did Mom still expect me to burst into tears over melting ice cream? Did I still expect Mom to make things better again? How would we get along for months on the road with just each other for company? How would we avoid getting in each other's way and who would make the final decisions? Would she see me as a woman on my own and not a five-year-old child, clinging to her hand, struggling to stand up in the snow?

Part Two

ROADWORK

CHAPTER 4

No, wait a minute, this can't be right! Mom and I left Kansas at five am, heading east on Interstate 70 in my Toyota Tacoma pickup truck. Our plan was to travel halfway across the top of Missouri and then turn south. We would drive through Arkansas and then into Memphis, Tennessee.

But something had gone wrong. I had lived away from Kansas for several years now. I wasn't familiar with the new highway structures and felt completely disoriented. The traffic had been growing steadily heavier as the sun began to rise and we were suddenly just pushed along, caught in a sea of cars and missing our exit. Now I realized we had just traveled in a big ole circle, a circle that was taking us right back to where we had started. Seriously, we started out heading east. I don't have a clue why we were suddenly facing the opposite direction. Two hours of traveling and we were only forty-five miles away from our starting point of Kansas City, Kansas!

I wondered for a moment if I should say something to Mom. She sat in the passenger seat, gazing out the window, and talking on about the excitement of traveling. Maybe this hadn't been such a great idea.

I gripped the steering wheel now and wondered if I would be willing to listen if Mom tried to tell me which direction I should go.

This would be the real test of my maturity. After spinning my wheels for years on my own, would I be willing now to listen to someone offering me the right path to follow? I took a deep breath. Just two hours into our journey, on the very first day of our very first trip across America, and we were just about to put it to the test.

I kept glancing to the right and left and into the rearview mirror. Will another driver give me a break? Can I get to an exit to turn around before Mom noticed? She was nervous about this trip during the planning stages. Telling her that we were already lost would probably make her a little crazy. Okay, it's okay, I won't say anything to her. I'll just turn the car around at the next exit.

"Oh, look," Mom suddenly said excitedly, "there's the Hallmark building again." She was silent for just a moment. "Wait a minute...'"

She was figuring it out. I should have known that she would recognize the downtown plaza of Kansas City, Missouri, just across the Missouri River from our Kansas City, Kansas home. When I was a child, we used to drive around the plaza every Christmas season, looking at all of the light displays. Now, we were driving past the Hallmark building heading west. Just another ten or so miles and we would be crossing the bridge over the river and be right back in Kansas City, Kansas.

"Jamie," Mom asked me cautiously. "Why are we going back home? Did you forget something?"

I shrugged my shoulders and helplessly moaned, "We're lost!"

"No, we're not! We aren't lost," Mom insisted, which was true. Technically, we weren't lost. We knew where we were, just not quite sure how we got there or how to get back on track to where we wanted to go. "We're just...going back to Kansas! Why are we going back home?"

However, before I could even think of an answer, Mom offered an idea. Why not just pull off the highway and have breakfast? This seemed like a good time to stop. I silently took her suggestion. I finally maneuvered my single cab pickup truck over to the right and gladly exited off Interstate 70.

Over breakfast at our local McDonald's back in Kansas, Mom remained silent as I took a long look at the map. She had been surprisingly calm about the whole situation. She said nothing as I studied the road atlas over my second cup of coffee. Mom just sipped her coffee and took small bites of her cinnamon roll. Yeah, she didn't say anything at all...good...she didn't criticize or give advice...great...Darn it, why isn't she saying anything!? Why isn't she frustrated or angry? Why isn't she insisting on looking at the map and planning our route? But nothing, she said nothing. Mom just sat back and let me look over the maps.

I had driven from New Mexico to Kansas many times. I had always stood on my own two feet and found my own way. But now, lost just out of our own driveway, I suddenly wished Mom would take control. I wanted her to tell me which way to go. Alright, this is really messed up and I don't know how we are going to last for months on the road together. I swallowed more of my bitter coffee along with my bitter thoughts. I didn't want to ask for help...and Mom didn't want to volunteer it, which is amazing because I had always felt that Mom had strong opinions about my life before. Now, she was just content to let me find the way. I took a deep breath before saying, "I think I have it figured out. I think I know the highways we need."

And all she said was, "Let's go then." She didn't even ask me the route. Did she suddenly trust me that much? Don't! I wanted to scream. No, no, I just have to pull it together...okay, let's go.

Mom and I were traveling without GPS systems and cell phones... just like the days of my childhood. Mom and I roam; GPS systems don't always work well for hopeless wanderers. We would have to take our chances with just the road atlas. We left the restaurant and pulled back out onto the highway. Now, I felt like my eyes were wide open. I wondered for a moment if getting lost was just anxiety about the upcoming adventure. I began to relax now and suddenly could see our way clearly.

Once we were on the open highway, Mom concentrated on an activity that helped her pass the time. She loved fighting and racing truck drivers. She would get upset if truckers were blocking our path. She encouraged me to speed up around the semis and then she would give them the "evil eye" when we passed by. Twice, she was convinced that the truckers were coming after us, and would duck down in the passenger seat, playing her own imaginary spy game. I just let her play like a six-year-old so I could concentrate on the traffic.

I was more concerned with the cars that would speed up and zip around us, zigzagging in and out of highway lanes. Finally, as a white car came zooming up from behind and whipped around us, I just happened to say in the direction of the passing car, "Yeah, go on ahead. We all see how big your peepee is." Mom started laughing so hard I thought she was going to choke. She couldn't believe I had made that comment but it was true. That's why most drivers speed, right? Speeding and whipping around other cars just makes people feel powerful and important. Well, my comment became a common saying for us. We pointed out all of the drivers who were just showing their peepees and let them pass on by us.

We traveled for several hours through Missouri and Arkansas, turned a small curve on the highway, drove across the mighty Mississippi River...and there was the Memphis skyline directly in front of us. Funny, but this was the first time I had ever taken notice of an American skyline and Memphis completely dazzled me. Maybe just because it *was* Memphis, but I was overwhelmed and excited.

Besides the skyline, I felt a sense of reverence looking at the St. Jude's Children's Hospital that loomed large in all of its pink glory in front of us. Mom has always been a big supporter of that particular hospital, unselfishly sending a donation every month.

I don't really know where or how it started, but I do remember ever since I was a child, Mom always prayed to Saint Jude, who is the patron saint of lost causes. Maybe that says something right there. But St. Jude was the saint Mom always turned to with prayers of help and hope. I still carry with me the medals and figurines that Mom used to carry in her car. I remember as a child, whenever we were leaving home, our family always had to chant, "Saint Jude, please, protect us," before Mom would even start the car. Mom encouraged us to pray before every car trip, even if it was just to the grocery store around the corner. We participated in this ritual this morning before leaving Kansas. It must have worked. We were safe and in Tennessee.

Mom and I spent the night in Memphis. We had planned to go to Graceland the next day. Mom had always been a big Elvis fan and, as a child, I remember cuddling up with her on many nights when my dad was away and watching the King on the late night movies.

Mom and I excitedly woke up our first morning in Memphis, dressed quickly, and began driving around town looking for Graceland. We started out lost again. We drove around aimlessly for a while until we finally decided to stop and ask for help. We pulled into a parking lot where we saw a middle aged, African-American man walking towards a small, white building. Due to all of my past travels, I have no qualms screaming out for help to people on the street. It's the longer conversations and relationships that give me trouble.

"Excuse me, excuse me," I called out to the man from my window. As he continued to walk away from us, I parked and climbed out of the truck. I ran after him, screaming, "Excuse me. Could you please help us?"

"What do you need, my child?" he suddenly turned and asked quietly.

"We're looking for the King," I heard Mom call out as she walked up behind me.

The man gestured behind him to the white building which I suddenly realized was a small community church. "Oh, no, no, no," I tried to correct the situation. "She means Elvis."

The man stopped moving completely now, looked us over, rolled his eyes, and whispered, "Oh, good Lord." I had to bite my lip not to laugh. I realized then that the words "king" and "Elvis" had taken him by surprise. I think he would have been much more encouraged to help us if we had said we were looking for "salvation" instead.

As we stood in front of the small church, I suddenly realized from the way he was dressed in his suit and white collar that he must be the pastor. Mom and I must have been a sight. There we were climbing out of a pickup truck, faces beaming, eyes shining, holding a map, and looking for the King. The man graciously and simply offered us directions and then turned to walk away.

"Thank you, thank you," we called out but the man just waved his hand, kept his back to us, and kept walking. He stopped and tensed for just a brief moment when Mom called out, "God bless you." His whole body visibly shook. Then he waved his hand once more, not turning back around to look at us. I stood still for a moment until Mom touched my arm. "C'mon, c'mon, let's go." I climbed back into the truck and we were off again, following the directions we had just received like heavenly guidance.

We didn't have to go far, just turn a few corners and there was Graceland. Mom and I parked and climbed out of the truck. We bought our tickets and then went to stand in a long line for one of the small buses that would take us up to the mansion. As we waited our turn, we noticed that everyone in line in front of us was having a picture taken in front of a wall mural that looked like the front gates of Graceland. Mom and I watched for a moment and then turned to each other. Dealing with body issues, we both hate having our picture taken. No, we don't want our picture taken, we both agreed. No, that's okay. We don't need a picture. We were getting closer to the front of the line, but we still decided that no, no, we were not going to have our picture taken. We confirmed it with each other several times as we slowly moved ever closer to the front of the line.

A family of four directly in front of us didn't seem too enthusiastic about the picture, either. With a wave of her hand, the young photographer gave them directions, instructing them to stand in front of the mural. The father shook his head and waved his own hand sideways back and forth in front of her, "No," he told her, "we're not interested in a picture." Suddenly, the petite, young photographer glared at him. Her eyes narrowed dangerously as she took several steps towards him. She was directly in his face as she said, "Now, you listen to me. You gonna walk over to that wall there, and you gonna pose, and you gonna smile, you gonna smile real big, and you gonna like it! You hear me?"

The man stared down at the photographer's angry snarled face in total shock at first, then placed his hands on the shoulders of his wife and guided her, with their two young kids trailing reluctantly behind, to the mural. He assembled his family together in a tight little knot, turned around, and smiled real big. The photographer snapped the picture and then turned to the rest of us standing in line. "You all listen to me! You all gettin' your picture taken whether you all likes it or not!"

Uh, Mom and I were next in line. We weren't feeling entirely rebellious or defiant that day. We were actually used to following orders. We were used to smiling through our discomfort. We had grown up trying to stay out of trouble. Mom and I looked at each other, shrugged, and then slowly went up to the wall and posed. We smiled real big, too...and we later bought the picture as well. We weren't going to argue. We didn't want any problems with anyone that day.

Mom was just happy to finally be at Graceland, a dream come true for her. She became an Elvis fan when she was a young girl of sixteen and first heard him on the radio singing "Love Me Tender". She fell in love with his voice and bought all of the Elvis records she could find. She hadn't seen a picture of him at the time, though. She had no idea what he looked like...neither did my grandmother.

Mom came home from school one day to find all of her Elvis records smashed and destroyed. She was absolutely heartbroken, especially when she found out why. My grandmother had heard Elvis's music, saw my mother's developing infatuation, and had become alarmed. From the sound of his music, Grandma thought he was black and was horrified that her teenage daughter had developed a crush on an African-American man. This was, of course, the 1950s, and interracial relationships were definitely not acceptable. Grandma decided it was best to nip Mom's developing devotion in the romantic bud. A week later, Mom finally saw a picture of Elvis in a magazine and suffered through her heartache again. As she looked at his dark hair, dark eyes, and white skin, she realized her beloved records had been destroyed for nothing. Mom had been devoted to Elvis ever since.

Growing up, I remember Elvis's music constantly being played throughout the house. Though Mom adored Elvis, she loved a variety of music and usually had records or the radio playing most of the time. She had a beautiful voice and would sing along with her small collection of records that included the Platters, Johnny Mathias, and Gary Puckett and the Union Gap. Mom's love for the Platters and Johnny Mathias didn't seem to upset my grandmother, who seemed to have reluctantly accepted her youngest daughter's carefree musical obsessions.

While I was a child, though, Mom's favorite song was Deep Purple's "Smoke on the Water." That particular song would be played repeatedly while I was growing up. It is the only rhyme or rhythm I actually remember from my childhood. I don't remember any nursery rhymes or lullabies, just "Smoke on the Water" and Elvis.

I loved watching Mom at Graceland. Her eyes widened with amazement as if she were visiting Wonderland. She moved from room to room, grabbing each doorknob with both hands and rubbing at it vigorously.

"Mom, what are you doing?" I whispered to her as I watched her consistently perform this ritual.

"Well, this was his home, right?" Mom responded as if she was making perfect sense. "He had to have touched the doorknobs some time." I laughed and then reached out and rubbed my hands over the nearest doorknob, too. I'm rather surprised we didn't get thrown out. Mom and I behave sometimes like toddlers first learning about the world. I think a lot of people choose to overlook our somewhat obnoxious behavior. We were just excited to be at Graceland and honoring Elvis.

Mom's devotion to Elvis was eventually challenged when she discovered Josh Groban. At the age of sixty-eight, Mom became a "Grobanite." She continually played his music in the house, in the car, everywhere.

As proof of her devotion, one day, while we were sitting in the lobby of a Jiffy Lube somewhere in Georgia, waiting on an oil change, I started mindlessly flipping through an old issue of *People* magazine. Suddenly, I nudged Mom and held the magazine up to her. I had come across a full two-page article on Josh Groban. Mom grabbed the magazine with a bit of a scream and quickly read through the item.

"I want this!" she insisted. "Can I take it?" She looked around, over her shoulder, and then began to slowly tear the pages out.

"Mom," I stopped her. "Don't do that!"

She looked up at me with big wide eyes. I exhaled deeply. Alright. "Um, excuse me, sir," I called out to the mechanic standing behind the counter on the other side of the room. "Can she have this?" I held up the magazine and for a moment, he just stared at me.

"What...what does she want?" he finally asked.

"She wants these two pages out of this magazine. Can we tear them out?"

Again, he stared at us and then shrugged his shoulders. I took that for a yes and tore the pages from the magazine, handing them over to Mom. When the car was ready and we went up to the counter to pay, the mechanic asked us what had been so important. Mom showed him the pages and whispered in an awe-filled voice, "It's Josh Groban." The man said nothing but just rolled his eyes. Mom and I get that response a lot. Mom folded up the pages and stuck them in her wallet and that's where they stayed until the very last moment. I loved this romantic side of my mother. I wish her own marriage had fulfilled her dreams.

The words "I never wanted to marry your father" just suddenly popped out of her mouth as we were on our way to Nashville the next morning. Mom and Dad had meet through mutual friends. Mom just shook her head as she said, "If I had only known then. But, you know, people are usually nicer when they're out for fun. You don't really know someone until you live with them. I don't think we ever really fell in love." Mom gave a deep sigh. "I think we both just kind of looked at each other and thought, 'Yeah, well, that'll do.' I think we just kind of ended up together through a process of elimination."

On the day of her wedding, as Mom walked down the aisle, she looked at my dad…and believed she was making the biggest mistake of her life. She had wanted to cancel her wedding earlier but went through with the ceremony just to please her family, who saw Leslee Jean going nowhere with her life. She was already twenty-five years old, too old to remain single. Mom had felt obligated to agree to the wedding. Her family believed marriage would be the cure for her anxieties and depression. Instead, my mother would find herself locked in a loveless marriage that caused her to sink into deeper despair.

My mother's assertions about her wedding made me think of her engagement portrait. It was absolutely stunning. So stunning, in fact, that the photographer used copies of it in all of his advertisements, displays, and portfolios. Mom's dark hair is pulled back into a chignon at the nape of her neck. Her eyes are shining green-yellow with a tender excitement. Her shoulders are bare except for a pink, lace fluff that surrounds the front of her body. Her skin is pure and glowing with a young woman's blush. Did she have any premonitions at that moment of the sorrow, the heartache, she would soon experience?

As a child, I would gaze at the large framed portrait and wish I had known her then. I wish I had known my mother when she was a dreamer and had her whole life stretched out ahead of her. No, I only knew her as tired, broken, and lonely. I had seen her in her silent, contemplative movements. I had seen my mother bruised and broken from where my father had left her sprawled on the kitchen floor. I had seen my mother in her moments of depression, becoming catatonic and emotionless. I had watched as my mom's body grew older and the light began to dim from her green eyes. I only got to know her after my father had systematically broken down her spirit.

The resulting damage was obvious. Mom would soon lose what small amount of confidence she had when she entered this marriage. She would argue with a compliment, dismissing kindnesses with a wave of her hand and a shake of her head. She would decline to spend any money on herself, keeping just a meager wardrobe of two pairs of jeans and a few button-down work shirts. She refused to attend social events and hid in the bedroom whenever friends and relatives came to visit. She would continually put herself down, commenting on her own faults and weaknesses with a viciousness that could have been considered a hate crime.

I have often wondered what Mom's life would be like if she had been born in another place and time other than Kansas in 1933. When my father was away, my mother would sing around the house. She would smile then, look at me, and say, "I should have been a singer." She would make a great meal and declare, "I should have been a chef." She would move the furniture around the house and say, "I should have been a designer." She would talk a lot about "should have beens"… but never was. So, instead, she remained, for almost forty years, a sad wife to an angry man, raising a family that was fragmented, and moving around furniture to relieve her frustration.

My mother's humiliation continued to grow when she realized that she would never be the only woman in my father's life. Somewhere on highway 40 in Tennessee, she looked away from me and continued staring out the window as she stated, "The first time you realize there's another woman, you cry. Then you just get used to it." I wasn't surprised by her words. I remember my father being away from home at night. I remember the voices of strange women on the phone. It was difficult, though, to realize that my mother got used to abusive behavior. That's what she had accepted for herself.

I kept my eyes on the road now as I asked Mom, "Why did you stay?"

She shrugged her shoulders again and answered, "Where was I going to go? I didn't have any skills. How was I going to support my children? Besides, Dad always said if I left I would never see my children again. I didn't want to take that chance. Everybody was always threatening to take my children away."

My mother's words inspired a deeply buried memory to surface into my conscious brain. I struggled to keep my mind on the present moment but the recollection kept bobbing up like a floatation device. It couldn't save me, though. It would instead drag me down deeper.

One afternoon, when Mom took my sister, Carol, and me to have our eyes tested, we innocently informed the doctor about all the notes our teachers had been sending home for weeks because we were having trouble focusing on the chalkboards. After the exams, the doctor called my mother into his office for a private conversation. My sister and I sat together with Grandma Edith on the green plastic chairs in the waiting room, holding hands and staring at each other with wide eyes as we heard the doctor's loud angry voice reverberate from the inner office. Mother emerged a few minutes later with tears pouring down her twisted, horrified face. She quickly gathered us together and rushed us home. I would found out years later that the doctor had threatened to report Mom to Social Services for child neglect. Mom hadn't neglected us, though. She had been carefully saving up the money for our glasses from the meager grocery allowance Dad had given her every week. He had refused to give Mom any additional money because he was paying for an apartment for his current girlfriend. For weeks after the encounter with the optometrist, Mom lived in terror that Social Services would show up at our front door. It hurt to know my mother would continually suffer the fallout of my father's infidelities.

I couldn't imagine being trapped in my mother's situation. Feeling incredibly free and thankful, I studied the passing scenery as we traveled on to Nashville. Nothing, not my past, not my heritage, not my parentage, could hold me back. I was now free to live my own life the way I pleased. Now, I appreciated even more traveling through Tennessee. After years of living in the deserts of the Southwest, I was thankful, in so many ways, for the lush foliage rolling passed my car window.

The highway to Nashville is littered with billboards advertising all kinds of attractions, from two headed snakes to the Grand Ole Opry. Mom and I read every road sign and debated about where to stop. My mother's excitement energized me. I watched the enthusiasm that glowed on her face and thought of her engagement portrait, which remained forever fresh and tender, the hope refusing to be extinguished. I knew, in some area of her brain, she was still that dreamy young woman.

Everywhere we went, Mom made souvenirs out of everything she touched. Brochures and flyers, restaurant napkins and placemats all found their way into her purse, which was bulging open by the time we made it to Nashville by nightfall.

The next day, we explored Nashville on foot. Or we tried to. Mom and I had asked at the front desk of our hotel about the Grand Ole Opry. We really wanted to see it, to walk on the stage, to know what had been home to Loretta Lynn and the great Patsy Cline.

I asked at the front desk where the theater was and the clerk waved her hand. "Oh, honey, you are close to it. You can walk there." Mom and I stared at each other. We can walk there? Sure, why not.... that would be fun!

We started out walking in the direction that the front desk clerk had pointed out to us. We walked...and walked..and walked...Okay, something was wrong. Where the heck were we? We had started out walking down a wide sidewalk in front of the hotel before coming to a busy highway. Next thing I actually remember is that it was an hour or two later, and we were contemplating climbing a chain linked barrier that was suddenly blocking our path. We stood for a moment staring through the diamond shaped openings in the fence. Okay, this simply could not be right. We stared at each other for a moment before Mom pointed to the left. "Let's go this way," she stated. Why? Because it was the only way not blocked by the fence! We walked through a field for several more minutes until I noticed that Mom looked like she was about to keel over. Sweat poured down her face and she was huffing a little heavier.

"Mom, are you okay?" I asked cautiously.

She just looked at me and stated, "Where are we?"

I shrugged my shoulders and before I could honestly admit that I had no idea, I suddenly noticed Mom was gazing off in the distance. "A bus," she whispered quietly as if she had just seen a religious image.

"What?" I whispered back as I looked around and saw nothing. I reacted as if Mom was seeing a mirage from walking through the desert for days without water.

"There," she pointed in the opposite direction. "A bus! C'mon!" She took off across the field, running so fast her small body was a blur in front of my eyes. She waved her arms and hollered for the bus to stop. I raced behind her waving my arms exactly as Mom was doing, my voice blending with hers as we shouted and hollered. "We're lost," I heard Mom screaming out. "Please stop. We are so lost." As her words floated back to me, I saw the bus begin to move slowly away.

Mom found a burst of speed from somewhere in her tiny body. I was reminded of all of those stories about petite women pulling Buicks off of small children trapped underneath. Mom literally was going to stop a moving bus...and she did it! As I was still dragging my tired body across the center of the field, Mom was now standing directly in the path of the progressing bus, forcing it to slow down and come to a full complete stop.

"Jamie, c'mon!" she screamed to me as she raced to the bus's now opened door. "We're looking for the Grand Ole Opry," Mom announced to the driver.

He glanced at Mom, taking in her sweaty face and labored breathing, before looking up and watching me pull myself the last few steps out of the field. He laughed then and said, "The old one or the new one?" Mom stared at him in surprise, totally speechless. The bus driver, a large man with a beautiful smile and gorgeous deep brown eyes, chuckled for a moment and then said, "Get in. I'll take you there." Mom took my hand and together we climbed up onto the bus.

Mom and I were the only two people in the vehicle. The driver went on to explain, "I just got off duty, but don't ya all worry about it. I'll get ya there. You're only about a mile or two away." He drove us down the street and right to the front door of the Grand Ole Opry. He refused any payment from us. "Don't worry about it," he told us. "Just have some fun."

Mom and I thanked him profusely and stepped off the bus and up to the door of the building. The Opry was closed, but we stood outside peering through the dark windows, our noses leaving gentle smudges against the glass. We took turns posing for pictures against the outside banners that featured all of the illustrious singers like the great Patsy, Loretta, Willie, and Dolly.

I love music. It is a form of communication that fascinates me. Growing up, I couldn't talk but I loved to sing. My inability to verbally express myself caused me to become fascinated with all kinds of communication. I am continually awestruck by art, books, dance, music. When life is hard, I learned to create beauty on my own, to design a reason to stay alive. Mom and I felt a new energy engulf us as we walked around the Grand Ole Opry and Opryland for most of the afternoon before calling a cab to go back to the hotel where we crashed into a deep sleep.

The next morning, the front desk clerk chatted happily with us as we checked out. "So, did you all get to see the Opry?"

"Oh, yes," Mom answered and then told her how lovely it was. As Mom went on to describe it, the clerk looked at us in surprise. "Oh, so you went all the way out to Opryland!" she exclaimed.

"Well, yes," Mom answered, "and we were a little surprised that it seemed like we were walking for miles. You told us it was close by."

"Right," the desk clerk answered. "You should have gone to the Ryman Theater. Not all the way out to Opryland." She tried to keep the laughter out of her voice when she saw the confused looks on our faces. Mom and I look that way a lot lately. "There are two Grand Ole Opries actually. The one you must have gone to is the brand new one. It was built a few years ago along with the hotel, mall, and amusement park. The Ryman is the historic theater where the Opry originated. All the greats played there....Wait! Don't tell me you walked all the way out to Opryland when the Ryman is right down the street?" Okay, we weren't going to tell her but the reddening of our faces and the hanging of our heads gave us away. The clerk laughed, "My goodness, how did you miss the Ryman? It's the big red building right down the street."

Mom and I had walked right by it and didn't pay any attention. What exactly had we been expecting? I don't know. But the thought that we could have been at the Ryman in ten minutes instead of going on a two-hour walking odyssey to Opryland made us both feel a little queasy.

Mom and I were silent as we climbed back into the truck and didn't say anything until we drove past the Ryman which suddenly caused us both to talk at the same time. "There it is. Why didn't we see it before? What were we thinking? Should have known, man, should have known." And then we were silent again as we drove out of Nashville.

We finally came to rest in Sevierville, Tennessee, at the Landmark Hotel which sits right on the banks of the Mississippi River. Mom and I checked in and went up to our room. Usually, the first thing Mom looks for when entering a hotel room is a coffee pot. She loves to have her coffee early in the morning (about four am!) and will sometimes get completely dressed just to go to the lobby for coffee. She doesn't like to be seen anywhere with no make-up or her hair undone. That never bothers me. I walk around everywhere all the time in my sweats or pjs. I don't care what people think.

This time, however, when we entered the hotel room, Mom walked right past the coffee maker and headed to a door cut into the back wall. "What is this door for?" she asked me.

"Probably a closet," I answered with a shrug of my shoulders. I followed her to the back of the room as she flung open the door. Suddenly, we found ourselves on a white, wooden balcony overlooking the river. We looked out at the trees, the water, and the ducks. There were ducks everywhere, quacking and waddling all over the bank. Mom and I spent the evening sitting on the balcony watching the sunset and, like the other hotel guests, feeding the ducks bits of chips and bread.

As Mom and I watched the small, playful ducks, we were shocked when one of them started to bark. One fluffy white duck that stood amid all the other fowl began to growl like a dog. I grabbed Mom's arm and pointed it out to her. "Do you hear that? The barking is coming from that duck!" As the duck continued to howl, all the other ducks turned in unison and literally began to march towards their boisterous commander. When they were all crowded together in a massive circle, the ducks suddenly turned as one body and began to march off the bank and into the river. No sooner did the last duck put his little webbed foot into the water, Mom and I spotted a woman walking a German Shepherd along the banks. As soon as the woman and the dog passed by, all of the ducks began to waddle out of the water and calmly move back to their places on the riverside. Mom and I just stared at each other in surprise for a moment before we started to laugh. What an incredible display of animal intelligence and intuition.

We stayed at the Landmark for two days and the ducks continued to be our main source of entertainment. One evening, someone had put out several large watermelons for the ducks to enjoy. They loved it! They couldn't get enough of it! The ducks tore into the fruit, their sharp beaks smacking against the rind as they gobbled it up. They were still eating when Mom and I finally went in to bed.

The next morning before we left the hotel, we decided to have a quick cup of coffee on the balcony. We stepped out the back door, looked down at the ducks...and couldn't believe what we were seeing. Watermelon rind was all over the bank. The fruit had been completely demolished. The ducks, who had been so lively and active, now seemed unable to move. They had eaten so much of the watermelon the night before they were lying around on the embankment, most of them on their backs with their bellies extended, their little tongues lolling out to one side of their mouths, unable to get up. Their white feathers seemed ruffled and wrapped around their small bodies like crumpled bed sheets. It looked like the aftermath of a duck toga party! Some of the ducks would roll over and struggle up to their feet, take a few waddles, and then tumble back over again on to their backs. The ducks had overindulged on the fruit the night before and were now stumbling around as if they were having watermelon hangovers.

Mom and I finally told the ducks goodbye and continued on our journey. That morning found us driving through the Great Smokey Mountains which are part of the Appalachian mountain chain that runs along the Tennessee and North Carolina border. The name "Smokey" comes from the natural fog that covers the mountains and looks like smoke from a distance. Was it smoke, fog, or a fresh breath of exhaled air on a chilly autumn morning? The peaks were so green and alive, I could actually feel them breathing. I studied the landscape and I felt myself breath deep and full and easy, too. I was enjoying moving carefree through the mountain passes. I felt so free as I swung around the trails...

"Stop!" I suddenly heard Mom scream. "Stop!"

"Mom, what is it?" I asked concerned. I glanced over to the right to see Mom leaning slightly forward with her head in her hands.

"I'm sick," Mom groaned. Oh, man, I had forgotten that Mom always had problems with an inner ear disturbance due to a busted eardrum she suffered when she was hit in the head with a baseball bat as a teenager. Mom never told me any more details than that. Even though I don't know exactly what happened, I had seen the results. Mom would suffer migraines and vertigo for most of her life. She would suddenly become dizzy and lose her balance. She has never been able to fly and can get sick in any fast moving vehicle. Weaving around the peak trails made her feel a little queasy. I would have pulled over but couldn't find a convenient place to stop. Mom gripped the door handle as we continued slowly now around the trails, hanging on until we finally made it down out of the mountains. She seemed to calm down when we hit Gatlinburg and then relaxed when we stopped for the night in Ashville, North Carolina.

Leaving Ashville the next day, I wasn't in the greatest of moods. Maybe I was just tired or maybe I was just feeling overwhelmed. Maybe I was feeling uncomfortable from hearing Mom's stories yesterday. Maybe I was feeling guilty because I thought it was my fault Mom became sick as we drove through the Smokey Mountains. I had been thoughtlessly having fun careening around the curves and dips of the mountain roads. My dark mood grew worse when I got lost trying to find the highway that would lead us through North and South Carolina and then into Georgia.

Several hours later, I began to breathe a little easier when we suddenly found ourselves in Jonesboro, Georgia, which was not our original destination. We didn't even know such a place existed. We were shooting for Atlanta. We wanted to see the CNN building and take the *Gone with the Wind* tour.

Mom and I both loved *Gone with the Wind*. When I was about seven years old, Mom took my sisters and me to a revival showing of the classic film at our local movie theater. Did I love this masterpiece the first time I saw it? No, I hated it! Twenty minutes into the film, I was restless and bored. Several times, I turned in my seat to look at Mom and demand, "When is this going to be *over?*" Mom always took my siblings and me to see a lot of big movies like *My Fair Lady* and *Thoroughly Modern Millie*. I was always thrilled to see glamorous people up on the screen suddenly breaking into song and dancing spontaneously. I lived in a fantasy world anyway, so this made perfect sense to me. But *Gone with the Wind* just lost me right from the beginning. I begged continually throughout the film (almost all three hours of it) to be taken home. Mom made me stay and I cried and whined all the way through the burning of Atlanta. It wasn't until years later, during my rebellious stage, when I was reading all of the classic books by great authors like Pearl Buck and Harper Lee that I finally turned my full attention to *Gone With the Wind*. I read the sweeping novel and was totally captivated by it. The book thrilled me and then I watched the movie three or four times, cherishing every minute. I guess I just needed to be a little more mature to appreciate Margaret Mitchell's amazing ability to tell a story. So the *Gone with the Wind* tour in Atlanta had been at the top of our list of things to do when we first started out on our southern adventure.

There was one big problem. We had found ourselves trapped in a huge traffic jam just a few miles away from our destination. The problem was not just the heavy traffic but several highway lanes were closed due to construction. Mom and I slowly moved with the traffic but we couldn't get to our exit. We flashed our blinkers, waved our arms out the windows, cried, screamed, cussed, and prayed, but the other vehicles fell into line like bricks in a wall blocking our way off the highway, which was bumper to bumper and guard rail to guard rail full of cars. We just couldn't move. We actually looped around Atlanta four times and just could not get to the exit we needed. We circled Atlanta as if we were in some endless holding pattern. Finally, when we were rounding the city for the fifth time, we gave up and took the first open exit we could access to get off of the lost highway of Atlanta, Georgia. We found ourselves heading south on highway 75 to Jonesboro where we finally stopped for the night.

Gone with the Wind is set partly in Jonesboro, and Mom and I were pleased to see how celebrated the book was here. The next morning, we decided to take advantage of where we had happened to land and went on the Margaret Mitchell tour. The women leading the tour were dressed in costumes from the late 1800s and proudly embraced the fact that Mitchell was born in Jonesboro as they showed us everything from Mitchell's childhood playhouse to the public train she rode to get around town. So, even though we didn't make it into Atlanta, we fell in love with the little town of Jonesboro. In fact, Mom and I found almost all of the towns in Georgia enchanting.

Mom especially loved Savannah, Georgia, so much she was ready to fight for it. One morning, as we stepped out of the hotel, Mom noticed a young man hard at work landscaping the front lawn. Mom smiled sweetly at him and energetically said, "Good morning. This is such a beautiful place."

The man looked at Mom as if she was crazy and then stated, "It's hot and it stinks!"

Mom was horrified and turned to look at him with her hands balling up into tight little fist. My nearly five foot tall mother was about to take on a man well over six foot in a battle over how beautiful Savannah, Georgia, is. Oh, the poor man. He had no idea the terror he had just unleashed and the tongue-lashing he was about to receive. As I pulled Mom away, she sputtered about how shocked she was that somebody did not find Savannah enchanting.

We continued walking down the street staring at the moss on the trees in the squares. The best part was visiting the small shops that lined the pier. All of the little shops served decadent foods like rich ice creams, caramel corn, and pralines. We ate so many free samples as we stumbled from shop to shop that we didn't even have dinner that night. We waddled along the pier feeling just like a pair of ducks after eating way too much watermelon. Mom and I weaved our way around the port before stumbling back to the hotel. I was exhausted but too terrified to sleep.

When Mom and I first rolled into Savannah, we had stopped at a local gas station where I bought a map of the city. We were amused to see that the road map was decorated with little ghosts. Each ghost represented every location in the municipality that had experienced a haunting. When we checked into our hotel, Mom mentioned this to the front desk clerk. He laughed and told us that Savannah is considered the most haunted city in America. "We've even had several guests report ghost sightings in this hotel," he explained to us. "We've had the paranormal experts out here three times now."

Mom was absolutely delighted with this news. She ran ahead of me down the hallway, hid in doorways and around corners, and jumped out at me as I approached. Every time, I would scream, throw the luggage, and run in the opposite direction before pulling myself back together and continuing down the hallway to our room. I'm very sensitive to supernatural happenings and have had visions of angels, healing experiences, and spiritual encounters. Though I would come to greatly appreciate it years later, at this time in my life, it was completely overwhelming and I was still figuring out how to deal with it all. My constant pleadings to Mom to knock it off didn't stop her. She jumped out at me when I opened the door to the hotel room, when I came out of the bathroom, when I rolled over in bed. She wouldn't stop and I was kept in a constant state of terror until we finally left for Florida two days later.

One of the first places Mom and I wanted to go when we arrived in Florida was to the beach. At this time, I had not seen either ocean before and was excited to see the Atlantic. I was totally unprepared, though. I hadn't brought any shorts or a swimsuit with me. I think I was the only person (except Mom) on the beach in jeans, t-shirt, and tennis shoes.

I don't know why I was so totally unprepared. Well, yes, actually I do. I have to stop being so anxious and excited about traveling and moving and exploring and discovering. My excitement tends to make me not think rationally about the things of this world. My experiences and wanderings cause me to make myself different. I cry sometimes for not fitting in and yet know that I go out of my way to make myself unique.

So while everyone else was running around in skimpy swimwear and bronze dark skin, I sat on the beach fully dressed and wearing a baseball cap to block the sun off of the pure, white skin of my face. It didn't matter to me. I didn't want to miss this experience.

I kicked off my shoes, rolled up my jeans, stood up, and walked out to the ocean. I stood there, letting the cool water lap at my legs and felt the slimy muddy sand between my toes. The whole situation seemed so surreal to me. Just last week, I had gone out to lunch with my friend, Laurie, in New Mexico. Afterwards we walked along the banks of the Rio Grande for a while before kicking off our shoes and wading into the cool water. We gathered stones and splashed around for a while. And now, here I was. How did I get from the Rio Grande to the Atlantic Ocean in such a short time, just a matter of days? But most of my life has been that way, full of unexpected surprises and coincidences

I looked out at the ocean now and felt myself grow small and tender. I felt my body being swayed back and forth, the swell almost rolling me off my feet. I felt my body was easily forgotten in the wake of the waves…and yet my spirit felt as endless as the ocean, as wide as the sky, and I knew there was no horizon where my spirit ended and the world began. Yes, so that's how I could have been walking in the Rio Grande just last week and having my feet washed by the waves of the Atlantic Ocean today.

It was during the journey through Florida that I felt connected to everything and everyone in the Universe. The ocean was just one part of this overall union. I found myself feeling at one with the sky, the road, the scenery, and the other travelers. One of the best things about being on the road is the sudden friendships that develop with the other drivers even if it is just for a few miles. Traveling across the panhandle of Florida, Mom and I built a friendly relationship with another traveling family. Oh, we didn't know their names. We never even talked to them. We just would smile and wave at each other out of the car windows. It started when a teenage boy waved to us from the left rear window of the crowded station wagon. We waved back and I felt safe traveling with our new friends until they finally exited the highway about two hours later. It was comfortable and relaxing to feel like we had friends on the road. There was a connection even though Mom and I had no idea who they were.

Not all drivers in the south were friendly. As we traveled through Florida, Mom began to play her "conspiracy game" again with a truck driver who suddenly seemed to take Mom's innocent diversion a little too seriously. As we passed the semi on the left side of the two-lane highway, the driver became annoyed with Mom who was pumping her arm out the window trying to get him to blow his horn. When we pulled back into the right lane, the semi suddenly pulled to the left and sped past us, sailing back in front of us with just a few inches to spare.

"Go around him," Mom insisted.

"Mom, no, let's just stay behind him," I said as I followed him in the right lane. And then the trucker slowed down…way down to where we were traveling at a crawl. So I moved my pickup into the left lane and began to pull up around the semi. The semi began to speed up, refusing to let me pass. As Mom hooted, cheered, pounded on the ceiling, and stomped the floorboards, I increased my speed in an effort to zoom passed the semi. I was just beginning to pull ahead when I noticed something. Oh, man! Blue and red flashing lights in my rearview mirror!

"We have a cop behind us. Mom, we have a cop behind us!"

Mom was cheering so loud, she didn't seem to hear. She suddenly stopped her commotion when she realized I was slowing down. "Let's go," she hollered to me.

"Mom, there's a cop behind me! How fast was I going? Oh, my gosh, I'm going to get a ticket! I've never had a speeding ticket before… Oh, my gosh…"

"Just pull over...pull over," Mom started screaming at me.

Thankfully, the truck had slowed way down. I scooted over in front of him into the right hand lane, got a few feet ahead, and then pulled over to the side of the road. I took a deep breath, glanced back, and saw the semi traveling down the road towards us. "Where is he?" I shouted to Mom. "The cop? Where is he?" I could only see the semi coming towards us. "The cop, Mom? Where did he go?" I was turned to look behind me as the semi now moved away from us down the highway.

Mom suddenly grabbed my arm. "There he is!" she hollered. "Look there!" I turned back around to see the cop car now on the left hand side of the semi, flagging down the driver. "He wasn't after us! He went after the truck! Woo-hoo!" she hollered out.

I started laughing. "We're safe. We really are safe! The cop was after the truck! He didn't want us!" Mom and I hollered and danced in our seats for a moment before I started up the pickup again and pulled out onto the highway. Around a bend, we suddenly came upon the semi on the side of the road. The police officer and truck driver were standing just outside of the cab of the semi. Mom couldn't resist. She leaned out the passenger window. "Hey," she hollered, "hello..." and as we drove past, she pumped her arm in the air a few more times before throwing a few kisses.

"Mom, stop," I warned her, but we were both proud of our victory. Mom did, however, agree to tone down her efforts in the Trucker Wars after that event.

There was another battle in Florida, though, fought long before we had arrived, that made us both feel uncomfortable and hopeless. I convinced Mom to stop at one of the Civil War Battle Sites. Mom didn't really want to stop at Olustee. I think she was a little worried about what we were actually going to encounter. I convinced her that we had to see at least one battlefield since we were both very interested in the Civil War. We parked in the dirt parking lot and started across the field. The landscape looked like a scene from historical movies about the Civil War that I had seen before. I looked around at the wide-open ground with just straight, painfully thin, white trees scattered around. The thin barren landscape would have provided very little shelter. I could imagine soldiers marching around the trees, trees that offered meager refuge from the enemy. I shuddered as I walked forward because, oh, my gosh…the ground… every step I took…oh, man…it felt like I was…

"I feel like I'm walking on blood," Mom suddenly spoke, her voice echoing gently around us. Her words caused me to freeze in my steps. My gosh, that is exactly what I had been thinking! That very statement had flashed through my mind before Mom had spoken out loud in the gentle stillness. I was amazed that we had had the very same thought at the very same moment. But even more amazing was the ground. I don't know how to explain it. It is rather beyond description. The ground was a grayish ash color. It didn't look solid. It did not feel firm. It felt soft and squishy as if saturated with fluid, a thick fluid, like blood. The sensation was overwhelming and mind-blowing. Mom and I stared at each other for a moment in silence before turning around as if we shared the same thought again and had the same body. We literally raced back to the pickup. We drove out of the parking lot and headed back to the highway, not speaking at all, both of us contemplating what had just happened. It was a few miles before we could begin to talk again.

Subdued, Mom and I rolled into Alabama. We decided to stop at the Ave Maria Gardens, hoping that walking through the grotto would wash away the grief of the battlefield. Known as "Jerusalem in Miniature," the grotto displays 125 miniature replicas of well-known historical landmarks created by Brother Joseph Zoettl. Mom and I roamed through the grotto looking at the beautiful reproductions of cathedrals and basilicas. We ended our tour in the small gift shop.

As we were looking around the store, I noticed a vehicle pulling up in the parking lot. The bus was decorated with the name of a local school for handicapped adults. Several of the people coming off the bus were in wheelchairs; others were being guided by attendants who led them into the shop. I was standing on the opposite side of the room, across from the front door, Mom, and the handicapped adults. One of them was a middle-aged man. He was extremely tall, well over six feet, and very thin. He wore jeans, a red windbreaker, and a blue baseball cap. He lumbered towards Mom and loomed over her. My tiny mother only came up to the middle of his chest. She had to crank her head back on her neck to look up at his face as he stood before her. Nervously, I started towards them, and felt a slight panic as the man suddenly lifted his hand, gently laid it on Mom's shoulder, and stared into her eyes. Then he peacefully said, "God bless you, my child." He pulled his hand away then and lumbered off with the rest of his party. I finally made it over to Mom's side where she stood looking stunned. She didn't move at all; she just stood staring straight ahead.

"Mom? Mom, are you okay?" I asked as I touched her arm gently.

She turned slowly around to look at me. "Did you see his eyes?" she asked me. "They were glowing. They were so golden." Then she smiled a slow sweet smile. "I was just touched by an angel," she whispered.

We didn't talk at all as we walked outside, climbed into the truck, and drove away from the grotto. Mom seemed lost in the experience for a while. I don't really know what exactly happened, but Mom was quiet and serene as she leaned back in her seat, just watching the scenery roll by as we headed towards Mississippi.

Mississippi was a fun state for us. We stumbled onto a lot of entertaining places. That's the excitement of driving—we can watch the passing scenery, looking for signs of interesting things to see, and stop when we want to have some fun. That's how we stumbled into Tupelo. We saw a highway sign advertising the boyhood home of Elvis. Well, of course, we had to stop. We pulled off the highway and traveled through a few side residential streets until we came to the corner where the small white house was located. It was an adorable two-room home that had been built by Elvis's father, Vernon, in

1935, just before Elvis was born. Mom and I joked that we could have happily lived in this house if only it had a bathroom. I don't need a big home myself. I liked the comfort and coziness of this tiny house.

After talking to the docent for a few minutes, Mom and I walked around the yard for a while. Mom was in her element. She danced on the lawn and then posed for pictures with the bronze statue of Elvis as an eight-year-old boy. She laughed and talked and played, a completely free spirit. I don't know if her joyfulness came from believing she had just been touched by an angel, if she was thrilled to be in Elvis' home, or if she had just never felt so much freedom before. I actually was pleased to notice a real change in Mom as we traveled.

My mother always hated to have her picture taken. She was very introverted and wasn't very social. She always felt that she wasn't good enough or pretty enough or special enough. She was completely different on the road with me. She talked to everyone, argued with truckers, danced in the streets, and posed for pictures in every place we stopped. I have more photos of my mom during our travels together than I have over any other period of her life. Mom was finally allowing herself to have a good time. I loved this playful side of my mother, which I saw occasionally in my childhood. I wish there had been more moments of reckless abandonment in our home. The fun moments we did share, however, were precious. Now, I began to treasure this trip with my mother and happily snapped pictures to commemorate the moment when my mother gave herself permission to be happy.

Mom had a great time in Tunica, Mississippi, as well. She loves casinos and often plays the slots at the casino boats in Kansas City, Missouri. My parents used to bet who could win the most money while gambling. My mother and father were fierce competitors. Like me, Mom just needed to prove that she could be good at something. For most of her life, she always felt that she had something to prove. Though she never won any substantially large jackpots, just winning a few dollars made Mom feel a little more confident.

Mom was excited to stop in Tunica, which is known as the Las

Vegas of the South. We walked into the Hollywood Casino which I was excited to see. I don't gamble. I find it rather boring. I'm fascinated, however, by bright lights and exotic design. Usually, while family and friends play, I just walk around, sipping a soda, and people-watch. The Hollywood Casino, which displayed scenes and props from many different movies, seemed fascinating. I really tried to enjoy it, but I ran into a problem right from the start.

Mom and I walked in the front door and found ourselves suddenly standing in front of a full scale, lifelike replica of the Titanic standing on its end; its bow down in the water and its stern up in the air. Way up in the air. The model was huge. I had seen James Cameron's *Titanic* and recognized this model as the scene where the boat was standing on one end and people were sliding down the deck and into the water.

I stared at the ship in total alarm and horror. My heart started pounding so hard I thought it was going to tear itself right through its protective tissue. I started sweating profusely. My knees shook so hard, I thought I was going to stumble off my feet. I felt my chest constrict and I couldn't breathe. My stomach lurched and I thought I was going to be sick. I don't know why the replica upset me the way it did. I was attracted and horrified at the same time.

There was something about the size and shape of that replica that caused such anxiety inside of me I couldn't control myself. I was launched into the fight or flight response the minute I saw it. While Mom played some of the machines, I stayed in the bathroom, sitting on the floor, and crying. Thankfully, we didn't stay long. I finally calmed down again when we were back on the highway. I have always been a big believer in reincarnation and wondered for a moment if there was some connection. Maybe I'm just being romantic. Maybe I just connected to some childhood trauma. But either way, I was relieved to be driving away from Tunica and heading towards Louisiana.

As we turned towards New Orleans, my nervous system was finally cooling down as Mom's began to heat up. Now, she was on edge and very unnerved. Her anxiety level was beginning to zoom out of control. She had been peaceful until we approached the bridges that would carry us over the Gulf of Mexico. The bridges over the Gulf were not very high and as we crossed them, over what seemed like many miles, water from the Gulf swelled up, splashed against our truck and pushed us from side to side. It didn't help that the bridges were crowded with traffic, which was very thick and jammed up for miles. We finally found the cause of the situation after we slowly traveled forward a few more feet. There, on a small narrow strip on the side of the bridge, four young adults were frantically waving their arms and trying to get help. Their whole car was completely engulfed in flames. Fire was burning from the inside of the car that sat forlornly on the shoulder of the bridge, and, unfortunately, the fire trucks had to fight through the traffic to get to it. Mom and I prayed as we drove by hoping everyone was safe. It was a dangerous location for this to happen. It took us about an hour before we finally were able to leave the Gulf bridges behind.

From the moment we drove into Baton Rouge, we became hopelessly, impossibly lost. We had been lucky until this point. Yes, we had been lost before, but eventually found our way. Baton Rouge was really the only place where we became so inexplicably off course that we were both in tears and screaming at each other, the traffic, and life in general. Mom and I always wanted to be off the road before dark. But now, we rolled into Baton Rouge after nine o'clock and desperately looked around for some place to stay. We had no idea where we were and we didn't know where to go. We couldn't find a hotel anywhere and the traffic again was thick and heavy. I began to panic and Mom, at first, told me to relax, be nice. I was only making things worse. Then she told me to watch my mouth as I yelled rudely at the other drivers. I asked them to get over, move aside, go faster, get out of the way. Okay, honestly, that is putting it nicely. Instead, I cussed and screamed. I was exhausted and frustrated. I couldn't wait to find a place to stop. To make it worse, a gentle rain began to fall. At times like this, I am much better traveling alone. I would just pull off the road and sleep in my truck. I drive late at night. I drive in the rain or tornadoes. I don't care where I am or what may happen when I travel alone. But now, I had Mom with me and I didn't want to cause any problems for her. I was nervous with Mom in the car. I wanted to make sure that she was safe. I couldn't just keep driving around aimlessly with Mom sitting right beside me.

Finally, up ahead, what is that? At last, a hotel! I don't remember the name of the place. I just remember what it looked like. It was a very beautiful, pleasant, clean hotel with a wide-open lobby that was decorated with brass and gold. We walked up to the front desk and asked for a room. They had only one still available. As Mom started to fill out the registration slip, I just casually happened to ask how much it was for the night. Um, what was that...$400?!? Mom and I left the lobby, climbed back into my truck, and headed to the opposite side of town where the front desk clerk had assured us we would find a Super 8 hotel.

I was back to swearing and cussing, and apologizing to my mother out of the corner of my mouth because of my language. She was silent for a while until she finally shouted, "There, up ahead, there it is, the Super 8!"

Then, as I tried to pull into the lane to get to the hotel but couldn't because of traffic, I suddenly heard Mom scream out, "Move your stupid ass!" at the car next to us. She continued to cuss until we pulled over to the left and I heard the other driver honk loudly as I cut him off. And suddenly, Mom said it, the phrase I had only heard my father use up to that point. "Blow it out your ass!" I didn't even turn to look at Mom. I stayed focused on the hotel like a teleological missile until we finally pulled into the parking lot. We had made it.

As was our usual routine, Mom went to bed early as I sat on the floor in the bathroom and read until I was so tired I was falling asleep with my nose in the book. We were usually up and back on the road by five in the morning at the latest. Leaving Baton Rouge was no different. We got up the next morning, bouncing out of bed with boundless energy, the nightmare of being lost the night before well behind us. I showered and dressed quickly, slipped back into my jeans from the night before and a clean, but not very fresh, shirt from my backpack. We drove away from the hotel and went next door to the gas station where we filled up the tank before deciding that we should also go inside and grab some food for breakfast. I walked around the convenience store, anticipating all of the best road trip foods... cookies, cupcakes, doughnuts. However, I roamed the brightly lit shop and didn't find anything overly tempting. As I walked an aisle I had been down previously, I happened to notice something on the floor. It was a soft piece of black cloth that looked rumpled and dirty. Mom came up beside me. "I don't really see anything very appetizing."

"No," I agreed. "It is kind of nasty in here, too. Look, there's something on the floor down there." I nodded down the aisle.

"What is that?" Mom asked as she walked over to the piece of cloth and nudged it with her foot. "It's a sock."

"A sock!" I echoed and wandered over to look. "Why would there be a dirty old sock in the middle of the store?" I asked her with a disgusted shake of my head. A sock! A sock? It looked like one of my socks...Oh my gosh, it was one of my socks! How could I have left a sock in the middle of the...and then I began to realize something. I had yanked off my jeans last night so exhausted I wasn't paying any attention. My socks had become tangled in the legs of my jeans but I didn't care. I had just swept off my socks when I had pulled off my jeans. I hadn't really thought about it but when I put on my jeans this morning, they felt a little bit uncomfortable. This sock must have still been in my jeans and had fallen out of my wide pant leg as I had walked down that aisle.

I was really embarrassed as I realized the store was becoming a little more crowded with people coming in for coffee as they were heading off to work. I didn't want to pick up my sock in front of everyone, so I began to slowly nudge it down the aisle until I had slide it into a position around the end of the row where I could bend down to pick it up without being noticed. Good, I didn't think anyone saw me as I scooped up the sock and stuck it in my pocket...and suddenly I looked up and caught Mom's eye as she was standing at the front of the store. She started laughing as she said to the clerk, "She lost her sock! Isn't that cute? She lost her sock in the middle of your store." Then suddenly, people standing in line at the counter began to chuckle. Mom turned to them. "She lost her sock," she said to the gathering crowd. "Well, that's just like when she was three-years-old, and we were in the old K-mart store in Kansas and she had to go to the bathroom..."

Horrified, I stalked out the front door and to the parking lot as Mom continued to hold a captivated audience at my expense. I climbed into the truck and slouched down in my seat, hoping not to be recognized. When Mom finally climbed into the truck about fifteen minutes later, I started it up and headed for the highway without saying a word. Mom was laughing so hard, though, I don't think she even noticed. Instead, she continued telling stories about my childhood that she thought were "so cute" but continued to cause me discomfort. She continued to talk and laugh as we rolled into New Orleans.

Thankfully, New Orleans changed my mood and I found myself beginning to smile. Mom was amazed by the cemeteries where all the crypts rested above ground. This is necessary because the water is so close to the surface, strong rains could wash up the caskets. Street performers, singers and dancers, mimes and jugglers lined the brick cobbled roadways. Always fascinated by architecture, I loved walking through the French quarter and seeing the baroque designs of the buildings.

Mom and I wandered through the open-air markets looking at the large straw bins of beads, spices, fruits, voodoo dolls, and local crafts that were for sale. As we casually strolled down one aisle, we were almost knocked to the ground by three large Caucasian women who were racing around us to one of the big straw voodoo doll baskets. They vigorously began to dig through the dolls until one of the women triumphantly held a small doll up in her hands. "Look, look," she called to the others. "This one looks like Momma!" The women passed the doll back and forth, examining it carefully to decide if it did indeed have their momma's features. Mom turned to look at me. "Don't even think about it," she warned. Of course, I couldn't imagine what it would be like to want to put a curse on my own mother. I tried not to obviously stare at the women as I wondered what their childhoods could have been like if they had the desire to torture their own mother. Did their mother tell stories about them in crowded convenience stores, too?

After our stay in New Orleans, Mom and I traveled north, stopping at a few plantations along the way. We didn't, however, make as many stops as we had before as we traveled through Louisiana, Arkansas, and Oklahoma. After seven weeks on the road, we were exhausted and decided it was time to head back to Kansas.

It was in Oklahoma, however, where my pickup truck received its authorized name. We were rolling through the gorgeous countryside when I just happened to pat the dashboard of my pickup truck lovingly. I was proud that the truck had carried us so far without a single problem. While showing the truck some love, I just happened to say, "Roll on, little doggie." It was a strange thing to say and I had no idea why the thought had even entered my mind. It made Mom laugh, though. From that moment on, the truck was forever known as Dog or Doggie. I guess it was official. She was now part of the Zunick family. We were known for naming our vehicles.

I was bombarded by memories as we drove through Lawrence, Kansas. I had been away from home for a really long time. It felt strange being back. Everything was so familiar and so different at the same time. This is what I miss the most by traveling around so much. I miss the sense of community, the sense of home and familiarity, the putting down of roots that people feel when they stay in the place of their childhoods. I don't know if that is a situation I will ever experience.

I crave adventure, change, and exploration. I do miss the familiar, the sense of home, the connection to the past, and witnessing the growth and changes in the lives of family and friends. I sometimes wonder what it would be like to be born, to grow, to carve out a life, and be buried all in the same town. I wonder what it is like to be somewhere where family and friends will visit you both when you are alive and when you are not. What is it like to be somewhere where you are so familiar with the world around you? I have no clue right now where I will be when I eventually die, who will be around, who will make the arrangements, who will visit my grave...

I shook the thought away. For now, Mom and I were back in Kansas, finally back home...until the next morning.

CHAPTER 5

When I travel by myself, I take chances. I fearlessly sail down the highways, zooming in and out of traffic with the stereo blaring. I have driven bravely through tornadoes, rain, snow, and dust storms. However, with Mom in the car with me, I was much more careful. I stayed in one lane, watched my speed, and turned down the music. I was protecting her. I didn't want to do anything to cause Mom injury or pain on our journeys. Mom, of course, had only one complaint about my driving. She claimed I was too cautious. She would urge me to go a little faster and move around slower traffic. I would just grip the wheel tighter and keep my eyes on the road.

This is what it was like traveling with my mom. We had decided that I would do the driving while she continually checked the maps and made sure we were headed in the right direction. However, I didn't find out until we had been on the road for a while that Mom didn't really care where we were going.

For instance, traveling west on Interstate 40 (it could have been any highway actually), I see an exit coming up for a highway heading north. "Mom," I would ask casually, "is this the exit we need?"

She looks out of her passenger window, shrugs her shoulders, and says, "You're the one driving, honey. You decide where you want to go."

"No, Mom," I tried to explain. "I'm not asking if you want to go that way. I'm asking if that is the way we need to go. We were planning to head back north towards Kansas. Is that the highway exit we need? "

"You decide, dear," she would answer. "I'm just along for the ride."

"Mom, please," I would plead, "look at the atlas and tell me if we need that exit." And then, "Hurry, Mom. We only have a quarter of a mile left before we're at the exit. Mom...do we need it? Mom, is that the right exit? Mom....Oh, well, never mind, we've passed it."

"Oh, here it is on the map, honey," she would announce triumphantly as she pointed to a page in the atlas. "Yes, that's the exit you needed." Thanks, Mom.

Traveling on another highway (again, any highway), I spot a road sign that announces some kind of environmental attraction. There, advertised on a billboard, at the next exit, a national park that claims to have a "naturally made bridge and world famous waterfall." "Mom, do you want to stop and see the nature bridge?"

"Oh, gosh, no," Mom answers. "You know I hate bridges."

"I know," I told her. "But this one might be interesting. The sign also said there was a waterfall. Are you sure you don't want to stop to see that?"

"No, I really don't want to stop by the bridge." Okay, we drive just feet away from the exit where Mom now sees a second billboard announcing the attraction. "Oh, a waterfall and a natural bridge..." We pass by the exit. "That would have been interesting to see. I would have enjoyed that." I just grip the steering wheel a little tighter, my knuckles turning white, and say nothing.

Maybe it was because we were both exhausted from being on the road for so long. Maybe we both were dealing with old issues that still needed closure. Whatever the reason, small issues would flare up between us from time to time.

One morning, Mom and I were preparing to leave Ashville, North Carolina. We both were quietly getting dressed until I suddenly looked at Mom and said, "That's a pretty shirt." Maybe I was just trying to break the silence between us. Maybe I was trying to give Mom some confidence and reassurance. I don't know because, honestly, she was actually wearing one of the ugliest shirts I had ever seen.

"Oh, you like it?" Mom answered. "Here you can have it." Before I could respond, Mom was stripping off the long sleeved denim shirt that was stitched across the shoulders and back with patterns of bright blue, yellow, and red flowers. She tossed the shirt on the bed next to me and began digging in her suitcase for another shirt.

I sat staring at the shirt for a moment. I was really horrified by Mom's actions. Besides thinking the shirt was ugly, I was extremely uncomfortable that Mom would give me the shirt right off her body. Mom had so few possessions, taking her shirt made me feel incredibly guilty. "Mom," I told her, "I really don't want this shirt."

"No, it's okay," Mom answered, as she slid on another shirt and began to button it up. "I really want you to have it. Come on, get dressed. Let's go."

"Mom, please, take the shirt back," I begged her. I got up and moved over to her suitcase, sticking the shirt inside.

"No, no, no," Mom answered. "I want you to have it." She removed the shirt from her suitcase and stuck it in mine.

"Mom, no, don't do that," I said, pulling it out of my suitcase and moving back to hers. "I really don't want it."

"No, don't do that," Mother stressed as I slid it back into her suitcase. She pulled it back out and began to move over to my things with the shirt in her hand.

Thirty minutes later, we were in my truck driving out of Ashville. I was quiet and grumpy, driving around looking for the highway, while wearing a long-sleeved, stitched denim shirt. Finally, Mom looked over at me. "Oh, come on, Jamie," she moaned. "Why are you so upset?"

I kept my eyes on the road and sighed deeply. "I really didn't want to take your shirt."

"Oh, honey, it's fine," she laughed. Then suddenly she said, "Besides, I really didn't want it. For gosh's sakes…that has to be the ugliest damned shirt I ever did see."

I took my eyes off the road for a brief moment to glance at my mother. "Seriously?" I shrieked. "Honestly? You think this shirt is ugly."

"Oh, my gosh, yes…" she stressed.

"Then why did you buy it?"

"I didn't," she said. "Your brother gave it to me for my last birthday. I really tried to like it, I really did. I took off the tags and tried to wear it a few times." She sighed deeply. "It's just so ugly."

"Then why did you give it to me?"

"You said it was pretty," she simply answered.

"I don't think this is pretty," I breathed heavily. "I think it's horrible. I hate it."

"Then why are you wearing it?" Mom asked simply.

"BECAUSE YOU…" I started and then stopped. Why was I wearing it? I had just finally giving in to our argument in the hotel room so we could get moving. Why didn't I just tell Mom before that I thought it was ugly? Why didn't I speak my mind? Could I really blame my mother now for my situation?

"My goodness, that is an ugly shirt," Mom said again. And then paused for a moment before saying, "But it looks good on you, dear."

I pulled off the highway at the next exit. Ten minutes later, we were on the road again with a full tank of gas, large cups of coffee, and a new white t-shirt. The blue denim shirt was tossed into the station dumpster. Problem solved.

So now, here I was headed back on the road again with my mother on our way to Kentucky the morning after we had just returned from a seven-week tour of the southern American states.

"Can't believe we missed Kentucky," she sighed deeply. "How did we do that?"

I shook my head. "I don't know, Mom," I answered not taking

my eyes off the road. "Why are we going anyway? I mean what is in Kentucky?"

"Kentucky...Kentucky....Kentucky Derby?" Mom mused before sighing deeply. "Anyway, what does it matter?"

I certainly had to agree with her. We were just going to see what we could see. How would we know what's out there if we didn't go look? We had to go find out. Just to know.

"I want to see the blue grass." Mom's voice suddenly cut into my musings.

"What?" I asked shocked, turning my eyes away from the road for a moment. "What are you talking about? Mom, do you even know what bluegrass is?"

"Well, I've always heard about the Kentucky bluegrass," she answered. "It's in Kentucky....I want to see it."

"You know, Mom," I told her, "that it's a flower. It's not actually grass. You know that there is really no such thing as blue *grass*."

"Maybe," she conceded with a nod. "But, see, that's why we need to go to Kentucky. How do we know for sure if we don't go look?"

By that afternoon, we were driving aimlessly around Kentucky just to say we had been there. We finally stopped in Paducah for the night. Why had Kentucky been on Mom's mind when we had forty other states we hadn't visited either? I don't know. I think it had just been an excuse. I don't think Mom had been ready to stay home. She had had a small taste of adventure and wasn't ready to stop yet. Mom and I were stuck on the traveling, on the exploring, on the discovery of America. In just seven weeks time, we had grown accustomed to life on the road. It was during the Kentucky road trip that we had made a pact. Mom and I vowed that we would physically drive through every state in America.

The next morning, we circled back to Tennessee before driving north through Virginia and West Virginia, checking them off in our road atlas. We dared each other to stop in a small town in West Virginia called Point Pleasant. I don't know whatever possessed me because Mom had terrified me all through Savannah, Georgia. But I was curious if the legend of Point Pleasant was true. The legend claimed that large, winged creatures, known as "Mothmen" haunted the town and sent warnings to people of tragedies to come.

The drive to Point Pleasant was unusual. For several miles, we drove through a forest in thick soupy deep fog, which gave the whole region a creepy, unsettled feeling. We finally pulled into Point Pleasant around nine in the morning and even though the fog was lifting, the town still seemed to be underwater. It wavered and flowed, never standing still, but not in a romantic sense. It seemed to be a small, depressed town that reverberated with an unbearable sadness. I seemed to be looking at Point Pleasant through a veil of tears. It felt as if half the town had gone to sea and the other half was awaiting its return. No one seemed to smile or say hello. Mom and I parked and walked around the small square for a moment before finding ourselves in an ancient cemetery. Many of the tombstones dated back to the 19th century. My heart seemed to break into small pieces with every step we took. Without saying a word, Mom and I looked at each other and climbed back into the car.

I suddenly felt very ashamed of myself as we drove over the Silver Bridge before heading back out of town. The Silver Bridge had collapsed in 1964 after reported sightings of the "Mothmen" predicted the catastrophe. I wish I had stayed away now. I felt like a horrible voyeur into the lives of these people. I'm sure the town had been besieged by people who wanted to experience the legend. I also was aware of the fact that I could be misjudging this hushed town based on the questionable information I knew about it. How unfair. I had only known one thing about Point Pleasant based on a legend. I felt ashamed and just wanted to leave. Mom and I drove away and kept moving until we stumbled into Cincinnati.

We drove into the city at twilight. My breath was swept out of my chest when I saw the lights from the surrounding buildings glimmering on the Ohio River. For a moment, I wasn't sure if I was looking at an illumination in the water or stars in the sky. The effect was dazzling and purely delightful. There is a possibility that Cincinnati is different at night than during the day and that some areas are not safe; however, this first impression left me fascinated with the city. From what I saw that night, I would consider it one of the most beautiful cities I have ever known. Cincinnati deeply affected the artistic, right brain side of me that has always been attracted to vivid colors and bright lights. However, Ohio also excited my logical left-brain as well.

From what Mom and I could tell as we stared out at the state from our car windows, Ohio seems to be one of the most organized states I have ever seen. The portions of it we saw were clean and orderly. Whenever I drive through Ohio, it always seems to me that someone has very meticulously and conscientiously set all of the homes and businesses in a neat, methodical pattern. Ohio is a giant chessboard with perfect exact little squares and all the players know which way they specifically need to move for the win. Though I may be passionately restless, there is a part of my spirit that aches for that order and significance. Ohio just basically makes sense to me.

Unfortunately, Mom and I couldn't make a lot of sense out of the Cahokie Mounds in Illinois. I had been staring at the map when Mom and I made a stop for the bathroom and to refill the truck's gas tank. We had been driving for several hours and I was ready to walk around a little, to see the sights of a town. I saw in the atlas a small notice about the Mounds. Wow! This could be fantastic. I love history, and this promised to be an amazing historical site. The Cahokie Mounds are located where the Illinois, Mississippi, and Missouri rivers meet. It was supposedly acres of land that had been inhabited by ancient man. So cool!

I was excited as Mom and I climbed from the car once we had arrived at the location. We paid our fee at the visitors' center and started following the concrete path to view the Mounds...and that's exactly what we saw. Just mounds...everywhere...just clumps of earth and dirt with little signs insinuating that this was the foundation of primeval buildings that had once stood on this piece of soil. There was not a single broken down building, prehistoric ceremonial site, or carved engraving to be seen anywhere. We literally were just looking at mounds of dirt that we could have seen anywhere. I felt nothing mystical here. I didn't feel the energy here that I had felt in such places like Mesa Verde, Chaco Canyon, Bandelier, Grand Canyon....I felt nothing at all here. No, wait, what's that over there? A mound... of dirt...let me stand on it for a moment. Let the energy rise up into my feet and through my body. Let me dig a little deeper within my soul to feel a connection.

No, nothing...no...I really tried though.

After standing in front of the third mound, Mom begged to leave, but I pushed her on. I begged her to keep following the path. There had to be something more here. I was eternally optimistic. I wanted to keep searching. Mom and I continued to walk around endless dirt heaps while we were dripping with sweat and panting from thirst. Mom was taking deep labored breaths and mopping the water off of her face with a soggy, torn tissue but I still refused to quit. Wait... look...what's up there? A large hillside, standing about five hundred feet tall with a long concrete stairway right in the center. This was it! I thought excitedly. This was the promised land we had been searching for. There certainly wouldn't be a stairway to nowhere...right? Now, we were going to solve the true mystery of the Mounds. I started racing up the stairs while Mom stood exhausted at the bottom.

"Jamie, wait," she panted. "I don't know if I can make it up those stairs."

"Mom, come on," I cajoled her. "This is going to be great. I promise you it will be worth the climb." Please, Mom, come on! I wanted to scream. I was ruthless in my search for history. I heartlessly gave no thought to Mom's physical exhaustion and pleaded with her to catch up. "Let's go. Come on," I cheered her on. I ran up ahead as Mom took each step slowly one by one. I began to feel overwhelmed as I kept climbing, but the thought of the splendor I would see at the top was more than worth the sweat and exhaustion. Just twenty more steps.... fifteen....ten... five... almost there...three...two...one. Behold!

Grass... mud ...that's all I saw. I had climbed all that way just to look at more dirt, a whole valley of it. I stood there for a second, stunned and surprised. Several minutes later, Mom was by my side. She turned to gaze out at the open vista and then turned to look at me. The question "why?" was firmly planted on her glazed features. Why did you make me climb all that way to look at more dirt? her expression accused me. You promised, her tearful eyes shouted. You promised it would be worth the climb.

I shrugged my shoulders helplessly, not knowing what to say as I watched the sweat rolling down her face and heard her huffing for breath.

"Well, let's go," I sighed, turning back towards the steps.

"No, wait a minute," Mom whispered, "I need to rest."

So we sat down on the top step of the monument. We sat there underneath the hot sun, feeling the cool breeze...and that's when I got it! It doesn't matter whether we saw ancient structures or not. The earth has been around for billions of years. The world has grown, people have come and gone...and we still walk on this same ground. We still feel the warmth of the same sun and feel the same cooling breezes. We are one, connected for always by the same environment. Maybe, because we are so connected...

"You ready to go?" Mom suddenly asked.

"Yeah," I whispered. We got up slowly and began the journey back down the steps and over to the truck. We drove away without saying another word, still a little confused by the whole experience. Though the mound situation was a little upsetting, Mom and I still fell in love with Illinois.

While many of the states blend together in my mind, I still have fond feelings for each one. Every new state we drove through, Mom and I declared was our favorite and we talked of living there someday, which meant we would have to move at least forty-nine times.

The northern territory of America is inspiring. Mom and I gazed out the car window and were surprised to consistently find ourselves surrounded by endless amazing beauty. We roared through Michigan and the Wisconsin Dells where many fun activities, like water parks and casinos, screamed out to us from the side of the highway like energetic cruise directors. We explored the Mall of America in Minnesota. We are not shoppers and basically just roamed the many levels of the shopping emporium just to say we had been there. We couldn't wait to run back to the car and travel through the countryside, just to gaze out at the many beautiful, foggy, pure lakes. Having lived in southwestern deserts for several years, I was fascinated to be in a state with so much water.

Nebraska reminded me of water, too. This state has the most amazing rolling hills I have ever seen. I had believed before that "rolling hills" was just a descriptive term like "purple mountains majesty." I had been wrong about the mountains and soon learned, from traveling through Nebraska, that there actually are hills that spool like ocean swells. As Mom and I traveled through the state, we were pounded by wave upon wave of grassy, gorgeous hillsides. I could easily imagine being not in a car but a ship as we sailed through the tumultuous seas of land and grass.

We just drifted easily along for a few hundred miles until we finally came to rest in the small town (population 112 in 2002) of Medora, North Dakota. I do not always do well in small towns. I love having my privacy and my space but I need to be in touch with the energy of a city, which is rather strange because I am so self-sustaining. Maybe it's because I am not a laid-back kind of person. I am very high-strung. I'm always running to somewhere, always feeling like I have too much to do in such a short amount of time. Sometimes I feel like I can't live fast enough. Sometimes I feel time slipping away from me and I am desperate to hold on to it and control it at my whim. But, unfortunately, managing time is one of the few situations in which I tend to join the modern world...faster, faster, faster, race against time.

Arriving in Medora was like stepping back in time. I wondered for a moment if we had just driven through a wormhole somewhere in the universe. For all of my rushing around and need for city energy, I fell in love with Medora. If this was an alternative universe, I began to wonder what reality actually is. The main part of town actually looked and felt as if we were walking on to the set of an old western movie as we ambled down dusty, unpaved roads that were bordered by wooden plank board sidewalks. In all of the saloons, cafes, and general stores, the locals were friendly, kind, and anxious to tell the history of their beloved town. With pride in their voices, they related the story that Medora was founded in 1883 by a French nobleman known as the Marquis de Mores who named the town after his beloved wife. Medora, however, was not a weak, wilted woman looking for a man to rescue her. There are many legends of her bravery, including an encounter with a grizzly bear that she killed with a single rifle shot. Stories of strong women always fascinate me. Mom and I toured the Chateau de Mores, which is the large home the Marquis had built for Medora. We had become enchanted by the town and the surrounding territory. Upon leaving Medora, Mom and I found ourselves drifting into the Badlands of South Dakota.

I am an earth person so the Badlands was the ideal place to open up my heart and free my spirit. Teddy Roosevelt first came to this area in 1883 and fell in love with this rugged land. He called this area "the romance of my life." Looking at the painted peaks of land that were created from water and wind, I could certainly understand his feelings. The whole area inspired adventure in me.

Venturing further into South Dakota, Mom and I drove around Mount Rushmore and stopped for a moment to stare at the figure of George Washington hanging off the side of the mountain in the Black Hills. After a brief discussion, we decided not to go up to the actual site where the four presidential figures reside. We had heard that the figures of the presidents had been carved into land that was actually owned by the American Indians. So, instead, we traveled just a few miles away and went to view the Crazy Horse Monument located in Crazy Horse, South Dakota.

The Crazy Horse Monument is said to be the largest mountain sculpture in the world. Lakota Chief Henry Standing Bear had appointed sculptor Korczak Ziolkowski to begin the monument in 1948. Although Ziolkowski died in 1982, his family continues to work on the mountain. The monument will be 563 feet in height when it's finished. It was an amazing exhibition to see even if it was only partially completed at the time Mom and I were there.

Mom loved South Dakota so much that she was even pricing houses in the area. I didn't think she would ever move there on her own, but South Dakota was a dream for her. South Dakota would be one more state added to our dream home list along with North Dakota, Ohio, Tennessee, and Nebraska, to name a few. I suddenly became aware of the fact that Mom and I were actually doing more than just traveling. We were looking for a safe place, a peaceful home, something neither one of us had ever really experienced. That's what was keeping us on the road.

Five weeks after we first started out on our venture to Kentucky, we wandered back to Kansas, ready to rest for a while....for a short while...because after just one day back in Kansas, we were back in the truck, heading towards New Mexico.

Mom and I claimed we had a practical reason to drive to New Mexico the morning after we had returned from our Kentucky expedition. We had returned to Kansas to find an audit notice in the mail. I had lived in New Mexico and had successfully operated my own massage office for several years. The state tax department just needed a document that separated out my business income from income I made as an independent contractor at local spas. But instead of mailing the documents to New Mexico, Mom suggested we drive them there. I gave no argument. We were in the truck the very next day at four am, driving away from Kansas, this time heading southwest.

The six years I lived in New Mexico were the most enchanting of my life. I loved sharing Santa Fe with my family and friends. Every time someone would come to visit me, I would prepare endless agendas of all of the sights I wanted my guests to see. I was literally the tour guide from hell. I kept a very strict schedule of where we should be each hour of the day. I realized now that I may have ruined moments of discovery and enchantment for my guests, but I was so anxious that they would miss some wonderfully charming part of the town that I seriously kept everyone running every minute. When Mom and I arrived back in Santa Fe now, it was as if I had never been gone. This particular trip was not about discovery but renewal.

I love driving through New Mexico and witnessing the ruggedness of the land. I was entranced the first time I actually saw purple mountains. I thought the whole thing was just a myth, an illusion, just a line in a song of our country. But mountains, due to all the granite they contain, shine purple when bathed in sunrays. I first saw this phenomenon as I was walking around Santa Fe, lost in my own personal thoughts. I suddenly looked up and was facing a wall of purple light. Seeing a miracle was that easy. I literally felt as if the wind had been knocked out of me as I stood shock still for a moment staring up at the mountains. I live for moments like these. New Mexico is full of them.

The Loretto Chapel was high on the list of places Mom and I wanted to revisit. This small chapel in the heart of Santa Fe is the home of the Magical Staircase. Though I had heard the legend of the Loretto many times, it still inspires warm, loving vibrations in every chamber of my heart. Mom and I were both feeling the mystery and mystique of the chapel. We sat together in one of the pews with my head resting on her shoulder. We were both locked in our own silent prayers as we stared at the spiral staircase that led up to the choir loft. We just sat there, listening to the choir music and the broadcasted narration of the chapel legend that echoed around us.

The small building was completed in 1878 and became the home of The Sisters of the Chapel. The Sisters loved their chapel but found that they had one small problem. There was no way to climb up to the choir loft that was situated in the back of the small church. The original architects did not include a staircase, and a ladder was not appropriate since young women would be making the climb in long skirts. The Sisters decided to pray on the situation and held a seven-day vigil. On the final day of the vigil, a young man appeared and offered to build a staircase for them. At first, the Sisters were skeptical because the man only brought with him a single hammer and few other tools. But because there was no other option, the Sisters decided to take a chance. The man went alone into the chapel and began to work. A few months later, the Sisters awoke one morning to find the carpenter had disappeared as mysteriously as he had arrived. They were never able to locate him to pay or thank him for what he had created...and what he had created was truly inspiring. The spiral staircase has several 360 degrees turns but no central support. There are no nails, just wooden pegs, holding the structure together. No one has ever been able to identify the wood. Though tests have been done, the wood has never been matched to any that exist on earth. Now, people of course can have all kinds of theories about how this was accomplished...but what if...What if the legends are true...That it was St. Joseph who had arrived in answer to the Sisters' prayers.

What if...It's these mysteries that make life so remarkable. I don't think I would ever be happy completely knowing the secrets of the universe or the reason for life. I prefer having those "what if" moments. I love the times that make me think beyond what I know and what I can see. I live for those moments that make me look beyond myself. Is this what God is?

Mom and I also searched for God at the chapel in Chimayo. Even the journey there, through the hills and valleys of northern New Mexico, can make me feel closer to divinity. I love driving the long winding roads around Chimayo to visit the chapel that was built upon sacred ground. Legend has it that the dirt around Chimayo can heal people of their ailments if they believe in God's mercy. The entrance of the chapel is littered with crutches and wheelchairs that were abandoned by people who were miraculously healed.

Thousands of people also participate every spring in the pilgrimage to Chimayo. From all over New Mexico, the faithful walk away from their homes in hope of reaching the chapel by Easter day. I remember, every spring, seeing large groups of people walking along the highway during the day and sleeping in ditches at night. I admire their faith and courage, and I hope someday to demonstrate my own beliefs, live by faith. Maybe the day will come soon when I can share the life I have known.

When I find myself growing tired and wanting to give up, I just think of Mom's warrior woman demonstration. While we were in New Mexico, Mom and I were staying at the Camel Rock Hotel in Tesuque. I had made plans to go to lunch with my friend, Laurie, who I hadn't seen in a few months. I invited Mom to go with us, but she refused. She told me instead that she wanted to walk across the parking lot to the casino. I was nervous for Mom to go by herself, and tried to convince her to come with me instead, but she just brushed off my concerns.

"Oh, Jamie, it's okay," she stressed. "Nothing is going to happen to me."

"Yeah, Mom, but what if someone comes running at you and grabs your purse and…"

"No problem," Mom assured me, laughing. "I hide all my money and credit cards in my clothes. My purse is a decoy. If someone grabs the purse, that's fine. There's nothing in it."

"Yeah, but, Mom," I tried again, my apprehension causing me to be a real pessimist. "What if someone knocks you in the head and…"

"Ah," Mom sighed as if she was about to reveal an ancient battle secret to me, "I always carry my keys like this." She showed me then how she places her ring of keys in the palm of her right hand and makes a fist around it. She had placed her long car key in between her curled index and middle finger. She now held her hand out to me with the key "spike" sticking out. "See, I hold my keys like this, so if anyone comes at me, I stab 'em, see. I stab 'em like this." Mom began twisting her tiny body around the room, jabbing the air hard with her right hand. "See, Jamie, see, I can get 'em. I can get 'em." She suddenly grabbed the pillow off the bed and held it up in front of her. "See, Jamie, he's coming at me." She held the pillow up closer to her body. "See, and when he gets close enough, I stab him. I stab him just like that...and like this."

"Mom!" I squealed as she suddenly fell to the floor. She laid on the shaggy white carpet with the pillow resting on her chest.

"See, he thinks he's got me down, but he doesn't. I stab him, Jamie. And I stab him again." And once more she's jabbing her fist into the padding before rolling over with the pillow now underneath her. She pulled her small body up into a squat over the pillow and, to my horror, she then held her hands together, with the key sticking out between her fingers, above her head. She drove her hands down repeatedly into the cushiony softness of the pillow in a surprisingly real display of close range combat.

"Mom, stop," I hollered, appalled at the savage attack she was waging on the hotel linens.

Suddenly, she stopped and turned to look at me. "You want to fight me, too," she suddenly shouted. She jumped like a panther up on the bed very close to where I had been lounging back and charged at me with the key. "Mom, stop!" I jumped up and raced across the room as Mom leaped after me. "Mom, stop!" I ran into the bathroom and locked myself in. I could hear Mom now laughing hysterically.

"Jamie, come on," Mom teased, banging on the door. "I'm not going to hurt you. I'm just teasing you. Come on out. It was just a joke."

But I stayed in the bathroom for a while until I was positive Mom had calmed down. Once she was quiet again, I stepped out of the bathroom. I rushed over to the bed where she was relaxing. She was quiet now, so I leaned in to kiss her on the forehead. She surprised me by suddenly reaching up and grabbing my arm.

"Jamie," she whispered now. "You know I wouldn't ever hurt anybody. It's not in my nature to hurt someone."

"I know," I answered as I tried to ease my arm out of her surprisingly tight grip.

"I just don't want you to be afraid," she told me then. "I don't want you to be afraid of anything. I want us both to just live now. We've been locked away too long. God is here. He will protect us."

I smiled at her then. "I know," I whispered. "I know you'll be okay. I just want you to be careful."

I looked in her eyes and knew she would be fine. Her faith would see her through. She had been through so much already and had survived. I wanted to be a strong woman, too, fierce and determined, fearless and faithful…courageous…like my mother, sisters, and all the women who came before me.

This feeling became deeper ingrained in me when Mom and I visited Bandolier National Park the next day. Though we had been there several times before, I never tire of it. I loved the places that make me feel the wonder and innocence I never knew as a child. That's why Bandelier is one of my favorite places. Bandelier is a national park north of Los Alamos near White Rock. It was the home of nomadic Pueblo people who lived in the canyons over 10,000 years ago. I feel strong and invincible when I climb up to the caverns and come into contact with the way the ancients had lived. Bandelier is not to be seen and touched, but to be felt and experienced.

Chaco Canyon is endlessly fascinating, too. The canyon is located in the historic Four Corners, which is the intersection of Colorado, Arizona, New Mexico, and Utah. Chaco Canyon contains many public and ceremonial structures of the ancient Chacoan people who were known for their use of architectural designs, astronomical knowledge, landscaping, engineering, and geometry. This was an advanced civilization…

So what happened to the people? Where did they go? That is the mystery of Chaco Canyon. The people are gone and historians cannot say what happened to them. No one knows why or how this advanced culture suddenly disappeared. It has been said by some historians that the people must have been scared away because so many of the buildings, pottery, and tools were left completely intact. Everything was left behind when the people ran, but nobody knows from what… or where to.

I don't belong anywhere, and yet, I continually search for things not of this world. I walk through those ancient ruins, looking at all of the excavated materials that had belonged to the Chacoan people. A chill brushes through me…what could have scared a civilization of people so badly that they would leave behind their homes and all of their possessions? I felt a connection to the Chacoan people deeper than I have every felt before. I have left so much behind every time and everywhere I have gone that pieces of myself feel scattered across America. Is it fear that causes me to run, too?

I run from a fear of not living fast enough, of not having time enough. The people in Chaco Canyon usually lived to the age of just thirty-five. Did the fear of losing this life scare them…But it certainly wouldn't have caused them to run, would it? God only knows about the Chacoan people…God only knows about me.

CHAPTER 6

*W*hen I was a child, Mom usually had second-hand cars that were constantly in disrepair. Dad never saw any need to get Mom a new car. He never imagined that she would ever need to go anywhere important enough to warrant a better vehicle. He would buy new cars for himself and then pass his old cars over to Mom. The old cars would usually have a lot of mechanical problems that Dad refused to fix. Mom would normally find herself on the side of the road, trying to calm her four children, and praying for a kind stranger to offer us a tow home. I now sympathize with anyone who is struggling with car trouble and usually say a silent prayer if I am not in a position to help.

Mom and I had been lucky on our journeys. We didn't experience any hardships on the road—no car wrecks, flat tires, or running out of gas. I didn't even lock my keys in the car like I usually do. Sure, we got lost a few times but that was the extent of our problems. I felt blessed and credited our good fortune to Mom's daily prayers to St. Jude.

Two years after our return from New Mexico, Mom and I headed west on I-70, which took us right into the winding passes around and through the Rocky Mountains of Colorado. There is something so magical and thrilling about traveling in the mountains. I tried hard not to slam on my brakes as we rolled down steep hills. It is a little nerve wracking driving along precipitous roads and sharp turns with traffic zooming all around us. I held my own even though my knees knocked together and my knuckles turned white as I gripped the steering wheel. I watched a few drivers losing control of their cars on the turns and fighting to straighten their wheels as they sailed towards the next breathtaking turn. Other cars were leaving trails of smoke as the drivers burned their brakes, trying to control the speed of their vehicles as they rolled past us.

I didn't realize how fortunate we were until I was back in Nashville, Tennessee, about three weeks later. I took Dog in to have the brakes checked since they had been scraping and whining lately. "Oh my gosh, your brake shoes are bare," the mechanic stated. "You've been driving the last couple weeks on bare brakes. They could have gone out on ya at any minute." I never told Mom that we had been flying around the Rocky Mountains without brakes! Thank you, St. Jude.

Though the Rocky Mountains were challenging, it was actually in Vail, Colorado, where Mom and I ran into a little bit of trouble. We had been winding our way around the mountain passes and watching as the shadows grew long over the highway. We had no idea where we were going to spend the night. We just happened to land in Vail where we hopelessly searched for lodgings. All the hotels were completely booked up. We finally found one that had a room available...for five hundred dollars that night. Five hundred dollars!? The friendly front desk clerk responded to our surprise by saying, "Well, of course, all the hotel rooms, if you can find one, are going to be about five hundred dollars right now...you know...because of the trial."

Oh, the trial! Oh my gosh, Mom and I had stumbled right into the middle of the Kobe Bryant court case which was set to take place the next morning! How could we have forgotten? It had been in the news for the past several months. The clerk went on to discuss the case with us. She personally knew the young woman (cousin of a cousin's friend or something like that) involved and had a whole different take on the situation. Mom always found court cases fascinating and listened intently to the clerk's views. After talking for a while and getting good directions to a different hotel, Mom and I were ready to move on…if we could just get out of Vail.

Vail is full of roundabouts and, of course, heavy traffic. We were stuck circling continually around one particular roundabout while the other drivers honked incessantly at me until I finally was able to scootch my way over to an exit about twenty minutes later. While Mom continually encouraged me to be nice, I fought the urge to honk and swear for the whole thirty-five minutes it took us to finally work our way through all of the roundabouts and back out to the highway, which had only been about five miles away.

I felt no anger or disorientation, however, while we were in Utah. Oh, Utah has to be one of the most beautiful places in America. Northern Utah looks like an oil painting to me. The browns and greens of the surrounding mountains take my breath away. I can look out at the passing scenery and actually see the textures of the world. My eyes can actually caress the land and I can feel the movement of the grass and the breeze that blows through the trees. Further south, the ruggedness of the earth inspires me. I am continually fascinated by this gorgeous, vast landscape. I have a need to be surrounded by beauty, unique beauty, beauty that changes and evolves and moves and inspires. Beauty that is everlasting, yet consistently changing and surprising. That is Utah.

I imagine retiring to Utah some day. I can visualize spending the last few years of my life just staring into the robust earth of Utah and imagining all of the figures and forms I can see in the canyons, boulders, and mountains. This spiritual land has attracted countless seekers like Mom and me.

One afternoon, Mom and I were traveling through the Bonneville Salt Flats. Mile after mile of white grains surrounded us as we drove down the highway through this level dry land. I was fascinated with the mountains that rose up on the horizon to the right. As I kept the car moving forward, I would steal quick glances at the rugged landscape. Then, one last time, I glanced up, and suddenly gasped as Mom reached over and grabbed my right arm, her small nails biting into my flesh. She had seen it, too. I had glanced up from the road, up to the mountains, and there, standing at the top, was an angel. She stood straight, her hands folded in front of her and her large wings spread out behind her. Mom and I saw her for just a moment before deep clouds suddenly rolled in from both sides and covered the figure, obscuring our view. I knew how special Utah was then. The land doesn't just offer a spiritual awakening; it inspires and creates holiness, turning me into a true believer.

In deep contrast to Utah, Mom and I stopped in Las Vegas where the lights of the city diminished all of my quiet musings. I love Las Vegas, Nevada. The pageantry and the radiance trigger my imagination. I'm a very visual person so light and color always excites me. I was willfully blinded by the illumination of Vegas. Mom and I walked the strip and gazed in awe at the dancing waters of the Bellagio. Mom gambled in the casinos and danced in the streets.

That always surprised me about Mom. She tended to shy away in a lot of social situations. Mom was a bashful, unassuming woman who never did anything to bring a lot of attention to herself. At gatherings, she preferred to let others have the spotlight. But here she was again, her spirit overwhelmed. She danced, ran into people, apologized, laughed, and danced some more. Nothing stopped her from twirling her tiny body around in circles in front of all the other tourists.

Mom talked to everyone she meet on the streets of Vegas, which got her into a little bit of trouble from time to time. One afternoon, at Madam Tussaud's wax museum at the Venetian casino, she got into a small dispute with the usher at the front doors. We had just been wandering around the Venetian when Mom noticed a wax figure of Princess Diana. She went over to the big, plate glass picture window to get a better look. Besides Princess Diana, other wax figures like Lucille Ball stood in the lobby of the museum. The usher waved Mom inside so she could get a better look. Mom stood gazing up at Princess Diana before turning back around to speak to the young man.

"She's just beautiful," Mom whispered. "She looks so lifelike." The man just nodded his head without turning around. He continued to stare out the front window at the people walking passed the museum. "Look at her," Mom insisted. "It's incredible."

The usher had only one response, "No, I'm not turning around." He continued staring out at the sidewalk, at full attention, waiting to collect tickets.

"But why wouldn't you just look at her? She's so great, so beautiful. Turn around," Mom tried to encourage him.

"No," he answered again. "They scare me."

Mom stared at him in surprise, "Excuse me...what?"

"They scare me," he repeated. "I ain't looking at 'em."

"Hhhmmm," Mom approached him carefully. "You work here."

"Yeah," he answered, "at the front door. I ain't going in there. I'm going to be at the front door so I can run from 'em if I have to. I ain't going in there and I ain't looking at 'em."

"Honey, you're safe. It's okay," Mom tried to reassure him. She slowly reached out and touched his hand. "I promise you. I won't let them hurt you."

While Mom comforted the usher, where was I? At the front door ready to run. I wasn't going near them, either. Wax museums scare me, too. When I was about seven-years-old, my family was in Colorado for our usual summer visit. Our cousin, Jo, and Aunt Nancy took my family one afternoon as a "treat" to the Ripley's Believe It or Not museum. While my sisters and cousin were fascinated by the displays, I screamed, cried, and kicked with every step along the twisted passageway that lead through the bizarre exhibits. Seeing wax figures of three legged-lambs and a man with four eyes totally freaked me out. I remember clinging to Mom's hand (legs and arms, too), begging her to get me out of there; however, there was only one way in and one way out. I continued whining and pleading to leave until we were finally at the exit. Now, I was feeling the very same way. I stood up front next to the usher while Mom took one more look around the lobby. I only began to breathe a little easier when we walked back out into the hot desert air.

Mom and I continued walking down the crowded strip. I was walking a few steps in front of her because there were too many people and not enough room for us to walk side by side. As I moved down the street, young men approached me at every corner, waving brochures and flyers. I just shook my head no as I walked passed them. I knew what the "brochures" were for and I wasn't interested. I just kept my head down and continued walking. Finally, I stopped at the next corner, turned around…and saw my elderly mother walking along with a handful of flyers. "Thank you, thank you," she murmured politely as she accepted more brochures from the young men who had just approached her. I ran back and grabbed her arm.

"Mom, what are you doing?" I asked her. "Why did you take those?"

"Well," she answered, "these poor boys are working so hard out here trying to get some attention and everyone keeps ignoring them. I didn't have the heart to just walk by them." She turned on me then. "*You* were very rude to them!"

"Mom, look what you have," I whispered, pointing down at the brochures in her hands.

Seeing the photos of the naked women that graced the leaflets, Mom screamed and tossed them down onto the sidewalk. "I don't want those!"

"Then why did you take them?" I asked her.

"I didn't know they were for…" Mom started, and then quickly lowered her voice as she glanced around at all the people pushing passed us. "I didn't know they were for…," and now she whispered, "strip shows! Well, they must think I'm some kind of…of deviant, pervert…"

I looked at my mom in her little baggy jeans and blue windbreaker with her big, blue sunglasses hanging off the tip of her nose and choked back a laugh. I didn't want to hurt her feelings. "Yes, Mom, you are a real sex goddess," I told her. I scooped up the brochures and tossed them into the nearest trashcan, knowing it was a somewhat wasted gesture. Brochures and business cards displaying sexy adult images littered the entire sidewalk. I grabbed Mom's hand and started leading her away. Mom was now hanging her head, refusing to make eye contact with anyone, and declining all handouts with a shudder. Las Vegas had lost its shine and glitter. Mom was ready to move on. We left for California the next morning.

Mom and I literally drove aimlessly around California, not knowing where to go or what we were going to do. But then again, that's how we did most of our traveling. We ended up completely lost in the limbo of the California countryside until Mom claimed to have seen a road sign advertising a local Harrah's casino. She asked if we could stop there. Okay…if we could just find it. But we drove for about an hour and a half and suddenly found ourselves in San Diego…only I didn't know we were in San Diego at the time. I figured that out later.

We must have taken a wrong turn somewhere. We suddenly found ourselves at the naval base. I would have turned around if I had known where we were. I had no clue. We just happened to end up in a long line of cars trying to get into the commissary. Each car was thoroughly checked by several military men before being allowed access onto the base. I knew we were in the wrong place but there was no room to turn around. We were closed in on all sides by other cars and road barriers. Finally, it was our turn and the sergeant on duty barked out orders for us to stop. He came over to my window and asked for my military ID. I smiled and shrugged my shoulders, trying to help him find the humor in the fact that we were hopelessly lost. He wasn't laughing. He looked at us as if we were crazy. Okay, uh, thank you, sir…Yes, we will go now…thank you. Can I do a u-turn here? No, okay, up at the next light? Okay, thank you. I pulled up to the light and started to turn but thought that the lanes were too narrow to make a full u-turn. I turned directly onto the base. Ooops…shouldn't have done that. Suddenly, in my review mirror, I saw five military men running up behind my truck, screaming and waving their hands at me. Oh, my gosh, were some of them reaching for their guns? Their hands were on their hips as they ran behind us! I quickly made a u-turn and headed back to the entrance of the base. I gave a slight wave of my hand out the window as I drove passed the officers. Why did I do that? I don't know! I think I was just trying to tell them everything is under control. I'm leaving now. Okay…it's all cool. I drove right off the base, out to the highway, and headed north, not stopping again for a hundred miles or so out of fear of being shot. I just wanted to be as far away from San Diego as possible.

Mom watched as I hunched over the steering wheel, intently staring at the road, holding my breath, and keeping deathly quiet. I kept checking my rearview mirror to make sure we were not being followed. Mom then began to laugh. "Jamie, relax," she insisted. "We just made a little mistake. It's no big deal. We're okay."

I kept my eyes on the road and took a deep breath. "I know," I stated. "I just feel…just…stupid."

"Stupid?" Mom asked. "Why?"

"That was just a dumb thing to do," I answered, my hands tightening on the steering wheel. "I should have studied the map. I shouldn't just wander all over the place. I should have known where we were. I just made the biggest fool out of myself. I'm an idiot."

"Don't say that," Mom insisted. "You are not an idiot."

"Yes, I am," I insisted. "I'm just a stupid idiot."

"Stop it!" Mom demanded. "You are not stupid. You never were. For gosh's sake, you wouldn't have been called a genius if you were. I sometimes wish I had let the counselors jump you forward a few grades. Maybe that would have helped you…"

I took my eyes off the road for just a few minutes. "Mom," I interrupted her, "what are you talking about?"

"Oh, you know, honey," Mom sighed with a wave of your hand,

"when you were in first grade. All the testing you had to do…turned out you were a genius."

I pulled over and stopped on the side of the highway, somewhere in California. I was completely lost in all kinds of different ways. "I don't know what you're talking about," I said, staring now into her green eyes, my eyes. "When I was in first grade, Sister Alvera claimed I was mentally handicapped because of the way I talked…"

"Right," Mom agreed, "so I had to take you for all kinds of psychological and mental testing. Don't you remember?"

"Yes, I remember," I stressed. I have vague memories of the doctors at the clinic continually asking me endless questions and writing notes in their small leather notebooks.

"Right, well, remember, the psychologists claimed that the reason you had trouble talking was that your brain worked too fast. You processed information much faster than you could talk. You spoke way too fast to keep up with your brain. You picked up information faster than you knew the vocabulary, so you made up your own words. The doctors said you were near the genius level. They suggested that we jump you ahead two grades. I didn't think that would be good for you, as shy as you were, so I told them no. I wanted you to grow up slowly."

I sat there, staring out the window at the California countryside in stunned silence. "You never told me this."

"I thought you knew."

"How would I know? I didn't! I never knew this! You never said anything! You never even made me do homework."

"I didn't think you needed to. "

"I thought you just thought I was stupid and not worth the effort."

Mom stared at me for a brief moment before she was yelling back. "Whatever gave you that idea? What made you think that? I never thought you were stupid. I thought you were too sensitive. You just always felt things. You just always knew things. You would tell me about talks with angels and God. What was I supposed to do with that?"

I stared at my mom for a moment and suddenly realized something. When I was just six-years-old, I had accidentally overheard a conversation between my mother and grandmother. Mom thought I was in the bedroom, but I had wandered down the hallway and stood unseen at the threshold of the living room. I just briefly heard pieces of their conversation. "It's Jamie," my mother was saying, "I don't know what to do. She just knows things. She tells me her dreams and it happens the next day. She tells me things that she just can't possibly now and she's always right." I didn't listen to any more of their conversation. I turned around and tiptoed back into the bedroom. I had heard the fear in my mother's voice and thought I had again done something wrong.

Now, I turned to look at my mom again. "So, you weren't protecting me, " I began, "because you thought I was stupid..."

"Oh, no," mom protested.

"You were protecting me because you thought I was too..." and we both said the word together, "smart."

"YES!" Mom stressed as if I had just discovered uranium.

I stared at her for a moment and a thought jumped through my mind.....and that's when I understood my mother's fear. "The angel on the mountain in Utah," I said, "you saw it, too."

"Yeah," she sighed, and then shook her head. "Yeah."

I understood Mom's fear then. Her visions and thoughts had always made her feel different and unlovable. Was that the reason she would lock herself away in the bedroom? Was she seeing things and knowing things that scared her? She had been terrified when I started to show signs of the same abilities. Was she overly protective with me at times because she knew the hardships and tragedies I would have to face? I just sighed deeply now. "You should have told me," I said with a shake of my head. "This is my life. You should have told me."

We sat there in the truck in the mid-day heat for several minutes in total silence. After several deep breaths, my anger slowly began to dissipate as I started the car and pulled out onto the highway. I didn't know what else to do. I went back to what was familiar to me... driving the highways of America.

That was a good thing. We were both silent and just concentrated on the beauty of Northern California. The mountains looked like a patchwork quilt. Patches of green and brown blanketed the hillsides that were home to small farms and roadside fruit stands. The countryside felt like a comfortable coverlet resting on my troubled shoulders. The scenery and the breeze blowing in through the window erased the embarrassment from the base at San Diego and the shock of the revelations I had just discovered.

We finally stopped for the night in Woodland. I tried to relax but I couldn't sleep. Instead, I sat in the bathroom, trying to read but I couldn't keep my mind on the words. I suddenly couldn't help it. Large tears began to form in the corners of my eyes and slowly rolled down my cheeks. I grabbed a bath towel and covered my face trying to muffle my cries. If I was so *smart*, why didn't I know about my own life? Why didn't Mom tell me? How could I have just known? Should I have known? Then I started thinking back over my life. Yes, I had visions of angels as a child but I didn't think that was unusual. The first time something seemed unusual to me was at my high school graduation. I never studied, never did any homework. I just did enough work, I had assumed, to get by. I remember being completely shocked when I received high honors. Then there was graduating from college which was more about rebellion than accomplishment. I thought about my massage practice, running my own business with no help or support. I thought about my ability to feel energy, my intuition, my sense of "knowingness." I thought about working as a reporter and all of the newspaper articles I had written. I thought of my current occupation as a teacher of English and math at a Southern California tech college. Should I have known I was a genius? Yes, I should have known. Instead, I had concentrated on the people who called me names because they were so unsatisfied with themselves. Why had I listened to them? That was the way I had chosen to live. I had chosen to listen to the people who told me I was different, who insisted I was stupid, instead of listening to my own heart and head.

I had to fight for everything in my life, but strangely I didn't feel angry. I had only one thought. If I had known this before, would I have been happy? I had spent so many years, wasted years I realized now, being so angry! Did that emotion further cloud my vision, my sense of self? Can I make it different now? I cried for the strength and opportunity to move on with my life. I asked God to help me turn my life around. It was my responsibility now to renew myself and become someone different. I needed to start from now, from the knowledge I now possessed.

I finally got up off the floor and left the bathroom. I laid down in bed and fell immediately into an exhausted sleep.

I awoke the next morning at five am and Mom and I silently got ready to head out on the road again. Mom and I carried our luggage out to the truck and loaded it in the back. I closed the door of the camper shell, locked it, and then turned and threw my arms around my mother burying her in a deep embrace.

I surprised Mom who then wrapped her arms around me and we stood there in the parking lot of the Super 8 motel for several moments before Mom patted me on the back and whispered, "Come on, now stop that. Let's get going," she added when she saw the tears in my eyes. "We're good. We're okay. Let's go." I pulled away from Mom and shook my head. We climbed in the cab of the truck and headed north.

This was a perfect moment. Mom and I drove into Idaho before turning east to Montana and Wyoming. I have never seen such beautiful, blue, cloudless, wide-open skies as there were in these northern states. The earth stretched out before us like a promise of forthcoming good fortune. Our opportunities would be endless; our hopes and dreams as wide and vast as the land and heavens before us. California would soon be my home but for the moment, driving through Montana and Wyoming, I felt as if I belonged to the universe.

I will forever be a child of the coming together of land and sky. Why does all of America seem to be a second home to me? Strange that I can feel awkward in a group of people, but comfortable anywhere I travel in America. My future stretched out open, blue, and bold before me. I know where I belong....and I am beginning to realize who I am. I am an American daughter. I *am* a child of the earth and sky, forever knowing my home is always beneath my feet and over my head. I will always know where I belong.

CHAPTER 7

A year later, the wide-open skies of hope and good fortune had turned dark and gloomy. In April, 2008, I drove to Kansas from California completely disoriented and disconnected. I was distressed, depressed, and drained. I felt so exhausted I could barely make myself move. I was overwhelmed by my life, and by all the many changes that had occurred in such a short time. My past and future had collided. I was drowning in the old feelings of loss and loneliness.

I had just broken up with my latest boyfriend. The experience this time had left me unsure of myself. I was usually the one to walk away. I did this time, too, but instead of making me feel empowered, I felt beleaguered. I felt totally unlovable and ashamed. I was out of work, out of love, a complete and total loser. There was a knowingness inside of me of a moment past that I could not recall. I couldn't remember my own life anymore.

For once, I just couldn't seem to find my way and I didn't enjoy the feeling of being lost. I didn't know who I was anymore. So, thinking that I had no direction at all, I wandered back to Mom's Kansas home. Mom and I were on our way to New York and the east coast where we had never been before.

However, this time, Mom didn't seem to be excited about the

journey. She claimed that she would be just as happy to stay at home with me near and I had a feeling I knew the only thing she really wanted this time. She wanted me to move back to Kansas. But it was too late. I already felt that I had grown up and was too old to permanently run home to Momma. But where do you go if you are too old to run away and too broken to go home? I realized I was actually doing a little bit of both. The road is the only place I would feel myself again. However, I was spiraling down this time and this journey showed it.

Mom and I both were beating down and weary, tired from the journey before we had even started. But we still climbed into my truck on a crisp April morning and headed east into heartbreak.

The first splinter came just outside of Chicago. It was at a Cracker Barrel restaurant in Gurnee, Illinois, where Mom and I had stopped for lunch. As we started to eat our sandwiches, I began to notice something for the very first time. I stared at my mom from across the table and noticed that her hands shook as she slowly brought her food to her mouth. She couldn't hold her hands straight. Her hands vibrated constantly as she moved. I couldn't stop staring at her. When had this started? What had happened in the time we had been apart? How could I have not noticed the changes that were occurring in her body?

Mom had also developed a bad cough due to smoking. She claimed she only smoked when she was nervous. However, during all of our trips, she would light up at every stop we made and then she would proudly show me the length of the cigarette, trying to prove to me that she had taken just a few small puffs.

Now, I listened to a cough rattle through her chest as she covered her mouth and then reached for her water glass. The glass shook and wobbled as she carried it up to her mouth. At that moment, I began to regress. I suddenly saw myself relating to my mother through all the stages in my life. I saw myself as a young woman, angry with life and with my mother as if everything was her fault. I felt the rages that shook my own body and caused me to do things like slam doors and hang up phones in the middle of conversations. I saw myself as a teenager, often disrespectful and demanding, fighting for my independence and refusing my mother's words of wisdom. I saw myself as a child needing my mother to help me through teasing and bullying. I saw myself running to the safety of her open heart to hide from the world that thrilled and yet terrified me. I saw myself as a baby, nestled safely in her arms, sleeping and eating peacefully without a care. I don't know where the memories came from but they all came flooding back into my mind until finally I could imagine myself protected and growing within her body, cradled close to her heart. I could imagine for a moment, moving through her and how she gladly gave up so many parts of her life and body to me.

Suddenly, I was so overcome with emotion, I had to excuse myself from the table. I went into the bathroom, locked myself in a stall, and cried. Tears were just rolling from my eyes and I did nothing to stop them. I let them flow down my face without even wiping them away. I cried over her life. I couldn't explain it any other way. Other than that, I really had no other explanation. I remember times when my mother wasn't loved or respected enough by her family. Usually, any upset any of us faced always wound up as Mom's problem. She suffered through her children, at times, being disrespectful, sometimes downright rude, dumping all of our anger at the world at my mother's feet.

I thought of a story Mom had told me several years before. It shook me so hard now, I was almost having difficulty standing up. Early one morning, Mom was getting dressed. She made some comment to my father that made him furious. He took his hand and shoved her in the shoulder. It was a hard enough push that Mom, who was eight months pregnant with my sister, Carol, lost her footing and fell over backwards. She fell down hard on her backside as my dad turned and walked out of the room, leaving her alone to struggle back to her feet. At the time, Mom had only one worry. What if she had fallen so hard that she had hurt the baby? Would her baby be alright?

Mom would suffer a lot of confusion, disappointment, anger, and sadness with my father for forty years. She did without so much, never buying anything for herself. One day, she had saved up enough money from her weekly allowance to buy a pair of shoes that she desperately needed. They were just black sneakers that she had bought at a discount store for five dollars. That weekend, however, she suddenly realized, was our church/school's annual ice cream social. Not able to get any extra money from my dad, she did the only thing she could think of to make sure her children got to have fun. She returned the shoes in order to take her children to the social on a bright, sunny Sunday afternoon.

All of these memories flooded my mind as I stood in the bathroom stall crying. The tears streamed freely until I was finally able to take a few deep breaths. At last, I wiped my eyes, blew my nose, walked out of the bathroom, and back to the dining room where I sat down at the table across from my mother. She stared at me for a moment before saying, "Are you alright? You weren't sick, were you? You were in the bathroom a really long time."

"I'm fine," I informed her. I didn't know what else to say.

"Upset stomach?" she asked me as she patted my hand, and, suddenly again, I felt five years old. I just nodded my head. Funny, at any other time, I would have lashed out at her for treating me like a child. Today, however, I wanted to crawl into her lap, cuddle into her chest, and cry into her heart. But, of course, that couldn't happen. I couldn't tell her why I was crying. So I just sat there, twirling my knife on top of the table, while Mom's shaky, bent fingers picked up each French fry and moved it to her mouth. My profound feelings kept me patient this time. I let her finish all of her food before getting up from the table. Usually, I am urging her to hurry. "Just eat, c'mon, finish up. We have to get back on the road" was my usual lunchtime conversation. If Mom noticed the change in me this time, she didn't say anything. For once, she was able to finish her food in peace and I think that unusual occurrence kept her from asking any questions. She probably didn't want to risk getting me all fired up again.

We climbed back into the truck after lunch and I really wish I could have left all of the pain behind in the bathroom of the Cracker Barrel. But it followed us all over the northeast. We couldn't drive fast enough this time to get away from it. Our emotional pain was there with us everywhere we went. And it showed everywhere.

The weather throughout this trip was horrible. Storm clouds seemed to follow in our wake or were waiting to greet us everywhere we went. Just the day before, we had been forced to stop for an hour in a cornfield in Illinois. We just sat in our truck, among the tall stalks, until the rain cleared enough for us to roll on. Pennsylvania gave us the same chilly, wet reception.

But there was a blessing in the rain. Pennsylvania was so rich and green with tall, leafy trees and beautiful, crisp, emerald grass. Of course, with all the rainfall, it couldn't help but be anything but God-blessed green. We drove through the Poconos Mountains and only stopped when the rain forced all of its attention on us. But the rain didn't really matter. We drove throughout Pennsylvania with no clear direction and completely lost even when we asked for guidance.

For example, Mom and I decided that we really wanted to see the Liberty Bell...but we couldn't find it....and didn't really have a clue where to look. After searching on our own for a while, we came upon a tollbooth. As I paid the toll, I asked the booth operator for directions to the Liberty Bell. He held up a finger to me for just a moment as he put away the change I handed him. "He's going to tell us the directions, Mom. He's going to tell us," I whispered to her. I watched as the toll taker grabbed a pen and began writing down some notes. "He's writing it down, Mom. He's writing down the directions," I told her excitedly. I thanked the man as I took the slip of paper he handed through the window. "We got the directions, Mom. We got the directions," I stated, thrilled as I handed her the small slip of paper. "Okay, Mom, where do we go?" I asked as we started to pull away from the tollbooth.

She glanced at the note and said, "I don't know. What is this?" She was looking helplessly down at the paper.

"It's the directions, Mom, to the Liberty Bell," I told her.

"Are you sure?" Mom asked.

Trying to keep one eye on traffic, I took the paper from her and glanced at it. The writing was so scribbled across the page, the characters didn't resemble any letters at all. It was just random ink scratches on paper. I could make out just a word or two but that was it. Poor guy…he probably did try to help us but we just couldn't read his handwriting. We were still cruising down the highway, trying to decipher the scribbled note, when we sailed around a turn and suddenly found ourselves facing towards Atlantic City.

We didn't fight it. As if by magnetic force, we were drawn into New Jersey. It was getting late into the evening, so we decided to look for a hotel for the night. We could see some hotels across the freeway but couldn't figure out how to get to them. There were no exits anywhere. We finally stopped for directions at the tourist center that was sandwiched right between the west and east bound highways. Thank goodness, the older woman working at the center was able to give us directions. Back in the truck again, we drove around for a while…and suddenly found ourselves back in the parking lot of the tourist information center where we again stopped to ask for directions. "I'm sorry. We are so lost. We never did find the right way…"

"Oh, honey," the woman at the center answered, "I gave you the wrong directions." She wrote out a different course for us. Back in the truck, we drove around for a while…Oops, still wrong. After another journey around the highways, we were back at the information center a third time.

"Oh, honey, so sorry," the tourist center woman laughed. "I wrote down the wrong exit…"

We finally got to a hotel after throwing out the directions we received from the information center and just driving around on our own. When we parked the truck at the inn, Mom climbed out and slowly wandered off to the far end of the parking lot. I watched her, wondering where she was going for a moment. She looked so small and tender as she stood with her back to me. I walked up behind her.

"Mom, what is it?" She seemed so quiet, so contemplative.

She turned to me slowly. "It's the Atlantic Ocean," she whispered. I turned my gaze to where she was looking. Oh, I felt stupid now. I hadn't even noticed the ocean! My thoughts had been completely focused on the small, fragile, lone figure of my mother. Now, standing with her, staring out at the water, it seemed that the gray sky had slid into the even grayer ocean, and together they had just become one complete hoary nothingness out on the horizon. Because of the stormy weather, the archaic ocean seemed to blend right into the ancient sky. The ocean seemed to be completely swallowed up by the dark clouds. The horizon was invisible. The scene seemed so hugely vast and empty. I related to the ocean today. I am the sky. There is no distinction between me and the rest of the murky universe.

Mom and I stood there for a while, silently staring out at the sky and ocean as small drops of rain beat against our bodies. We were both lost in our own thoughts and seemed oblivious to the slight evening chill. When the rain began to drizzle down harder, Mom and I turned as one and walked back to the hotel.

After getting a room, we cleaned up quickly and decided to explore Atlantic City. However, even the bright lights and dynamic colors didn't lift our melancholy moods. I don't know if it was the weather, or our state of mind, but Atlantic City was our crashing place.

When we came back to the hotel, Mom changed into her pajamas and then sat in the middle of the bed with her knees pulled up to her chest and her arms cradling her body. I don't recall how the conversation actually started but she just looked up at me, her bright green eyes clouded over with tears that eventually ran down her cheeks. She looked at me and began to discuss her life. The revelations took me by surprise since I had been thinking the very same things in the Cracker Barrel bathroom. Her words were haunting and heartbreaking. She just seemed to be so broken and sad as she tried to justify her existence.

"I am who I am," she stated defiantly. "I don't care if people don't like me. I know that people make fun of me. But I have to be myself. I don't care anymore." Her words continued over and over in this manner as she rocked herself back and forth. Mom talked about being unloved for most of her life. She told me that she had always felt unwanted in this world. She confided that she always knew that she was different and didn't belong. Though I felt the very same way, I couldn't say anything. I didn't want to tell her, "I know how you feel." Would it be unkind of me to focus the attention on myself? Would she have taken the blame for my life? Would she have thought that she did something wrong? Instead, I kept quiet and let her have her moment. It's kind of a shock to realize a parent is only human, too. It's a little alarming to know that parents can feel the same hurt and confusion that their children can feel. Sometimes it is shattering to witness the emergence of a parent's humanity. Mom and I are the same. Human and broken. All I could think to do was hold and rock her as she cried until she was exhausted and finally fell into a deep, soundless sleep.

I couldn't sleep, though. I stayed awake for most of the night. I remembered those times in my childhood when I wouldn't see Mom for hours as she locked herself behind her bedroom door. It would be deathly quiet. No sound, no movement. Those quiet afternoons echoed loudly around in my head. I remember Mom's horrible bouts of social anxiety. She never wanted to attend our class plays or games or concerts. She rarely wanted to meet our friends, classmates, or co-workers. Like me, her connection with the universe, her intuition and sensitivity would keep her locked in her own private world.

Mom had told me before about the visions that would appear to her. We had endless discussions about reincarnation, angels, and faith. Mom would always end the conversations with "I can't talk to anyone the way I can talk to you." Maybe, that was the problem. Our struggle to keep our visions secret so we could be just like everyone else caused us to stand apart from everyone, different and lost. I think so many people struggle with the same situation. I think that's why there is so much violence and depression in the world. Very few people feel safe to live their true spirits.

I tossed around in my bed when I thought of my mother's confession to me one afternoon when we were somewhere in the middle of Arkansas. She once had put rat poison into ice cream and forced herself to eat some of it. She had just shrugged her shoulders and said, "I thought it would help me lose weight." I just stared at my tiny, five foot, hundred-pound mother and wondered what possibly could have been so wrong with her weight that she would feel compelled to eat rat poison. Of course, I didn't want to address the fact that there were bigger issues than just her weight.

I think I always had some inkling of Mom's emotional situation. I think that's why it meant so much to me to see her dancing in the streets of Santa Fe or Tupelo or Las Vegas over just the last few years. I was witnessing a social breakthrough of sorts for her. This relapse in New Jersey was bound to happen sooner or later. She had been on a high for too long. Depression is like quicksand. It is smothering as it pulls you under. It takes tremendous amounts of strength to pull back out. It is exhausting and overwhelming. I was so thankful that for now, Mom was sleeping peacefully, and I finally did the same around three in the morning.

Traveling out of New Jersey the next day, we rolled towards the harbor to see the Statue of Liberty. I always thought that the Statue of Liberty was located directly in New York. Now, I realized that it is in the harbor between New Jersey and New York. We parked on the Jersey side and went to buy tickets. There weren't any more tickets available for Liberty Island, so we were headed just to Ellis Island. Mom was a little worried about getting on the ferry. She was concerned that her inner ear disorder would irritate her and stop her from enjoying the experience. Halfway to Ellis Island, however, Mom relaxed against the bench on the ferry and watched the scenery passing by, a look of pure joy on her face as she felt the cool breeze sweep over her.

Ellis Island was very inspirational to both of us, especially when we were able to find the name of my paternal grandmother on the plaques that framed the front garden. Mary Zuniga moved with her sister to the United States from Croatia. They had left behind a brother who they did not see again for almost forty years. Mom and I stood together staring at her name and then walked around the garden reading the names of all the people who took a chance on a new life in America. For a brief moment, I believed I had found my people. I ran my hands over the plaques feeling more than just the etchings of countless names. I was feeling lives, dreams, and hope. I had never felt a tangible faith before, but I rested my hand against it on Ellis Island.

Mom and I roamed around for quite a while and gazed at the Statue of Liberty across the harbor in the distance. After a few hours, we joined the thick line of people waiting to board the ferries. I was a little disappointed that we wouldn't actually make it to Liberty Island to stand next to the statue, which I stared at wistfully as the crowd began to push ahead towards the docking ferries. I heard a harbormaster yell "New York," but continued letting myself be swept forward with the crowd.

Once Mom and I settled down on the ferry and were moving away from the dock, I heard the harbormaster again call out "New York." This time the words caught Mom's attention, too. "New York? Why is he saying New York? Aren't we heading back to New Jersey?"

No, we were headed to New York. Even though I tried to calm her down, Mom was so agitated that we were on the wrong ferry, headed in the wrong direction, that I finally walked over to talk to the harbormaster. No, there was no turning around now. We would have to get off at the next stop...Liberty Island! Yes, we were on the wrong ferry but headed to the statue. Mom remained in a state of agitation...until she happened to look out the open sides of the ferry and realized we were directly in front of the glorious figure. We were both completely awestruck.

The Statue of Liberty has to be one of the most magical entities I have ever seen. I never realized before how big it is! An amazing 305 feet! I stared at the icon in silent, awestruck fascination, nearly tripping over myself as we exited the ferry at Liberty Island. Mom and I ran around the statue for a few minutes, trying to take it all in, before climbing onto the correct ferry and heading back to the New Jersey side. Mom could not believe our good fortune. We actually had made it to Liberty Island, quite by accident, but we were there. We had gotten onto the wrong ferry but the "accident" had placed us in a magical place, right where we needed to be.

Now, I have a confession that I eventually told Mom about later. I knew we were getting on the wrong ferry! I had heard the harbormaster screaming out "New York," but I let myself get caught up in the excitement of the moment. I really wanted to see New York! I wanted to gaze upon it and feel its energy wash over me. I was a little disappointed that we didn't get as close to fabulous New York as I had hoped at that time, but then there was the Statue of Liberty in front of me and my disappointment was healed. I plot and plan and scheme...and then let go and see what the world has to offer. I am rarely disenchanted or disappointed.

I did get the opportunity to drive through New York the next day. It took a bit longer than expected. Mom and I were about to cross the George Washington bridge when we were caught in a huge traffic jam. It was a little surprising. Instead of being stressed, most people climbed from their cars and began to party. Music was playing and people, talking and laughing, ran from car to car. I had never seen people so happy to be stuck in traffic before. That never happens in *laid back* California! It was my experience that traffic in California caused a screeching of brakes, a honking of horns, a flashing of lights, a curse and a finger wave....and it's not just me! Tranquil Californians speed on the highways and demand free passage. I need to learn to be more of a New Yorker when I drive. Their traffic party attitude was certainly a lesson I needed to learn. Stuck somewhere? Relax for a moment, take a deep breath, talk to people, listen to music, listen to God...move on....if I could only learn to live my life that way...I need...Oh, wait a minute....Watch out!

Mom and I had been lolled into a false sense of peace and security. When the traffic jam, which had been caused by a car wreck, was cleared, the once happy crowd began to move in every direction. Cars were all over the highway. The air became filled with honking, cursing, brakes squealing...Mom and I suddenly were on high alert, on our guard, trying to weave and dodge around all the cars that seemed to be headed directly towards us. We held our breaths and barreled on through until we were finally passed the worst of the traffic. In a few minutes, we were finally free and rolling over the bridge.

Mom and I headed north to Buffalo. Niagara Falls was cold, but we didn't let that stop us. We stood staring out at the Falls in total amazement and I suddenly had an inspiring thought of where I wanted my life to end. Here...in Niagara...or Bandelier...or Chaco Canyon...or Mesa Verde....I want to end my life surrounded by so much beauty. That's what I am looking for in my life...not just a place to live, but a place to die. I want to let go surrounded by pure, awesome, heartbreaking beauty. Niagara Falls not only inspires a peaceful life but an amazing death as well.

As Mom and I rode the tram around the falls, we talked with a Canadian couple who confirmed that I was on the right path. They were a real inspiration as they regaled us with tales of their travels all around the world. When the tram stopped and Mom and I were stepping off, the woman smiled at me and whispered, "Don't ever stop traveling, honey. Don't ever stop dreaming." I wanted to hug her. She couldn't have spoken more eloquently to me. I wanted to thank her for the kindness of her words at a time when I felt so incredibly lost. The woman was a prophet encouraging me on my path and

I knew then that the only way to find my passageway was to stay completely lost. I need to keep searching and dreaming.

This thought became even more profound to me when Mom and I suddenly roamed around the falls right up to the border of Canada. We stood at the white, iron gates. Our hands gripped the thin poles. Mom and I were like two children staring through a toy store window. I gripped the cool metal of the gate and tried to push myself as far as I could through the bars. It was brand-new territory to explore and I couldn't seem to hold my heart back. Mom and I stood in silent awe as we stared at the trees and emerald green grass. That's all we could see, but we stared at it as if we had never seen nature anywhere before. It was Canadian land, bright and beautiful, and we yearned for a moment to be a part of it.

Yes, we were still exploring America. We loved our country, but had a fascination with the world that could not be tamed. We could not ignore the allure of roaming into this new frontier. After a few moments of staring at Canada and trying to flirt with the guard to let us through (he wasn't having any of it), Mom touched my arm and whispered, "Someday...come on, let's go." I reluctantly let go of the bars and trailed slowly behind her. I glanced back at Canada every couple of steps. With further dreams of exploration, we headed back to the car and drove towards Albany.

The majority of our time in the northeast was just a driving tour. It was too stormy and wet to actually stop and walk around anywhere. We drove halfway north through Maine and then swung around in the opposite direction. We cruised quickly through Delaware before landing in Boston, Massachusetts.

Driving through Boston had to be the scariest experience I ever had while traveling. The rain was falling hard, and the highway was packed bumper to bumper. Cars were speeding along through exit ramps and road shoulders, and almost running right over each other. At the time, I was shocked to see people using the exit ramps and shoulders as additional lanes. A few months later, I found out this was perfectly legal. I wish I had known it at the time. I wouldn't have been so nervous. But on the highway that day, I gripped the steering wheel tight and tried to keep my knees from knocking together as cars sped past me from every direction. For all of my driving experience, I couldn't stop the anxiety that built up inside me as we fought our way through the traffic jungle. I stuck to my basic driving principle: get into a lane, hold my space, and just keep moving forward. I ignored all of the other drivers that zoomed around us when they found a break. I just gripped the wheel and prayed. The system must have worked; we made it through Boston with just a few cusses, horn blasts, and fingers from the other drivers.

The traffic and stress calmed down as we traveled through Connecticut, New Hampshire, and Vermont. I fell in love especially with Vermont. My tumbled soul rejoiced as we drove through the mountain passes which were some of the most beautiful I had ever seen. Vermont is one of the most picturesque places I've ever known. It reminded me of Switzerland in all of her gentle majesty.

As we came out of the mountains, we stumbled into the small town of Woodstock. Mom took one look around the town and announced, "I'm moving here." I echoed her sentiment. Woodstock, Vermont is one of the sweetest, most colorful, most gracious towns I have ever seen in America. It was clean, beautiful, with the mountains beaming in the background. This is a town that is well loved and definitely inspired; the perfect picture of American life. Homes and families, white picket fences and town squares radiated in my heart in sharp contrast to my earlier desire to run off to Canada. Now, I wanted nothing more than to settle down in a quaint American town.

This feeling within me could have been inspired by Woodstock… or maybe inspired by the stories Mom told me as we rolled along the mountain trails. Mom began to talk again about our family as we moved through the northeastern states. I was happy to listen to her talk. Traveling is so healing to the soul. My journeys helped me find my own voice. Now, I listened eagerly to Mom as she told me countless stories of my childhood and ancestry...some I had never heard until now.

My family did not grow up close, even though most of us lived in the same area of Kansas. I only saw aunts, uncles, and cousins on special occasions like weddings and funerals. Holidays and birthdays were celebrated privately within the separate families. My father rarely spoke about his family. I never even heard him talk about his own father. I didn't even know my grandfather's name until I was about ten. It suddenly dawned on me that if my dad was a Jr., my grandfather had to have had the name of Joseph John Zunick as well. I don't know why my family never spoke of him. We were always very secretive. Grandma Zunick didn't even know that she had married a man twenty-five years older than she was until their eighth wedding anniversary. Grandpa Zunick hadn't lied to her. He just simply neglected to reveal his age and she just never asked. Privacy and secrecy are our family traditions.

It's sad, too, that my family doesn't brag, talk, or celebrate themselves. According to Mom, my grandfathers were considered two of the most loving, giving, hard-working men in the community and I didn't know either one. My paternal grandfather died years before I was born and I only knew my maternal grandfather for the first four months of my life. I look at old pictures where I am posed in his arms, and I wonder. I feel connection but not emotion. I am beginning to understand where I came from but don't understand why we remain hushed and enigmatic. Why not let the world know who we are, where we come from, where we are going? No, usually we are stoic and silent. That is my family.

As I get older, I feel their presence more in my life now. I want to know my family, so I was pleased that the road travel inspired Mom to talk. On our way out of Vermont, Mom told me that when she was about six-years-old, her mother finally bought one of the few pieces of furniture that the family owned. Grandma Edith had purchased a five-drawer dresser for about ten dollars. Grandma told her four children that they each could have a drawer for their own possessions. With what little they had, a drawer would be just enough for each one of them. Mom was thrilled to have a drawer because she finally believed she had something that was hers alone, that she didn't have to share with anyone else. In order to stake her claim on the bottom drawer and make sure no one else used it, she ran into the kitchen for a knife and then carved her initials as carefully as her little hands would allow her into the face of the bottom drawer. Of course, when Grandma saw it, she was furious. The only nice piece of furniture the family had was now marred with crooked, badly carved slanting letters. Mom laughed with forced humor in her voice as she told me she was thoroughly spanked and the drawer was taken away from her. The only thing she was proud to possess on her own was no longer hers. Mom had laughed again before adding, "It was okay. I had nothing to put into it anyway."

Both my mother and father had many strange habits and thoughts about money. I used to cringe when Mom and I would go out to lunch and she would insist on leaving the tip. Mom would pull a fresh, crisp dollar bill out of her purse and place it on the table. "There. Now, that little girl," Mom would say referring to the server, "can get herself something to drink. She can take a break with a coke." Mom would smile at me then, pleased with her generosity. I would just smile and insist on paying the bill with my credit card, adding a few extra dollars without telling Mom. After growing up in the Depression Era, and then having to fight for extra money during her marriage, a dollar was a lot of money to Mom.

My attention suddenly returned to my mother when she said, "Oh, your Grandfather Zunick was such a sweet man to me. He was the only one in the family to make me feel welcomed. Grandfather Zunick owned a little grocery store. I loved working there with him. I worked there for a while in the first few years of my marriage. He hated banks though; he didn't trust any of them. He actually kept all of his money in a hole he dug out of the basement wall."

She paused for a moment and then continued, "Oh, and your great grandmother, my Grandmother McCurdy, was an amazing woman. So fun, so full of life. She never took no for an answer and lived by her own rules. She did what she wanted to do and damn everyone else. I remember coming home from school when I was just about six-years-old, around 1940, and there was Granny McCurdy sitting at the kitchen table with her shot of whiskey in front of her and her big cigar hanging from her lips. She loved playing poker with the neighborhood men. She normally took all their money and drank them under the table!" I smiled and fooled myself into thinking that my female ancestry would be proud of my own independent nature.

Mom began to run out of stories by the time we hit Illinois. She refused to speak any more about herself. I think she feared another Atlantic City breakdown. I didn't push her. We drove along silently for a few miles until we decided to stop for gas in Pocahontas. I pulled off the highway onto the exit when it suddenly hit me. Pocahontas, Illinois...Gretchen Wilson's hometown! Gretchen is one of my favorite country artists and to suddenly stumble on to her hometown excited me. After filling up at the gas station right off the exit, I ran around and took pictures of the signs that welcomed visitors to Pocahontas, Illinois, "Home of Gretchen Wilson." I'm such a geek, I know, but I want to remain excited and pleased with the little particulars of life. Little things like this can thrill me after I had just seen the Statue of Liberty and Niagara Falls. These little moments make life so pleasurable...and, now, after four weeks of rain and tears and worries, getting caught in traffic, stumbling onto the wrong ferries (intentionally or not), crying in hotel rooms, Mom and I were beginning to relax and laugh again. We were in much better spirits now, even if the hotel rooms we stumbled across were in sad disrepair.

Mom and I had just driven into Indiana and started looking for a place to stay for the night. Along the highway, we had noticed a billboard for a hotel that advertised rooms for just thirty-nine dollars. Wow! What a great deal! Let's stop there.

We turned off the highway at the second exit as the billboard directed, and as we turned the corner, we saw the hotel in the distance. I pulled into the parking lot and we followed the same routine Mom and I had enacted all across America. I would drop her off at the front door and then park while she started the registration. I would join her in the lobby and we would go together to our room.

But this time, as I pulled up to the front of the hotel, Mom hesitated before getting out of the truck. "Uh, Jamie," she sighed to me, "This doesn't look good."

"Mom, what is it?" I asked even while I was noticing the broken beer bottles all over the parking lot and a man standing not far away, puffing on a cigarette, staring right at us, and watching our every move.

"We need to go," Mom insisted. She was nervous. I was aggravated. It was getting dark and starting to rain again. It had been a little tricky getting off the highway and onto the side street that led to the hotel. Traffic had been heavy and menacing. I didn't want to go looking for another hotel.

"Mom," I tried to reassure her, "it will be alright." She reluctantly climbed out of the truck and went into the lobby. I parked the vehicle and then, after climbing stiffly out, awkwardly jumped over wide potholes filled with water on my way to the building. I pushed open the door and saw Mom standing at the front counter. Or what was left of it. A wide portion of the dark wooden desk had been broken off and it was looking rough and splintered. I heard the young clerk tell Mom the price of sixty-nine dollars. I nudged her gently. What happened to the thirty-nine dollar rooms? Sold out. Sold out!? There wasn't another car in the deserted parking lot! How could it be sold out? But I didn't argue. I turned away and looked around the lobby.

The threadbare carpet's red and gold flowers peeked out daintily among the many dark and heavy stains. There was very little furniture besides a stained, dusty couch by the front window that was held into the wall with layers of duct tape. I turned away and looked in the opposite direction. I looked right at the door leading to the swimming pool. Well, more accurately, I looked right at the notice hanging on the door leading to the swimming pool. The notice read that the swimming pool was closed....closed by the health department due to contamination! Oh, my gosh, could there be *hepatitis* in the swimming pool?

I shook the thought away and started to follow Mom out of the lobby but not before noticing a sign taped to the fragmented front counter. "All refunds will be giving only within the first fifteen minutes after check in." Okay, what exactly was that all about and why would they have a sign like that on the front desk?

Mom and I walked outside. We had to cross the parking lot to reach the hotel rooms. We literally bunny hopped across the lot trying to avoid all the water-filled potholes and climbed the stairs up to our room. We stared at each other for a moment as we looked at our door. It looked as if someone had tried to kick in the bottom panel. We used the key to open the door even though I think we both could have crawled through the hole at the bottom...at the same time. We opened the door and looked in; neither one of us was willing to enter first. We stood in the doorway glancing inside at the overflowing ashtrays and beer bottles on the end tables, fast food wrappers on the floor, stains on the carpet and bedspread...Man, what was that on the bedspread?

"Let's go," I told Mom before turning around and running back down the steps to the parking lot. I hoped we were still within the fifteen-minute time limit. We walked into the lobby and right up to the front desk. "We want a refund. We aren't staying here," I told the young, heavyset man behind the counter.

He stared at me for a moment. "May I ask why?"

I could have made him a list. Dirty hotel room. Hepatitis in the swimming pool. A splintered front desk counter. But I just shook my head. "We can't stay here. We want a refund." I actually felt a little guilty. There were two men behind the counter. They were very young and I wondered if they were brothers who were trying to make a go of hotel entrepreneurship.

However, we were two women traveling alone and needing to feel safe. We needed to go. Thank goodness, we got our refund without any fuss, jumped into the truck and took off. Anxious to get away, we didn't worry about the approaching darkness, falling rain, or heavy traffic. We just needed to be away as quickly as Dog could take us.

Surprisingly, just three exits further along the highway, we found a nice, clean hotel with a beautiful lobby, free internet, and clean, well-maintained rooms. Mom and I were able to get a good night's sleep without worrying about anything or anyone crawling through a hole in the bottom of the hotel room door. Refreshed and renewed, we headed back to Kansas the next morning.

Though this had been one of the wildest, stormiest trips we had ever taken, I felt fresh and ready for any upcoming challenges. I was ready to return to California and settle back down into my life again. I don't know if it was the stormy weather or the tidal wave of our emotions, but I felt cleansed and pure again. My mind was clear and my heart was wide open. I was, in a sense, reborn. On this particular journey, I had experienced my own birth. Traveling was always my maternity leave. It was my time to get away and experience the emergence of life and restart the nurturing process. This time the emergence had not been easy. It had been full of pain and tears and memories. It had been nearly four weeks of heavy labor, but it had all been worth it. I had given birth to myself...and I suddenly found I loved myself as strongly as any mother would.

I knew where I had been, where I came from, even though, I had no clue where I was headed. But that is the journey of my life. I leave myself open to God's plan.

Part Three

HOMEWORK

CHAPTER 8

*I*t wasn't the way we had planned it. I knew my life was going to change that day, only it had moved in a direction I hadn't anticipated. I should have been at home, cleaning, preparing, dreaming. Instead, in tears, I was sitting on a plane somewhere over the southwest.

It all began as a usual bright, sunny, Southern California Sunday morning. I had planned to go to the gym and then return back home to clean my apartment. My plan came to an end around ten am when I walked out of the gym. I had been feeling happy with all of my endorphins, like tiny dolphins, swimming around my body, leaping, shrieking, and radiating out to all of my cells. My entire body, however, went into shock, completely stopped functioning, as I sat in my truck and listened to the message that was on my cell phone.

"Jamie, Mom won't be coming to California today," my brother, Anthony, informed me. "We had to rush her to the hospital. The doctors aren't sure yet but they think it's a brain aneurysm..."

I didn't even listen to the rest of the message. My hands shook as I called him back immediately. I don't recall hearing his phone ring because my head was spinning with all kinds of thoughts. Aneurysm... one word that can send my whole family into absolute panic. My father died of a brain aneurysm ten years before. My mother now.. no, not now...please, not now...Not when Mom had been planning that very day to begin her journey to a new life with me in California.

I had been living away from my family in Kansas for almost twenty years. I have lived in many locations during that time, including Tennessee, New Mexico, and England. In each location where I landed, I begged Mom to join me. I thought she deserved a new life of her own. She had finally agreed over a year ago to join me in California as soon as she could sell her house.

I think, for a while, the house may have been an excuse, hiding her anxiety of packing up and moving. She fretted about the economy and the housing situation and believed that it would be months, if not years, before there would be any interest in her small two-bedroom duplex. But in April, she called me excitedly with the news...the house had sold...and we both sat for a moment in silence....This was really going to happen.

The plan we had devised was rather simple. My sister, Carol, would drive Mom out to California and then fly back to Kansas. At first, I was rather upset that Carol had volunteered to do the driving. Traveling was something I had experienced so intimately with Mom, I wasn't, at first, willing to share. It wasn't just about the travel; it was my whole life. I felt like a part of my soul was being taken away from me. But when Carol and I talked over the situation, her comments made me stop and think.

"Jamie, Mom is moving a thousand miles away from the rest of the family. What if we never get to see her again?" I couldn't argue with her then. I know how that feels. Every time I leave Mom in Kansas and take off for another part of the country without her, an agonizing anxiety would shake through me for the first few hundred miles. What if I never saw her or any member of my family ever again? And, yet, I don't stop. I don't turn back around. A stronger vibration pulls me in the opposite direction. I can't turn it off any more than I can stop the blood racing through my veins.

So the plan was set. Carol would delivery Mom to California. But now on the very day that they had planned to set out on their journey, Anthony was informing me they wouldn't be coming. He didn't have a lot of information. He could only tell me that Mom had been taken to a local hospital in Kansas but was now being moved by ambulance to a better-equipped hospital in Missouri. His last words made me break into loud, uncontrollable sobs. "The doctors are saying, if you want to say good-bye," his voice cracked and shook out over my cell phone, "you need to come now. She probably won't make it through the night."

As I flew back to Kansas that evening, I couldn't shake the memories running through my head. Ten years ago, I had received a similar call while I was living in New Mexico. "Jamie, Dad just had a brain aneurysm. You have to get home now if you want to say good-bye." I sped to the airport then and took the first flight out to Kansas that I could get. I prayed I would arrive at my father's side in time. My sister, Theresa, met me at the airport. The first words out of her mouth as she threw her arms around me were, "He died this morning at 11:20 am."

My father's passing began in a casino in Kansas City, Missouri. Mom and Dad were very competitive and it wasn't uncommon for arguments to break out between them while they were playing the slots. In order to keep the peace, they always played on opposite sides of the casino. However, that afternoon, Dad had ventured over to Mom's side and told her that he had experienced a really bad, unusual headache. Mom asked him if he wanted to leave and he had stated that he was feeling better. The headache had just been very quick, sharp pains that were beginning to slowly dissipate now. He didn't want to leave yet. He had been winning! Dad wasn't going to let a headache interfere with his lucky streak.

About ten minutes later, however, two large casino workers walked up to Mom and asked her if she was Mrs. Joseph Zunick. Mom's first reaction was to stare at the men and wonder, "Oh, Joseph, what have you done now?" When Mom finally admitted her identity, the men asked her to follow them. Mom quickly walked with the men to Dad's side of the casino. There had been no explanation. Mom had no idea what to expect. They stopped in an aisle of quarter slots...and there was my father...lying on the floor...his bucket of coins knocked to one side and his body covered in raindrops of bright silver quarters. An ambulance had been called and Dad was rushed to the hospital. But there was nothing that could be done. The artery that had burst was too deep within his brain to be repaired. My father had retired from his job just three months before. He had mellowed over the years and wanted a home and family now. He was too late. So was I. He died two hours before I arrived.

Mom had just started living her life a few short years before. We just had four states left to visit: Oregon, Washington, Hawaii, and Alaska. I'm not sure how we were going to get to Hawaii and Alaska because Mom hates to fly. Oh, man, what was wrong with me? My mother could be dying right now and all I could think about was how I was going to get her to Hawaii and Alaska!

But thoughts like that spun through my head as I flew to Kansas City. I tried to read or scribble a few words into my journal, but I couldn't concentrate. My head spun with memories of my adventures with my mother, and I buried my head into my book, just to hide my tears, every time I felt overcome with sobs. I didn't want to explain to anyone what was happening. I didn't know if I could. I didn't really know myself. All I knew was that my mother went to the doctors on Friday complaining of a severe headache. The doctors claimed she was fine. Nothing more than a pulled muscle. I talked to her myself on Saturday and though she complained about a slight ache in her neck, shoulders, and head, she assured me she was fine and looking forward to her journey to California the next day. Then Sunday morning, I got the call from Anthony that landed me on this plane headed towards Kansas City.

It hadn't been easy. My flight had been delayed for forty-five minutes because one of the overhead bins wouldn't close. Everyone on the plane had to wait until the maintenance people could finally slam it shut and then sign off on all of the paperwork. Flight regulations... we could not take off until every door, including the overhead bins, were firmly latched. Forty-five minutes felt like a lifetime. This one small detail had caused me to burst into uncontrollable tears. I didn't stop crying for the entire flight.

The Kansas City, Missouri, airport was completely deserted when I finally arrived around 11:45 pm. Anthony was there to pick me up and was in a surprisingly calm mood. Mom had never lost consciousness as the doctors had predicted and she was sleeping peacefully. Visiting hours had long since ended for the day and we were all exhausted. We would go to the hospital in the morning.

Anthony and I arrived at the hospital around 7:30 am the next day. He led me into the ICU where we both quickly slipped on hospital gowns and gloves. Then I followed Anthony to the right side of the large room. He slid back a heavy blue curtain, and there was Mom, resting peacefully, her face straight up and her right hand resting across her heart. I didn't focus on the beeping machines that surrounded her. All I could see was the beauty of her face. I stood there, outside her curtain, marveling at the fact that my mother, for all she had been through, looked more beautiful than I had ever seen her before. Her skin looked so luminous, pure and soft; her hands smooth and steady; her hair, short and resting in spikes across her clear forehead. I wanted her to open her eyes and look at me, but she slept on while I stood there, marveling at this small woman who had given birth to four children. Never had she looked so restful and at peace...and that thought terrified me.

I didn't want her at peace right now. I wanted her running around the falls of Niagara and climbing the hills of the Cahokia Mounds. I wanted her rubbing the doorknobs of Graceland and playing the casinos of Vegas. I didn't want to wake her up and yet I prayed that she would suddenly open her eyes. I wanted to see that bright emerald sparkle again. Over the years, Mom had been developing her fighter soul. She was a survivor. I wanted her up now, on her feet, fighting for her life.

It wasn't until Anthony gently nudged me that I suddenly realized that I had been standing just outside the curtain of her small cubicle, shocked still, and trying to make myself small. Where was *my* fighting spirit? I followed Anthony quietly into the room as he moved up to her bedside gently calling out to her.

"Don't wake her up," I told him as I fought my own urge to shake her alert. Instead, I just stayed quiet and watched as Anthony leaned down a little closer to her.

"Mom?" he whispered, "Mom?"

Suddenly, her eyes popped open and she moved her legs with a small jerk. Her head turned in my direction as Anthony said, "Look who's here."

I stood with my hands resting on my hips and said, "This is not the way we had it planned." I meant it as a joke, but it was true. We had planned her California journey so carefully. We had made a plan... and God laughed.

Tears sprouted to her eyes as she started to say she was so sorry. She should have been on her way to California, but instead there I was on Monday morning in Kansas, standing in my mother's ICU room while she was lying in bed with various tubes and needles in her arms and hands. As I moved closer, I noticed the large purple bruises that marred the smooth skin on the inside of her arms.

Mom talked in a low voice, a soft voice that made her words sound like a prayer instead of a command. "You shouldn't have come," she admonished me. "You shouldn't be here." I knew the real reason she was saying these things. She didn't want to be a burden. She had been a wife and mother for so long, taking care of her family without complaint. I knew that to be in such a helpless position was almost unbearable for her.

Anthony left the room after a few minutes leaving me alone with Mom, who I hadn't seen in over a year. My mind raced through our last visit together. Oh, yes, that was the drive to the northeast where we battled rainstorms, viewed Niagara Falls, and drowned in tears in Atlantic City. It seemed so long ago as I looked at her now lying on her back, tubes in her body, and bruises covering her arms. Mom vocalized a few short moans from the severe headaches she was experiencing.

But I know her well...and I knew in her quieter moments, with nothing else to distract her, she plotted her escape from the ICU and her run for the California border. I watched her eyelids twitch every time she closed them for a few minutes and I knew she was thinking of faraway places. I gently talked to her as I brushed my fingers over her short, to-the-scalp, hair. I don't remember what we said to each other, but I don't imagine it really matters. It was just words, a moment that we shared until she fell asleep again.

I kissed her cheek gently and stepped out to the waiting room. Anthony and Carol were there together and they greeted me warmly. The rest of the afternoon was somewhat of a blur. I guess time spent in a hospital waiting room is always the same for everybody. Time stops and then speeds up and then slows down and then disappears. We sat staring at the pale green walls all afternoon and yet each minute was never the same. Each minute was filled with hope, despair, desolation, love, despondency, and then hope again.

My family and I spun through all of the emotions as we spent the day running back and forth to ICU every time visiting hours came up again. In between hours, we sat together in a corner of the waiting room, sharing memories, telling new stories of our lives, and laughing at everything. God only knows why we couldn't seem to stop the laughter, especially when my niece, Jessica, and my nephew, David, arrived. I wonder now how inappropriate our laughter may have seemed to other people waiting for news of their loved ones, but nervousness and lack of sleep wouldn't let us stop. In the midst of worry and heartbreak, it felt so good to be together, sharing both memory and tragedy, unsure of how this situation would change us all, but knowing it already had.

We still did not know exactly what happened to Mom. The doctors were perplexed. The fact that she was bleeding inside her head but never lost conscious had them somewhat baffled and they were reluctant to give any definite diagnosis. They began to believe that their original finding of a brain aneurysm was not correct but they had no other explanation.

The following day, the family was back at the hospital by eight am. We spent most of the morning in Mom's room. I loved the moments when Mom was awake. Every time she fell asleep, my heart would start pounding wildly as I worried that she was slipping away. I wanted to keep her awake. When she was awake, she was talkative, funny, detailed in her summary of the events that lead her to this place.

So, yeah, I loved having her awake...until the severe pain began to race around her head, causing her to cringe and cry out. I sat beside her, stroking my fingers over her forehead and through her short, spiky hair. Mom began to request my gentle touch every time the pain was great and the nurses refused to give her any more medication. My hands always tend to be cold which usually embarrasses me. But now I was pleased when Mom told me that my cool fingers helped to sooth the burning in her head. I stayed with her, stroking through her hair until morning visiting hours ended again.

That Tuesday afternoon, June 17, 2009, my family squeezed into Mom's ICU cubicle as Dr. Singh explained the situation. The doctors had been surprised that Mom's angiograms had not revealed anything. An angiogram is a test that checks the arteries for any problems. No problems or complications were detected. Their only diagnosis was that Mom had not torn an artery (an aneurysm) as originally thought due to all of the blood in her brain. Mom had actually burst a vein. It could still be dangerous, but usually veins heal over without any further difficulties. Mom should recover with full brain functioning.

I listened in a daze as my family members asked several question. I couldn't keep myself from glancing over at Mom as she slept peacefully. I wondered if she knew we were all there, discussing her as if she were not even in the room. I knew she would be very upset to know her situation was being talked about without her.

The doctors still planned to keep Mom in ICU for a little while longer, but every day she was getting stronger. She began to stay awake for longer periods of time. Over the next few days, the tubes were removed from her arms and hands and she began to sit up and eat on her own. Mom began to refer to the ICU as the "looney bin." She constantly complained that the nurses did not let her move or think for herself. She was uncomfortable needing their help for all of her basic human needs. She hated not being able to prepare her own food. Mom couldn't always eat everything the nurses brought to her and went hungry for most of the day. Sometimes, her hands were so swollen with arthritis, it was increasingly difficult for her to use the plastic silverware she had been given. She continually craved bananas and it took several requests to the nurses before she began to receive them with her meals on a regular basis. A lot of what Mom ate made her horribly sick and she continually vomited almost everything she ate, except for fruit or jello.

The pills she was forced to take were huge and, many times, she choked on them. The medication was needed to stop brain spasms that could eventually cause strokes and other brain dysfunctions. But Mom had never been a pill taker and hated having to take any kind of medication. The nurses soon realized that the only way Mom was going to take her medication was to pop the capsules open and dump the liquid into chocolate ice cream. That method allowed Mom to ingest the medication she needed.

Mom was especially uncomfortable with using the bedpans. The nurses did not want her moving out of bed, even to use the bathroom. Mom found this situation completely unacceptable and so she came up with a plan. She perfectly timed the nurses' rounds. She would stare out through the opening in the heavy blue curtain that served as her door. Once they had passed her room, Mom would get up and run to the bathroom, praying she could do her business before the nurses came back around. Many times, however, she was caught just stepping back out of the restroom, trying to wrap her gown around her body. Then, of course, the nurses would admonish her for getting out of bed and tell her again that she must use the bedpan. Mother would nod her head, but all along she was plotting her next desperate race for the toilet. The nurses were kind to her, though, and took her rebellion in stride.

My mother had been plotting other rebellions. One doctor was extremely rude to her. The day before she was moved out of ICU, Mom finally told him he had no bedside manner and she was amazed that he was allowed any interaction with patients at all. What she said must have cut him deeply because he began to be more gentle and patient with her after that.

There was another doctor, however, that Mom found difficult to be around for a completely different reason. He was known around the hospital as Dr. Richard Gere because of his close resemblance to the actor. He was a neurologist and Mom was continually trying to set me up with him. He, however, didn't even notice me as he made his rounds. Mom was perturbed by the situation and couldn't understand his lack of interest. Yeah, Mom was getting back to normal. She was fighting back, standing up for me. I was pleased to see her spirit returning as she regained strength enough to be moved out of ICU. She was on her way to a full recovery.

Mom would have to spend several more days in a regular hospital room before she was allowed to return home. On the day of my departure, she anxiously waited all morning for her MRI, positive that she would be declared healthy and would soon be released. But it wasn't meant to be. Mom was healing but was ordered to stay in the hospital one more day. We kissed good-bye and I headed to the airport to travel back to California. We were not going to give up. Mom would be with me soon. But our journey back to a normal life was far from over.

CHAPTER 9

Though almost two months late, Mom's dream of moving to California was finally coming true. It wasn't an easy getaway for her. The medical tests she had to submit to in order to be cleared by the doctors had seemed almost endless. Mom had constant MRIs and waited anxiously for the doctors to tell her it was safe to travel. The minute she received the all clear, Mom and Carol were on the road.

Mom asked me to plan out their route, which made me a little nervous. I continually told her to please ask Carol and her husband, David, to make their travel plans. "What if I get you lost?" I continually asked Mom. "I don't know if there will be road closures, construction, detours. You and Carol need to plan your own route." Mom and I argued over this for a few weeks. Why was she putting so much trust in me? Maybe because I had proven myself on the road. I don't know. Mom had every bit of faith that I would safely guide them to California.

Big mistake! I got them lost! On their way out of Arizona, I had given them the wrong highway number. Carol called me from Barstow, a large city about 110 miles northeast of Palm Springs, to let me know my directions were useless. Oops! They would be arriving in Palm Springs later than they had planned. Mom and Carol no longer trusted me now. They refused to take any more directions from me. Instead, they decided it was better to get information from a complete stranger they had meet at a gas station than to let me choose their route again. Well, at least now, they were headed in the right direction and about two hours later, they finally pulled into the parking lot of my apartment complex.

I ran out my front door and to their car. I grabbed and hugged Carol first. She had come springing out of the car; the long drive seemed to have energized her. I knew how she felt. I always felt the same zing after the long drives Mom and I would take. After a moment, Carol walked me around the car towards Mom who was slowly climbing out of the SUV. Her movements amazed me. Where was my mother who climbed mounds and ran through the caves of Bandelier? Where was my mother who danced in the public square of Santa Fe and jumped out at me in the hallways of a Savannah hotel? This couldn't be my mother! Who was this woman who was struggling to pull herself slowly out of the passenger seat of the vehicle? I only recognized the emerald shine of her eyes.

I couldn't believe that Mom had made the 1500-mile trip from Kansas to California. Her right leg was cramping and she stood awkwardly, leaning haphazardly to the left. Over the last several weeks, she had been injected with ink in her right leg. The ink had moved through her arteries, lighting them up like headlights on a busy highway, so doctors could check for clots or blockages during MRIs. The area near her groin had not healed the way the doctors had hoped, but Mom refused to complain about it. Not when California awaited her. Mom is still a road warrior, and her amazing, adventurous spirit carried her from Kansas to California without a complaint or whimper.

Carol, Mom, and I spent two days relaxing around Palm Springs before Carol returned to Kansas and Mom and I were on our own. We stayed around town at first, letting Mom adjust to her new surroundings and allowing her the opportunity to heal.

After twenty years, it was a bit of an adjustment to live with Mom again, especially in a small one-bedroom apartment. Right now, I didn't want to leave Mom on her own while she was new to town and still in variable amounts of pain. We tried hard to make this new living arrangement easy on each other, but there were small disagreements along the way.

For example, there was the night we got into an argument over the best time to take out the trash. I always liked getting the trash out of my home every night. I don't like having empty cartons or wrappings just sitting in the trash can over night. I was going to take the trash out about nine o'clock one night, which greatly aggravated Mom who thought that going out to the dumpster at that time of night was just asking for trouble. We argued back and forth for a while until I finally shut up and let her talk. I listened to her and then, when she stepped into the bathroom, I took the trash out anyway. Of course, Mom was very upset with me, thinking I had gone behind her back (which, technically, I guess I did) and went to bed without saying good night. I didn't feel good about this. It was a silly thing to fight about. But I had my own way of living and my own way of doing things, so we were bound to clash at times.

Sometimes the clashes got us into real trouble. One day, Mom wanted to go to the Harley Davidson shop to buy a Christmas present for my brother-in-law, David, who was an avid biker. However, it was "biker weekend" in Palm Springs and I tried to convince Mom that it wasn't a good time to go. She was insistent though and we soon found ourselves trapped in a huge group of bikers just lounging everywhere around the shop.

I was a little uncomfortable because I felt out of place, surrounded by all that leather and bike exhaust. My basic shyness caused me to shuffle around self-consciously and make little eye contact with people. Mom, however, was on a Christmas gift mission, so she seemed totally oblivious to the large, tattooed, pierced men and women who surrounded her ninety pound little body. She shopped for her gifts while I tagged along behind her. Finally, after thirty awkward minutes, she was ready to go. As we were walking across the parking lot, I was so focused on getting to the truck, I wasn't even paying attention to Mom as she ran quickly behind me, trying to keep up with my long strides. All of a sudden, I heard a huge sigh mixed with a gasp coming from somewhere behind me. I looked back and surprisingly found Mom flat out on the ground, face down.

I ran back to her and knelt down as she slowly and awkwardly started to get back to her feet. Most of the biker guys just remained on their Harleys watching our struggle to get up off the ground. Only one large biker dude stepped forward from the wall of black leather. He towered over us as Mom rose back up to her full tiny height. Her poor face was torn along her left eye and a scrape ran down the edge of her nose. The biker turned to look at me. He shook his head disgustedly as he continually asked, "Is this your mother?! Is this your mother?!" I answered "Yes" with a slight shake to my voice as we slowly began to back away to our truck. Great, we had to find the only large biker dude who was a momma's boy. He began to say something to me but stopped when my tiny momma threw herself in front of me, assuring the man that she was fine and didn't need his help. With her shaky fingers, she dabbed at the bit of blood that was staining the left side of her face and then flicked the drops away. She stared into the eyes of the biker, told him she was okay, and that we would be going now. They stared at each other for just a moment until the biker finally turned and walked back to his buddies who had started gunning up their bikes. Mom pushed me towards the truck. We climbed in and started heading for the highway. A wave of motorcycles rolled with us for about five miles until we reached our exit for home. Mom was able to laugh about the situation later, but I still felt horribly guilty. Even after she had fallen on her face, Mom had still been ready to take on a large biker dude for me.

So, yeah, we did have a few rough moments. But surprisingly, when Mom was settled in California, we got along better together than either one of us expected. We were slowly learning how to live together again after so long. Mom was excited about being in California. It was as if she had a whole new life. Or she had kept the old one but was just starting to live it again. Her spirit returned but her body was slow to follow. She was having slight headaches and would become quickly exhausted and nauseous.

I find myself rejoicing in her smallest victories. If she was able to sit up a little longer, walk a little further, I would cheer her healing process. At the same time, every time she faltered, every small stumble, would break my heart.

The first time we went to a casino, I tried to hold my emotions in check as I watched her play. Mom sat in front of a slot machine, dropped in her money, and pushed the buttons to spin the wheels. I watched as she occasionally placed her right hand up against the front of the machine, palm down, and pushed into it before pressing the button to set the wheels in motion. At first, I found myself chuckling softly. Everyone always seems to have his or her own unique rituals and superstitions for playing the slot machines. I have seen many people patting and stroking their machines for luck. But Mom's actions took me by surprise when I finally realized what she was doing. Arthritis had horribly twisted her fingers around each other, intersecting them in long, thin tangles. Her "ritual" wasn't for good luck. Instead, she was trying to reorganize the bones in her arthritic hands in between each spin of the wheels.

But even though her body moved awkwardly, her spirit flowed. She would, at times, behave as if she could not live fast enough. After a few weeks in Palm Springs, Mom really wanted to go up to the Jemez Mountains. I was nervous, at first, about the altitude and the pressure it could cause in her brain. As we swayed around the curves, she would laugh and then her tiny hands would reach up around her head. "My head," she would whine. "It's exploding!" Her words horrified me the first time she said them. I pulled over to the side of the road, terrified she was in agony. I was reaching for my phone to call 911, when her laughter stopped me. It was a joke. She was perfectly fine. I did not find it funny. We sat for ten minutes on the side of the road arguing about what was acceptable humor and what wasn't. I told her not to joke about something so serious. She told me to lighten up. We finally pulled back onto the road again, but now I was the one threatening to turn the car around if she couldn't behave. While I continued to fume, Mom ignored me and continued to moan, laugh, and call me a "tight butt" all the way up the mountain.

On my birthday in August, we took our first trip together out of Palm Springs to Long Beach, California, to see the Queen Mary. We roamed the ship just feeling peaceful and happy to be a part of a time gone by. Mom's happy adventurous spirit seemed to be returning as she posed for pictures and strutted down the boardwalks. My hope was beginning to grow as big as the ocean and as bright as the Southern California sun. I stood staring out at the water from the upper level of the ship and felt hope swell within me as I said my thank yous to God.

Any time I felt myself looking at the Pacific Ocean, I felt my soul flow quietly and gently through my body. I could feel my spirit move through the universe and sail away on every wave. One of my happiest memories of the Pacific Ocean was just before Christmas, when Mom and I traveled north along the Pacific Coast Highway to San Simeon. It was one of the most amazing views I had ever seen. It was a beautiful and dangerous drive. I had to keep reminding myself to keep my eyes on the road. I had to fight continually not to stare at the wild waves that splashed up onto the rocky shore. I wanted to watch the current roll in and then retreat back. The tide reminded me of my own life. The deluge of water continually made me think of my constant flow away and then back home and away again. If the vast ocean can transpire that easily, that naturally, what fear could possibly hold me back from living a life of rootless wandering. I want that flow, the gentle give and take of a life without resistance. I wanted to have that ability to just let go and let God decide the course my life would take. But lately, my oceans have been stormy. My tide refusing to just follow the pull of the moon. I pull against the natural gravity of things. I aspire to someday give up control and enjoy the freedom of drifting into my life.

People have told me before how lucky I am to have no ties. Nothing to hold me down. But my freedom is the very thing that keeps me trapped. I have too many options, too many places to go. I don't know where I'm supposed to be. I don't belong anywhere. Nothing grounds me. I just continue to drift. Maybe I am more like the ocean than I originally thought.

Mom and I drove to Cambria where we decided to spend the night in a hotel on a hillside. Our room was a cozy little cabin that was very warm and welcoming in the freezing cold December weather. After checking in, we drove downhill into the homey little town beautifully garnished for Christmas. It was so vibrantly decorated that tiny lights sparkled like brilliant midday suns, brightening up the nighttime streets, everywhere we looked. After a quick dinner, we drove back up the hill to our hotel.

However, I couldn't find our way back. The road warped in zigzag patterns around the hillside and within ten minutes, we were horribly lost. After another five minutes of driving around the hill, I suddenly realized I hadn't turned on my headlights! All the bright Christmas lights in the town had been shining so brilliantly, I hadn't noticed the lack of light from my car until we were lost on the hill! We drove up and down the hill above the town three times before we finally stumbled onto the hotel again. I should have been thankful we were safe, but, instead, I was embarrassed and sick over the fact that I could have gotten us both killed by the other cars that had passed by us, honking and zooming around the hillside.

Mom tried to raise my spirits that night, but her own mood was dark and distant the next day. Mom and I woke up early and headed towards San Simeon and the Hearst Castle, which has since become one of my favorite places. It amazes me how one person could envision something so grand and produce it as if by magic. The magic worked slowly on Mom, though. She was quiet when we first arrived at the reception area. She kept to herself and wouldn't really talk to me. I didn't know what was wrong but her silence terrified me. She seemed disoriented and sad even in this magnificent surrounding. She had completely shut down that morning. My constant questions about her health were met with a stony silence.

I never found out what the problem was, but, thankfully, Mom's mood began to lift after lunch. She seemed to relax and enjoy herself later that afternoon and we spent a lot of time laughing and playing as we toured the great estate. The bus ride up the hill to the castle really had us giggling. December weather had settled into the area. It was raining, cloudy and foggy. The road was difficult to see. Blindly, the bus driver slowly navigated the twist and turns of the road up to the castle. We were driving through clouds, which gave a surreal affect to the surrounding area.

I was a little aggravated with the Castle tour guide, though. Before the tour began, the woman had warned us as we entered the mansion to stay on the plastic runners that were laid down throughout the rooms. We were not to step onto the carpets. Mom was fascinated with the mansion and as she moved from room to room, she would be looking up in wonder at the ornate ceilings and walls and would accidentally wander off of the plastic sheets. The tour guide politely told Mom to get back on the runner in the first room. However, by the time the situation occurred again in the fifth room, the guide's patience diminished.

"Ma'am, ma'am," she hollered out at Mom as she waved her hand in a backwards motion. "You have to stay on the runner!" The guide sounded extremely irritated now, which angered me. Mom had begun to enjoy herself, and I was mad that someone would yell at her. So as Mom slowly stepped back onto the runner, I stepped off and stood on the red, threadbare carpet. I had a defiant look on my face as I waited for the tour guide to yell at me. But before she could open her mouth, I felt a tap on my shoulder from behind me. "Honey," Mom's voice whispered to me, "you have to stay on the runner." I turned around to find Mom directly in back of me. She had the same look on her face that she had shown me when I was a child and she was trying to stop me from throwing a tantrum. There was a slight irritated gleam in the green gold of her eyes. "Honey," she whispered again as she wagged her finger at me, "you have to get back on the runner. Come on now." A smile began to highlight her lips as I slowly moved back onto the plastic runner in front of her, my head hanging, my shoulders down, totally deflated. "Good girl," Mom whispered to me as she patted my back. I looked back at her and then decided to just let it go. Mom's eyes were shining with excitement as she pushed me forward to follow the tour group. Neither one of us left the runner for the rest of the tour. We were good and respectful then and went where we were told to go, which is rather unusual for us. Mom and I tend to like bending the rules, usually by accident. We don't mean to be disrespectful. We just tend to have our minds on other things and wander off. We tend to cause a lot of trouble that way.

This was obvious when we went shopping for a new car just a few months after Mom arrived in California. Mom and I became serious car shoppers and took our time deciding what kind of car we would like to have. We did our research, shopped around. We were two women determined not to be put off or scammed. We were not going to be treated like senseless, clueless broads. In fact, we may have gone a little too far in the other direction. We came up with a "good cop/bad cop" plan that we played out in almost every car dealership in Palm Springs.

Before the salesperson approached us, we would quickly decide which one of us would be good and who would be bad. If I was "good", I would be excited about the car, anxious to make the deal. Mom, however, would be the hard sell, pulling back, skeptical. I would be saying things in front of the salesperson like "Mom, this is a great car! It's a great deal! We should go for it!" Mom would be resistant. "No, no, no, dear. I don't think so. We should shop around." Mom and I would bicker between ourselves while the hapless salesperson would be looking back and forth between the two of us, trying to keep up with our conversation. We actually would be bargaining the price of the car between just the two of us without letting the salesperson get a word in. Then finally, Mom would sigh dramatically and say, "Okay, dear, you win. Let's make the deal." The salesperson would sigh with relief not realizing until it was too late that Mom and I had actually switched roles. Now, it was my turn to be defiant and difficult. We would continue this process until we had beaten down the salesperson to a cheaper price...then we would walk away saying we still wanted to shop around. I think several salespeople actually resigned after dealing with us. I do feel bad about one particular salesperson who tried to sell us a new Scion at a local Toyota shop. We were sitting at his desk in the showroom, bickering and switching roles back and forth, until he finally threw his hands up, gripped his short blond hair and began to pull it out of his head as he screamed, "I cannot deal with you women! I cannot deal with you!" He went running into the back office and a few minutes later the shop manager came out to talk with us. I couldn't help picturing the poor salesperson lying in a fetal position, sucking his thumb, in a corner of the back office. Though he kept his cool, the manager couldn't make the deal with us either and actually seemed relieved when we finally walked away.

Though we did eventually buy a new car, at a very good deal, Mom and I still didn't travel too far. We were staying a little closer to home now. Until Mom felt stronger, we stayed around Southern California, running through the Joshua Trees and watching the mountains move and sway every evening in the light of a brilliant sunset. Our lives were settling into an everyday routine. In the morning, I would teach classes at a local college, run home to check up on Mom, and then run back to campus for the evening sessions. It was over the holiday winter break that we finally broke out of the daily schedule and began to travel a little farther.

Our journey to San Juan Capistrano had a mystical feel to it. Mom and I debated for several days whether we should make the trip. I was exhausted from my hectic work schedule and really wanted to just relax. I must have really been exhausted. For once, I wasn't anxious to travel and explore. I wasn't eager to jump in the car and see where I would end up. I wanted to rest, to shut my door, and lock the world out. I just wanted to be still for a moment. I don't know why I was having these rare feelings. I don't know why I was feeling that I couldn't leave home right now. There was just a premonition, a feeling not to go far from home.

But Mom was having feelings and premonitions as well. One morning, as we sat at the dining room table, sipping coffee, Mom looked into my eyes and mentioned San Juan Capistrano again.

"Do you really want to go now, Mom?" I asked. "Or would you rather wait until spring to see the swallows?" The arrival of the swallows to the Mission on March 19th, St. Josephs' Day, was an event Mom and I had talked about several weeks ago. People come from all around the world to witness the miraculous return of the swallows on this day. The birds stay throughout the summer, building their nests around the old chapel. On October 23rd, the Day of San Juan, after circling around the mission, the birds leave for their winter home in Argentina. Mom and I had originally planned to go to the mission in March to experience the arrival of the swallows.

But now, December 27th, 2009, Mom looked at me and stated, "I want to go today," she whispered, her green eyes sparkling. "I'm afraid if I don't go now, I won't get to go at all."

I stared at her for a moment, chilled by her words. But within thirty minutes, we were showered, dressed, and in the car, headed northwest to the mission. The trip was a little difficult. The journey to Capistrano consists of a twisting highway that bent and curved around the mountains. It actually would have been a beautiful journey if we hadn't consistently been harassed by cars and motorcycles pushing up behind us and urging us forward at a frantic pace. We frequently pulled into the turnouts to allow the more impatient drivers to pass us. I wanted to enjoy the scenery, the natural beauty that surrounded us on all sides, but found this somewhat impossible because of the traffic. The magnificence of the drive down Highway 74 was lost on me as I found myself instead anxiously gripping the steering wheel until finally, two hours later, we arrived in San Juan Capistrano.

I had never felt so much peace in my life. The mission, even in its somewhat collapsed state due to the earthquake of 1812, was breathtakingly beautiful. Mom and I were breathing easier as we walked around the courtyard and explored the chapel and museum. Though Mom's words that morning about "needing to go now" had unnerved me a little, she had been right. The visit had set my mind free and my soul soaring. I wanted to stay all day in the warmth and love I felt in this space. I wanted to move into the mission, bury my heart and soul within its walls. Finding a place on this earth where I felt accepted and loved and yet knowing I could not stay was heartbreaking. I had found a home, but would have to leave, just like the swallows. Like the swallows, my natural instinct and desires would always pull me away.

Mom and I had become restless again after a few days. Mom, especially, couldn't seem to live fast enough. She now wanted to go everywhere and experience even more. My family seemed surprised by Mom's sudden need to get out, especially at night. Back in Kansas, Mom rarely went out in the evenings. Now, she would peruse the paper every morning, looking for events that we could attend when I had a free evening from classes. We would go out to dinner, movies, and concerts.

Mom was slowly healing in so many different ways. The headaches were easing and the pain and stiffness in her right leg had stopped. She was moving easier now and could sit for longer periods in the car. We were beginning to move in every direction again, suddenly knowing no boundaries and with no restrictions. We were happy and limitless.

…And then we crashed.

CHAPTER 10

I wanted to believe that Mom would continue to grow stronger, but I knew a change was coming. I could feel it in Mom's every breath. I would see it in my dreams.

One night, I had been sleeping peacefully on the couch in the living room. I suddenly awoke, turned onto my left side, and found myself staring at a shimmering angel. She appeared exactly as I expected her to look. She had large, full, white wings protruding from the back of her slender body and a halo wrapped around her golden-blond hair. In her smooth, silky hands, she was holding a large brown tablet. I stared in complete awe as the angel stood in front of me. Then she calmly informed me, "Your mother is on the death list."

I looked at her for a moment, stunned by what I had just heard. I asked what she meant with a nervous laugh and a shake of my head. I tried to convince myself that this wasn't real and yet I felt compelled to pay attention to her message. The angel stated again, "Your mother has been placed on the death list."

"No, no, that's not right," I whispered as I started to cry. I begged the angel to please take my mother off the list. I tried to negotiate for my mom's life. I tried to bargain that if Mom and I could just have a few more years together, that's all, I would let her go then. But the angel refused.

"It's too late," she whispered to me. "It's already done." Then slowly she began to dissolve into the air around me. I found myself suddenly staring into nothingness until I felt completely alone. I suddenly popped fully awake then. I was lying on the couch in the living room. The television was still on, just as it had been when I laid down to sleep about two hours ago. It was almost three in the morning now. Everything looked the same as it had been when I had first fallen asleep, except now I was shaking and crying. My heart was beating so quickly in my chest, I felt as if I had just run a marathon on steroids.

I got up from the couch and stumbled to Mom's room in the back of our small two-bedroom apartment. I stood in the doorway and looked in at her. Her tiny, slender frame was stretched out on the bed. She was so small, I felt as if I was gazing in on a napping child. Watching my mother sleep peacefully, knowing she was safe here, could not erase the images that had fluttered through my mind just a few minutes before.

I stumbled back to the living room couch and sat down heavily. My mother....on some death list? Why would I even imagine something like that? Feelings of shame and guilt washed over me as though, by experiencing such a strange vision, I had done something horribly wrong. I thought back to the images I would see as a child. Yes, they would come true but I didn't rejoice in them. Some of the visions could upset and terrify me sometimes and I was experiencing that anxiety again. What could possibly have been on my mind as I had drifted off to sleep? I knew there was more to the dream than I could possibly imagine right then. I couldn't relax and sleep again. I didn't want any more visions or wanderings. This particular one had scared me.

I hated leaving Mom alone so much during the day when I went to work. I worried that she would be cooped up in the apartment all by herself for hours. She had no way of getting around. She had surrendered her driver's license when she first moved to California because the traffic scared her. I couldn't imagine ever giving up my license. It was my link to the life that I had had and the life I wanted for myself. It was my whole connection to the rest of the world. But she was ready to let go. Mom was good about letting aspects of her life slip away when she believed it was the right time. She accepted change without question. I usually thrived on change as well, but suddenly I found myself resisting even the smallest modification to our routine.

Usually, I came home from work in the afternoons, picked Mom up for lunch, and then we would hang out together at the apartment for an hour, watching *John and Kate Plus Eight* or *Tori and Dean* before I had to run back to work. I would sit on the floor in front of the couch. Mom would sit behind me and weave my hair into tiny little braids all over my head. That was the only time I would let anyone mess with my hair. I usually can't stand to have anyone tease, cut, brush, or play with my hair. But this was different. Mom's touch would relax me....usually. One time she weaved my hair around so tightly, I couldn't get all of the braids out. It made me laugh every time I ran my hands over the braids. I would smile as I thought about the crooked fingers that had twisted and twirled my hair into place. I looked forward to these afternoons with Mom.

On January 28, 2010, Thursday, however, something seemed different. I picked Mom up and we went out to lunch. Afterwards, however, Mom felt queasy as her stomach continued to twist and churn.

"Mom, are you okay?" I asked her, a little concerned. "Are you getting sick?"

"No," she answered, "I'm fine. I don't feel bad at all."

I just smiled and let the situation drop. I don't remember Mom eating a lot while I was growing up. Her eating habits, however, would lead to my own food issues and disorders. I think we both stopped eating for the same reason—we were trying to make ourselves disappear. I think we both just wanted to slip away. But Mom's eating habits began to change when she moved out to California. She began to eat better and feel more comfortable with herself. She would laugh and say she was retired now and it was time to enjoy life, and that included food. The pressure was off, and she began to indulge a little.

Yeah, enjoy life…so here we were now with Mom's stomach growling and grinding after having a very simple meal. But, honestly, I didn't think anything more about it. Mom said she was fine, like she always said when she had the flu, or a cold, or respiratory complications from smoking, or a broken heart from endless disappointments. I was skeptical, but choose to ignore it. I wanted everything to be okay. So an hour later, I returned to work again for my evening classes, convincing myself that Mom was suffering from nothing more than an upset stomach.

But things were a little more complicated the next day, Friday, January 29, 2010. I went to work that morning for just a few hours before returning home to get Mom for our day out. Mom loved our moments together even if we didn't do a whole lot. She just lived her days…that's all, just lived her days.

Mom wanted to eat at a buffet today. She loved buffets because she always liked fixing her own plate and not having anyone wait on her. That sounds like Mom. She always gave to everyone else, took care of everyone else, but became self-conscious and uncomfortable when anyone tried to take care of her. Maybe enjoying buffets was part of the eating disorders, too. For myself, I preferred buffets because I didn't want anyone else touching my plate or knowing what I was eating. I can't stand talking about food. It took me a long time to learn to eat in front of other people. Sometimes I just don't like to eat at all. Mom, at times, could be a very picky eater, so I preferred going where she was happy.

On the drive back home from lunch, however, Mom suddenly yelled, "I don't feel so well…Stop the car! I'm going to be sick! Stop!" I quickly pulled into the nearest parking lot and Mom jumped out of the car before it was even in park. I sat in the car for a moment watching her. She walked around for a moment before sitting down on one of the parking space curbs. I should have gotten out of the car sooner but I was trying to pull myself together. I was feeling slightly unnecessarily annoyed. That was an awful feeling. I didn't say anything mean to Mom or sigh heavily like I normally do when I am irritated. I took a deep breath and pulled myself together before climbing out of the car. Why was I so annoyed? Because I didn't want my mother to be sick! Any time Mom became ill, with any ailment, it would send me into sheer terror.

I think this all began when I was about five-years-old. I have a vague memory of an afternoon when I was sitting at the table with my sisters drawing in our coloring books. Mom and Dad walked into the living room which attached openly right to the dining room. Mom sat in the old wooden rocking chair while Dad knelt down by her side. She picked up the phone and dialed. My mother then said into the receiver that she needed to make an appointment to see the doctor. While my sisters continued to chatter and color, my eyes were glued on my mother as she sat with her back to me. My ears opened wide to every word she was saying. I stared at her and my father intently and felt a heaviness in my heart that I could not even begin to understand in my childish brain. I clearly heard her say into the phone, "I have a lump in my left breast." I stared at my parents, listening and just knowing that this was not a good thing. I was always a very sensitive child and I don't know if I was acting in response to my parent's reaction or my own sense of mortality. My father was kneeling beside Mom and I could see his face perfectly as he stared up at her. His face was filled with worry and tenderness, looks I had never seen from my dad before or since. Maybe that was the reason I became paralyzed with fear. I just knew, from my mom's words and my dad's expression, that something was terribly wrong.

I don't think Mom even knew I had heard her until we were driving though New Hampshire nearly thirty-five years later. I finally asked her about it then. Why did it take me so long to ask? I guess, even though I was an adult, it was still terrifying to think of something happening to my mother. That she could be so ill in any way caused my heart to beat rapidly. In New Hampshire, she just shook her head at my questions about the situation. "It was nothing, really. I shouldn't have made such a fuss." That was my mother. Why should anyone make a fuss over her? But then she said, "It turned out to be just a fatty tumor, a cyst. Just had it removed. Nothing else ever came of it." She shrugged her shoulders as if it was no big deal and I was not to worry.

But still...sometimes I can't stop myself from thinking of the "What if..." of situations. What if something had happened to my mother when I was such a small child? I couldn't imagine being raised just by my father...a cold, strict man who never hugged and hardly ever laughed. A man who threatened to lock me up for the slightest imperfection. I shook the thought away as I looked at Mom now sitting down in the parking lot. Her knees were bent up to make a small shelf to hold her arms which cradled her head. My head was filled with the dream I had had just a few weeks ago. My mother on a death list...oh, God, no, please. So now I tried to push my fear and irritation away and walked over to where she was sitting.

"I'm feeling a little better now," she whispered as I sat down beside her.

"What was it, Mom?" I asked her, keeping my voice soft. Please just say you feel great; it was nothing; please suggest going to a movie or shopping. "What happened?"

"I don't know," she whispered, "I just felt like I had to be sick. Maybe I just got too hot in the car. I just needed some air." That was a possibility. Though it was still technically winter, Mother was not in Kansas anymore, but sunny, warm Palm Springs. Mom's body temperature lately had been running hot. She would continually have hot flashes and sweat heavily. She wiped her face with the end of her sleeve, slowly stood up, and crawled back into the car.

"Let me know, Mom, if you need to stop again," I told her while praying we would be able to make it all the way home without a further incident.

Once we were home, Mom went in to lie down while I headed up to the gym, trying to convince myself that this was nothing. Just a little queasiness. She would be fine...

Yeah, fine, except I've never known Mom to sleep so much. She never was one to lie around doing nothing. Mom was always cleaning, cooking, working hard. Always up by five in the morning....

January, 30, 2010, Saturday, Mom was sleeping in late. That was the first clue that I knew something was wrong. Mom finally got up around 10:30 am and came stumbling into the living room. She went right to the picture windows and opened up the blinds to let the sun in as she normally did every morning. She always loved to have the sunlight sweeping into the apartment. I preferred it quiet and dark. I never open the blinds.

As the light began to pour in, Mom announced to me, "I have the flu." However, she moved gracefully around the room, without any awkwardness or wooziness.

"Are you sure, Mom?" I asked surprised. Mom was prone to flu infections so I knew her behavior when she was afflicted. She would be achy, weak, unable to rise out of bed, unable to move, vomiting. This was different. She was moving in perfectly balanced motion around the small apartment. "I was queasy this morning," she informed me. "Vomited a little."

"You did?" I asked. Then hesitated for a moment, not really wanting to know. "Was it bad?"

"No," she responded coolly before she went in to the kitchen to get a cup of coffee. She filled the cup easily without even shaking and carried it to the kitchen table. This wasn't a normal flu response. Coffee would usually upset Mom when she wasn't feeling well.

"Mom," I asked cautiously, "how are you feeling now?"

"Actually," she smiled, "pretty good right now. I'm just exhausted.

I was up most of the night. I'm going to go back to bed and lie down for a while." She began to move back towards her bedroom as I sat at the dining room table, watching her carefully as she slowly walked down the hallway. Something was definitely wrong. Mom seemed to have no energy at all. She stayed in bed for the majority of the day even though she continually told me she didn't feel that bad.

Right...she didn't feel that bad...until the next morning. Mom woke up in terrible condition. She moved slowly about the living room telling me she was having horrible stomach pains and nausea. She asked me to go to Wal-mart and grab some anti-nausea medication for her. "Anything," she requested, "get anything that will work for nausea."

"Mom," I tried to gently persuade her. "Why don't we go to the emergency room? Maybe you need to see a doctor."

"I don't need a doctor," she insisted. "This is just the flu. I have been through this so many times before. I think I know how to handle it. Now, will you *please* go?!"

I didn't say another word as I grabbed my keys and purse and headed out the door. I went to Wal-mart and spent several minutes looking at all the different flu medications available. I was so afraid of getting the wrong thing. I looked at each individual bottle. Could this help? Would this liquid have the power to return Mom to her normal self? Could these small pills restore her eagerness to live every moment? I found it hard to put that much faith in a small round tablet, but what other choice did I have right now? I didn't know what would help so I bought a variety of flu medications—liquid, gel capsules, pills. I paid, prayed, and drove back home.

"Where did you go?" Mom asked when I finally walked in the door. "Where were you?"

"I went to get some medication, Mom," I explained as I held out the bottles to her.

"Okay," she whispered and then went back to bed without taking any of the medicine. I was surprised. I wanted her to have it! I wanted to be correct that there was some restorative power in the pills. But Mom just shook her head and headed back to the bedroom where she remained for the rest of the afternoon. I couldn't help but think of all the days of my childhood when Mom would stay locked behind her bedroom door. Again, as before, I remained quiet and waited for her to return. Mom stayed in her room for the rest of the day.

I woke up around five am on February 1, 2010, Monday, to get ready for work. Mom was still sleeping. She usually got up when I did and it had become our ritual to walk out together to the car. She did not get up this morning, though, to see me off. I went into her room to check on her before I left.

"Mom," I asked her, "are you okay?" I didn't want to wake her up but I needed to know she was alright before I left.

"I'm fine," she answered. "I'm feeling great. Just didn't sleep a lot last night. I want to relax a little more. I'll get up soon."

"Okay, Mom," I answered. "Do you need anything before I go?"

"No, I'm fine," she whispered. "Go to work."

"Okay, but I don't know how soon I'll be home this afternoon. We're having a faculty meeting..."

"I'll be fine," she told me, "Go."

"I love you," I whispered.

"I love you, too," she sighed back to me as I walked away. I gathered up my books and left, but still had a very uneasy feeling.

After my morning classes had ended, I called home. Again, Mom assured me she was feeling great. She had even gotten all of the laundry done.

"Mom, that wasn't necessary," I protested. "I could have done it."

"No, why?" Mom exclaimed. "I feel great!"

On February 2, 2010, Tuesday, Mom didn't wake up again to walk me out to the car. She wasn't feeling well. I went into her bedroom to check on her before I left for work. She assured me again that she was fine as I sat on her bed and leaned over her.

I went to work and called home on my first break. No answer.

Second call...again no answer. Oh, God, no...on my third call, Mom finally picked up the phone. She had been vacuuming the living room and didn't hear the phone ring. What?! She felt great and was going to clean the bathroom next. This wasn't making any sense at all.

That night I was asleep on the living room couch. Suddenly my eyes popped open and there was Mom standing in the living room, just staring at me. "Mom, are you okay?" I whispered. "What time is it?"

"About 3:15," Mom answered. She stood there before me with a gentle smile on her face and a softness in her voice. "I just needed to tell you I love you."

"I love you, too," I whispered.

"Okay, you go back to sleep now," she whispered, "and don't worry about anything. Everything is going to work out. Just believe that."

"Mom, why are you telling me this now?" I whispered.

She just smiled at me and shrugged. "I love you," she whispered as she turned away.

"I love you, too," I said as I watched her move down the hallway and fade away at the bedroom door. I laid back down to sleep but tossed and turned for most of the night. Mom's sudden presence before me was so surreal, so ethereal. I wondered how long she had been standing over me. I thought again about my angel vision and shuddered. Mom on a death list.

Suddenly, I remembered something else that happened just a few days before Mom became ill. I had been asleep on the couch in front of the TV. All of a sudden, my eyes shot open and I jumped right off the couch into a standing position, shaken and scared. I literally had felt an unusual pressure on the back of my neck. It was as light as a breath and no stronger than the movement of a feather but it terrified me. I looked around but saw nothing that could have caused the sensation. I had walked down the hallway to Mom's room, opened the door and peeked inside. Gently snoring, she was fast asleep in her bed. I stood in the doorway, just watching her sleep for several minutes. I felt tears sting my eyes as I looked at her, so petite and delicate, in her bed. At that moment, dread and fear filled my soul and I wandered what would happen if she wasn't here. I suddenly had the strangest thought, an awareness of the sensation I had felt. My heart buzzed with the impression that I had just felt my mother's last breath on the back of my neck. The thought unnerved me, but I couldn't fight what I was feeling. I had known then, or I had the strangest premonition, that something was about to happen.

I have traveled all over the world, some days never knowing where I was going or where I would sleep that night...but nothing made me more unsure of myself than these past few days with my mother. The days were drifting more off course and vanishing like a passing horizon out of the rearview mirror...and there was no rest stop. No shoulder of the road to pull over. Our days just kept moving us forward to our final destination, whether we wanted to travel along or not.

The uncertainty ended on February 4, 2010, Thursday. I awoke at 5:00 am as usual in an atmosphere of abnormality. Mom was still in bed. I got completely cleaned up and then went into her bedroom to say good-bye as I had been doing for the past few days. But this time, as I moved over to her bed, I heard her voice, so soft in the quiet room, I couldn't hear what she was saying at first. I leaned over her.

"Mom," I whispered as I knelt by her bedside, "are you okay?"

I heard her quiet voice again, but this time, as I listened to her two small words, I felt my blood run cold. "I hurt," she gasped. That's all she would say.

"Where, Momma?" I asked her tenderly. "Where do you hurt?"

"My stomach," she mumbled as her hand slowly rubbed over her abdomen.

"Mom, I'm going to take you to the doctor now. Let's go. Can you get down to the car? I'll help you."

"No," she whispered, "not yet. Go to work now. When you come home, we'll go."

"Mom, it's not a problem," I insisted. "Let me call Peter. I just got to let him know I won't be in for my morning classes and I can take you."

"No, please, just go to work. I'm so tired," she whispered. "Please, let me sleep. Please, I just need to rest. Then I want to shower and get cleaned up before we go. Please, go teach your class and I'll be up and ready when you get back."

"Mom," I told her, "please, let me just take you now."

"I can't get up now. Please, go!" she demanded. "Please, let me sleep."

"Okay, Mom," I whispered reluctantly. "I'll be home at noon. But call me immediately if you need me. Call me. I can be back in twenty minutes."

All she said was, "Go."

I moved to the door and turned to look at her again, "Call me, Mom. Please, call if you need me. I love you."

Mom just rolled over slowly, clutching her stomach, and went back to sleep.

I drove to work in tears. I was angry at myself for not forcing Mom to see a doctor sooner. But, it's so confusing. I want to respect my mother's right to choose how she wants to handle her own life and illness. But when do I step in and make decisions for her? When do I make demands on how she should handle her own situations? When my mother is still brilliant, observant, and lucid, do I have the right to make health decisions for her? So, instead I found myself just praying and waiting for her to finally decide to go to the doctor. I didn't know what to do. This particular illness confused me. How could my mother be so sick at night, listless in the morning, and energetic in the afternoons? I don't understand, God.

I went through my morning classes in a daze. I did everything I needed to do but my mind just wasn't on it. I watched the clock, and when 11:30 am finally rolled around, I ran across campus, jumped in my car, and raced back home to the apartment. I was a wreck not knowing what condition I would find my mother in. Would she still be in bed? Would she be sick?

I parked the car at the apartment complex, jumped out, ran around the courtyard, and up the stairs to the apartment. I inserted my key into the lock, praying the whole time. Oh, God, please, don't let her be sick. I took a deep breath and opened the door....and there was Mom sitting on the couch in the living room. She was fully dressed and ready to go.

"Mom, are you okay?" I asked as I looked at her. She looked great. She told me she was feeling good. Now, I got really worried. I was afraid Mom would change her mind. I was afraid she would say that there was no need to go to the doctor. But to my surprise and relief, she still agreed to go. Okay, now, I knew something was really wrong. Mom was voluntarily going to the hospital? That certainly wasn't like her. She slipped on her shoes and we started out of the apartment to the car. I teased Mom that this was actually her first day out in almost a week. We walked to the car and she settled into the passenger seat. Mom was complacent and calm as if we were headed out on another day of exploration. I was tense and scared. I didn't even want to start the car. It wasn't the journey but our destination that made me hesitate. I took several deep breaths and turned the key.

As I started driving towards the hospital, I became impatient at the first corner turn and honked my horn at the car in front of me that had sat through a green light. Mom told me to be nice, her constant reminder to me whenever we are in the car together.

I had just turned the corner and headed towards the hospital when Mom looked at me and said, "Okay, if I don't make it through this...if I don't survive..."

"Mom, stop," I told her. "You're going to get through this. It's probably just the flu or something. You are going to be fine."

But she just shook her head. She was adamant. Now, I understood why she was so calm. "This is what I need you to do when I die. Get several copies of the death certificate. You are going to need to take care of the accounts and social security. You will find my will in the top drawer of my desk. Make sure you show that to the attorneys. It is what I want."

I tried to hide my reaction as I shuddered internally. A few years ago, Mom had said that seventy-five was a good age for her to die. I think I held my breath throughout her entire 75th year. Last December, when Mother turned seventy-six, I breathed a sigh of relief. But now, here we were, just five weeks past her seventy-sixth birthday, heading for the hospital with Mom telling me what to do if she never came back home.

I begged her to stop. I didn't want to hear it. But she continued on with her final demands. "Okay, Mom," I finally said to calm her down and ease her mind. "But you are going to be fine."

I parked in the emergency room section and we went inside. After registering at the front desk, we sat together in the lobby, waiting for Mom's name to be called. She pulled a pack of peanuts from her purse proudly showing me that she had found something she could eat that did not make her vomit. I was relieved she was finally eating something, even if it was just a small package of peanuts. Mom had been feeling so nauseous over the last few days, she had stopped eating. The peanuts seemed to be a small victory.

After about twenty minutes, we were finally called to the back by a medical assistant who took Mom's general information, blood pressure, and pulse rate. Mom was feeling surprisingly good at this point and was laughing and talking as she answered all the questions that were continually thrown at her. Finally, the assistant finished the general check-in, handed Mom a cup, and said, "Okay, you need to give a urine sample now."

Mom stared at the cup helplessly as we walked down the hallway towards the restroom. She threw up her hands in frustration. "This is ridiculous," she stated. "Why do I have to pee in a cup now?"

"They want to make sure you're not pregnant," I answered, to which my seventy-six-year-old mother gave me such a look of disgust,

I quickly stopped laughing. Oops, maybe I had pushed her good humor just a little too far.

Once that assignment was completed, we were asked to sit in a packed little room off the long hallway. Mom was perched on a desk chair that had been pushed up against the wall. We had been in the ER since twelve-thirty that afternoon and it was three-thirty when the Physician's Assistant finally walked over to Mom. The PA spoke to her and efficiently scribbled notes on a chart. Mom told her about feeling nauseous and explained the ache she was feeling in her abdomen. The PA pushed Mom's jacket aside...and that's when I saw it...Oh, my gosh, Mom's abdomen was so swollen she looked six months pregnant! I stared at her in shock. All this time, how could I have missed this? Mom was always a small woman, so small she normally shopped in the children's section. Any small amount of weight would show on her. How could I have not noticed the roundness developing in her belly? True, Mom was always a modest woman and wore loose fitting clothes. But now here I was staring at my mom's swollen abdomen and cursing myself for not having paid more attention.

I still was somewhat unaware of the seriousness of the moment... or maybe I was just in denial. When we went into the X-ray room, I was fascinated with the whole process. I watched the techs move around the large room adjusting the equipment and settling Mom on the table. Because of my massage background, I was familiar with a lot of the medical and anatomical terms the techs were using. I asked questions and paid close attention to what they were doing. Mom's attitude was just as casual as mine. She laughed with the techs and told jokes. She did a modest, silly strip tease when asked to remove her shirt. She let the techs work with her without complaint. We talked and laughed and teased...little did we know....

After a rather long wait for the doctor to review the images, we finally, after almost four hours, received an answer. There was an obstruction in Mom's colon, but no one had any idea what it actually was. The doctors wouldn't have any idea until after the surgery they scheduled for Mom on Saturday morning…Surgery? Oh, my gosh…But I was assured it wouldn't be any problem. The surgery was necessary to check if the obstruction was an infection, a mass, extra tissue, or cancer.

Cancer? Wait a minute.…But no one had any answers yet and couldn't calm my fears. Images of myself as a little girl listening to my mom talk about a breast lump shot through my head. But I didn't have any more time to think about it.

Now, we were rushed through admissions. Mom was settled into a bed in a small cubicle in the back of the emergency room where she was separated from her fellow patients by thick, blue curtains. We would be stuck here until an actual hospital room was available for her. Mom encouraged me to go back to work. I had a night class that started at 8:10 pm. It was about 6:30 at this time. She assured me she would be fine. I thought I needed to be with her but she wanted to be alone. Reluctantly, I kissed Mom good-bye and promised to return in the morning.

The next morning, February 5th, 2010, Friday, I drove to the hospital, eager to see Mom and make sure she was okay. We talked for a while and agreed that she would just have the surgery and everything would be fine. It would be that easy, right? I stayed with Mom for the rest of the day, watching her going through more CAT scans and other random tests.

On February 6th, Saturday, I arrived at the hospital around 7:30 am. Mom's surgery was scheduled for 8:00. I wanted to be there for her. I didn't want her to go through this alone. I wanted her to have a hand to hold as she was being prepped for surgery. I wanted her to hear soothing words that everything would be okay before she was put to sleep. I wanted her to know she was loved before she had to face one of the biggest challenges of her life.

Mom was in rather good spirits. We both had just assumed that she would have the surgery, the blockage would be gone, and she would be fine. So, while we waited for the orderlies to take her downstairs to the operating room, Mom began to tell me the story of what happened the night before. It seems that the doctor wanted her system completely cleaned out before she had the surgery the next morning. The nurse on duty received the order to give Mom an enema.

"So the nurse and I went into the bathroom and she was about to give me the enema when she suddenly confessed to me that she had never given one before! I was her first. So she is trying to get the enema in and we both started laughing. It was hysterical. Neither one of us knew what we were supposed to do." I didn't really care what story my mother was telling. I just wanted to hear her laugh.

A few minutes later, the orderlies came in to take Mom down for surgery. I stayed right with her as they wheeled her into the operating prep room. I held tightly to her hand, not wanting to let go. We were taken into a room that looked to me almost like a boiler/storage room. Large pipes ran along the walls and shelves were stacked with blankets and buckets of materials. The nurse asked Mom general questions about her health and what kind of medication she wanted for the surgery. Mom agreed to have an epidural.

There was one problem, though. Mom has a fatty tumor on her back that I found myself explaining over and over again to all of the medical personnel. That was a little strange because, honestly, I don't really know what it was or how it happened. All I know is that Mom had a lump on her back due to being hit with a baseball bat some years ago. One of her vertebrae had slipped into the surrounding tissue during the incident and it had caused a fatty tumor to grow. There was general concern about the situation so the doctors decided not to give her the epidural. Instead, she was just going to receive general anesthesia.

I kissed my mother good-bye and was lead out to the lobby where I was told to wait until the surgery was completed. The doctor would talk to me soon. I sat alone and tried to read for a while but it was difficult. I couldn't keep my mind on the words in front of me. The letters seemed to float around on the page. I was concerned about Mom's progress and needed to know what the doctor was actually finding.

About an hour later, Dr. Nelson finally came into the front lobby to speak with me. He told me that he had just removed a large tumor from the right side of Mom's colon. It was probably cancerous but he really wouldn't know anything until the oncologist had the opportunity to look over all of the test and the tumor. With that he abruptly turned and walked away, leaving me with questions that went unanswered.

I quickly stepped outside to call my brother and sisters. I told them the situation and they asked me to keep them posted. I said I would and fought the urge to scream at them. "Come out here," I wanted to shout. "Take care of this. I can't do this. I don't know what to do. Help me." But I didn't. I swallowed the words. I suddenly knew I couldn't show any weakness. I was going to have to maneuver my way around this sudden hazard all on my own.

I had been lost in America before. I had battled truckers and tornadoes and haunted hotels. I had traveled by myself through dust storms and rough back roads. But now...I had never felt so alone before. I was completely lost on the journey and in the storm...and for the first time, my instincts were not suddenly kicking in. I couldn't see my way through. For the first time, I felt the strain of being totally on my own without even the chance to call my mom for help.

I went back into the hospital and spent the rest of the afternoon, sitting in Mom's room, watching her sleep. I left later that night and went back home feeling totally alone. Surgery, chemo, radiation, and she would be fine, right? It was going to be hard but she would survive. My Aunt Nancy had colon cancer several years before and she had survived. Aunt Nancy was a strong woman who had lived through so many tragedies herself and had come out stronger for them all. She had survived and so would her sister, my mom. Yeah. It was going to be okay.

CHAPTER 11

I was shocked speechless the first time I saw Mom after her surgery. She had tubes that went up her nose. One of the tubes went down into her intestines; the other constantly supplied oxygen to her lungs. I stared at her, trying to choke back my tears. I had always tried to make believe that everything was fine, even through abuses at home and bullying at school. I used to thing I was good at pretending. Now, it seemed so incredibly hard to behave as if this was normal and everything would work out fine. I fought with myself and the rest of the world to keep up a sense of normalcy.

When she saw me, Mom shifted her body slowly and awkwardly because she had a hard time keeping her balance, even when lying down. She would slide to one side of the bed and struggle to pull herself into a comfortable position. Mom adjusted herself carefully in the bed with my awkward assistance before looking into my eyes and asking me what was wrong with her...and suddenly it dawned on me. Nobody had told her. Where was the doctor? Doesn't he do that? Why hadn't the nurses explained the situation to her? Were they leaving it up to me? Was it my responsibility to look my mother in the eyes and tell her she had colon cancer?

Mom asked me again what the doctor had found during the

surgery. I hesitated…and then shamefully lied. I told her that I didn't know. I shrugged my shoulders and said that the doctor should be in to speak to us soon. He never showed up, though, and Mom's questions became even more demanding. I couldn't get the word cancer out of my mouth. I mumbled to her that I was still finding out the details. I couldn't find the strength to tell my mom about her condition. Maybe our tradition of family secrets made me feel like I had to keep this one.

"Jamie," she called out to me again. "What was wrong with me?" I choked up and thanked God I was saved at that moment by the nurse walking in to check Mom's blood pressure. I waited quietly while the nurse completed her duties and then followed her out of the room.

"Um, excuse me," I called out to the nurse as she hurried down the hallway to the next patient. When she turned around to look at me, I stated, "My mom keeps asking me what they found during the surgery. Is the doctor going to talk to her?"

"He hasn't yet?" the nurse asked innocently.

"No," I answered. "Is someone going to come in to talk to her soon?" Then I honestly confessed in a low voice, "I don't know if I can do it. I don't know if I can tell her. I just…" and then I started to cry.

The nurse told me she would get the doctor on the phone and walked away to the nurse's station. I didn't walk immediately back into Mom's room. I turned myself to the wall and allowed tears to run unchecked down my face. Finally, after a few sobs, I wiped my eyes and took several deep breaths. I wanted to compose myself before I walked back into the room. How could I possibly explain my tears to Mom?

Doctor Nelson wasn't too happy with the situation, either. In fact, he sounded downright annoyed when I answered the phone that rang in Mom's room just a few minutes after I came back from my breakdown in the hallway. I had explained quickly to the doctor that Mom needed to know about her condition after the surgery. I thought he would speak to her but instead he gave a deep, angry sigh that emphasized his frustration and said, "I already told you it was a tumor and that we need to speak to the oncologist about the situation." Then he was gone. He hung up before I could say anything more.

It was left up to me to tell Mom what was happening. I replaced the receiver slowly and stared at my mom as she continued to ask me questions. I cleared my throat several times. My mouth felt so dry and thick I could barely speak. I didn't know what to say and finally choked out a few words. "Well, it was a tumor, Mom. The doctor thinks it may be cancerous, but right now they don't know anything about it. They want to talk with the oncologist first before they will tell us anything else."

Mom seemed calm with the information as if it was the answer she had expected. Surprisingly, she just shrugged her shoulders, sighed, nodded her head, and drifted back off to sleep. It was the very last time she would ask for information. There was a quiet acceptance about her situation that scared me. I wanted her to be angry. I was furious. I wanted her to be, too. But, instead, she just continued to sigh deeply in her sleep.

The oncologist finally came in a few days later to speak with Mom. He explained that the whole tumor, which had been the size of a grapefruit, had been removed; however, without chemo there was a 20% chance of a return.

Chemo? The word sent a shiver up my spine. I couldn't image my mother going through chemo and the thought made me nervous. I was already structuring our new lives in my head, though. How was I going to make sure she received the care she needed plus work full time? We would have to work it out somehow. What choice did we have?

I don't know if Mom was feeling the same anxiety that I was or if she was beginning to fight the reality of the situation. Her quiet acceptance was beginning to blaze into a fighting rage. After the oncologist left the room, Mom was already refusing treatment. She was uncomfortable with the oncologist. She told me that she did not want to see that doctor again. I didn't argue with her.

"Let's get you out of here first," I explained to her, "then I will help you find a doctor. We'll find another one you are more comfortable with," I promised her. I had no idea how to go about finding an oncologist for Mom on my own, but I would have promised her anything at that point…and I would fight for her, too. Mom smiled gently then and drifted back to a peaceful sleep. She never spoke about the cancer again.

Even though Mom seemed to deal with her diagnosis on one level, she continually fought against other aspects of her illness. Mom hated the tubes that were in her nose. She had to have a continuous supply of oxygen. Plus, there was a thicker second tube that went up her nose and down into her intestines. The purpose of this tube was to pump out fluids and wastes that were building up in her digestive tract. Mom was constantly trying to pull the tubes out. It was frightening to see her yank on the tubes to remove them. The nurses were continually yelling at me to keep the tubes in Mom's nose. "Don't let her pull them out!" they would roar at me. But wrestling with Mom over the tubes was like playing tug-of-war against Hercules. Mom was determined to remove the tubes and our constant battles left me continually exhausted.

I walked into Mom's room one afternoon to find her tangled up against the bars on the side of her bed. Her whole body was pulled into a tight knot in the upper left corner of the mattress as if she were trying to find a place to hide. She was lying there slowly pulling out the tubes. The thick, intestinal tube was halfway out of her nose.

"No, Mom," I told her as I ran into the room. "No, you have to leave the tubes in." I was surprised at the strength that Mom demonstrated. I wrestled with her for a moment, losing the battle due to her determination to get the tubes out of her nose.

I went running out of the room looking for the nurses but I couldn't find anyone in the hallway. Terrified, I ran to the door of the nurse's station, which was a small room situated in the middle of the 15th floor. I turned the doorknob but found it locked, so I knocked on the door. Through the windows, I could see a nurse inside the small room. She looked up, made eye contact with me for just a moment, and then waved me away. I knocked on the door again which only made the nurse angrier. She grimaced at me and then flung her hand in my direction as if swatting away a pesky fly. Hysterical, I turned away and ran down the hallway. I didn't find a nurse until I was on the other side of the ward. I stood at the door of another patient's room as the nurse turned to look at me.

Anxiously, I explained my mom's situation. I was having a hard time catching my breath due to my upset and anger now. Were the nurses even checking on Mom? How could she have ended up in the position in which I found her? I was speaking so fast, I'm surprised the nurse could understand me. When I had finally paused for breath, she told me, "Well, she isn't my patient but I will help you." I thanked her profusely as we walked quickly back to Mom's room.

Mom had the tube almost all the way out of her nose when we entered. Two more nurses now came running in and as I stepped out of the way, they placed Mom back into position on the bed and slowly put the tubes back in place. Fifteen minutes later, when the nurses had finished, I walked back to Mom's bedside. Mom looked at me with her eyes almost accusatory. "Why?" she seemed to be saying, "Why did you let them do that to me?"

The nurses were angry with me, too, for not using the call bell. I kept forgetting about it! For the first few days, every little moan or whimper from Mom would send me racing from her room and down the hallway, screaming at any nurse or medical assistant that wandered into my path. It always annoyed the nurses and one of the them decided to finally make her point. Later that afternoon, after my mother had been resettled and I was sitting by her bedside, the nurse came in to take Mom's blood pressure. She didn't speak a single word to me; yet, when she had finished, she picked up the remote with the call bell and threw it into my lap before stomping out. It was a gesture that clearly didn't work. Mom's next moan and gasp again sent me tearing through the hallways searching for help. Damn the call bell! It took several more days and more "subtle" hints from the nurses before I finally got the hang of ringing the bell.

After this latest crisis was over, I sat by Mom's bedside, holding her hand and brushing back her hair, which made her mad. Mom told me with her hair brushed back no one would recognize her. I smiled at that and brushed her hair back over her forehead. For the rest of the afternoon, I stayed by Mom's side. The day had overwhelmed me and later that night I flopped down exhausted on the cot that had been placed besides Mom's bed. Mom had asked me to stay and I just couldn't refuse her anything right now. I was exhausted but I just couldn't sleep. I was wide awake. I closed my eyes, though, and pretended to sleep as the nurses came in and out of Mom's room every few minutes.

I finally got up at 4:30 am when the light above Mom's bed flipped on. While the nurses cleaned Mom and checked her vitals, I quickly showered, dressed, and left the hospital. I arrived at work around 5:30 am. I was grateful to be at the school completely alone. I was exhausted but amazed how this had become my normal life. I was at work every morning between 5:30 to 6 am. I would read, study, make copies, and get ready for my first class at 8 o'clock. I would teach until noon and then run to the hospital to be with Mom for the afternoon. I would leave at 5 pm to be back at work for the evening classes and then return to the hospital when classes were over at 10 pm. Mom was usually asleep by the time I arrived but it didn't matter. I just needed to be there for her. I would settle back down on the small cot by Mom's bed and sleep fitfully until 4:30 am when the nurses were into their full routine and the day would begin all over again. This had become my life. Funny, even the strangest events can become so quickly normal.

CHAPTER 12

$\mathcal{M}$om had awakened from her surgery believing she was in Holland. The nurses claimed that when Mom woke up in the recovery room, she looked at the nurses running around in their surgical robes, head covers, and shoe booties and believed that she was traveling through the Netherlands. The nurses thought it was hysterical. I thought it was understandable. Mom was a traveler, an explorer, an adventurer. Of course, she would travel in her sleep.

Every day when I came to visit her, she would tell me where she had been the night before. The first morning she told me of her adventures, I was confused. She smiled up at me and said, "Last night, the nurses took me to Palm Desert."

"Mom," I questioned her closely, trying to understand what had actually happened, "why did they take you to Palm Desert?"

"The nurses claim that they have a better senior facility there."

"How did you get there?" I asked.

"In an ambulance," Mom stated very matter-of-factly. "I fell asleep here in Palm Springs and when I woke up in the middle of the night, I was in a different room. When I asked the nurses about it, they told me I was in Palm Desert. They had come into my room about midnight and pushed my bed downstairs. They made me go to sleep

189

and put me into an ambulance and I woke up in Palm Desert. Then they put me back to sleep and when I woke up again, I was back here."

Mom's story made me angry. Why would the nurses move her? Shouldn't the hospital have notified me? Mom had been so convincing in her details that I interrogated the first nurse who happened to walk into the room to check Mom's vitals.

"Why did you move her? Why didn't you call me? I have the right to be told if you take her to Palm Desert in the middle of the night!"

The young nurse just smiled at me when I paused for a moment to catch my breath. "Oh," she smiled, "so she went to Palm Desert last night!" Thankfully, the nurse continued on before I could take another breath to snap at her again. "Yesterday, when she woke up in the middle of the night, she thought she was in Kansas. And then it was Hawaii. She travels everywhere when she sleeps."

"Wait a minute," I asked then, "so she was never moved?"

"Of course not," the nurse answered. "I guess she dreams a lot about traveling."

"Yeah," I answered, "I guess she would." The thought made me smile...and gave me some hope. If Mom still thought about traveling, dreamed about going to all the places where we had been or had talked about visiting someday, then she would fight to stay alive, right? We still had to go to Hawaii, Alaska, Oregon, and Washington. During the day, we talked about this constantly. I thought it was an incentive for her to fight to survive.

The most engaging place Mom traveled to in her sleep was Mexico. Mom awoke one afternoon to tell me she had been loaded into an ambulance and taken to a farmhouse in Mexico City where she stayed the night with a young Hispanic couple and their tiny baby. She talked about playing with the baby and how nice the family was to her. She told me several stories about the infant who she absolutely adored. I just listened to her, asked her questions, and nodded my head from time to time. I didn't even try to convince her that it was all just a dream. If she believed she was in Amsterdam, or Palm Desert, or

Mexico…what difference did it make? I just assumed it was nothing more than the pain and medication taking her lively mind to places that she physically couldn't get to right now.

I wished I could have gone with her on her mental journeys. I didn't want to go home. Why? Because one night, while sitting with Mom in her hospital room, she suddenly woke up, turned to me, and said, "Jamie, Jamie, did you finally get all the mice out of the apartment?" What?! Mice in the apartment?! We never had mice in the apartment.

"Mom," I whispered, "what mice in the apartment? Mom, what mice?" But she didn't answer. She had already rolled back over and gone back to sleep. Mice! I was afraid to go home!

Mom, however, would lie in her hospital bed and believe she was at home. One day, she looked at me and then suddenly tried to throw back the sheets and climb out of bed. "Mom," I tried to stop her from getting up. "Stay in bed."

"But it's time to fix dinner."

"Don't worry about dinner, Mom," I told her. "I'll take care of all the cooking."

She flopped wearily back against the pillow, sighed deeply, and stated, "Well, I guess I'll really need a doctor then." Where did she find the strength to criticize my cooking even after her surgery and partial recovery?

Another time, Mom kept asking me where the dining room table was. She thought she was at home and was shocked that she couldn't find the table. I didn't let her confusion slide by this time. I tried to tell her that she was in the hospital, but wasn't successful. Mom continued to lift her head from the pillow every few minutes to search around the room for her wooden dining table and four chairs.

The illusion I really struggled with, though, was the afternoon Mom went looking for a cake in her bed sheets. Mom was hungry because she wasn't eating the hospital food. It tasted horrible to her and she refused it. But she still wanted something to eat. Her hunger forced her to believe that a fresh, white-frosted cake was hidden somewhere in her bed. I watched as she lifted the sheets several times and tried to move the heavy, tightly wrapped blankets. She was adamant that she had set the cake on the bed to cool before she could eat it. Now, it had suddenly disappeared. I did the only thing I could think of at that time. I dove underneath the blankets, raised the sheets, and searched for the vanilla cake. Of course, my search was futile, but I was tenacious. I searched for that darn cake until Mom finally fell back to sleep.

That story was actually easier to handle than other ones I would hear. Mom would tell me stories that the nurses were abusing her. She told me that she got into a fight late one night with the nurses who were refusing to let her see the doctor. Once the doctor arrived, the nurses refused to give him Mom's medical charts. Mom supposedly fought off the nurses, who retaliated by ripping diamonds earrings from Mom's ears and running away with them. I listened to Mom's story and when she had finished, I showed her the little bowl beside her bed that contained the small post earrings she had worn into the hospital before her surgery.

"Your earrings are right here, Mom." I held the bowl out for her to see the tiny pieces of metal and glass. "The earrings are safe. I have them." A little confused, Mom looked at the earrings and then praised me for getting them back for her. For the first time since entering the hospital, I was Mom's hero. In her mind, I had battled the nurses for the return of the earrings and won. She was proud of me.

That was an easily solved problem and Mom was comfortable around the nurses again...except for one. Mom kept holding up her hands to show me the small cuts she said were on her fingers. I noticed tiny bruises from the pinpricks Mom was receiving periodically to check her blood sugar levels, but couldn't see any other problems. Mom claimed that one of the male nurses was using a pocketknife to open up her fingers to draw blood. I asked the nurse about it when he came into the room that afternoon. When Mom argued back against his denials, he very calmly apologized and promised to never do it again. Mom relaxed and the issue never came up again. However, I got in the habit of checking Mom's fingers every day I went to the hospital. Though I knew it was probably just a hallucination, I wanted to be sure no one was hurting her. I was relieved that I never found any cuts, but I still continued to check every day.

Witnessing Mom's delusions in the hospital was difficult, but, to be honest, the stories fascinated me. I became very intrigued with my mother's fantasies. I loved the liveliness of her words. I wanted to be right inside of her head. I wanted to observe where she was traveling every night. I wanted to see the world that she was creating. I wanted to know how her mind was generating her illusions. Where did they start? Was it from pain or medication? Could it be the stress of the surgery? I wanted so badly to know. I would sit by her bedside every day as she acted out her dreams. It didn't scare me at all. I was totally fascinated with her words and movements.

At the same time, I was shocked to see my beautiful, intelligent mother, who would work countless crossword puzzles every morning and avidly watch the news every evening, reduced to looking for cakes in her hospital bed. I continually reminded myself that it was just another area of her intelligence. What surprised me was how freaked out the nurses were. They constantly commented on her behavior and hallucinations. Their response shocked me. They worked in a hospital. Why did they constantly behave like they had never seen a sick person before?

I didn't try to convince Mom that her illusions weren't true. I really didn't see the point. What purpose would it serve any of us? What exactly is the truth? Truth is an extremely individual mental activity. Each person develops reality within his or her own mind. The certainty of any situation is not universal. Everyone interrupts life based on their own experiences and personalities. There is no truth, only trust—trust in a fair universe and trust that other people will behave honorable. How could there be any one all consuming reality about anything? I know what I believe, but does that make me right? No, it only makes me *me*.

From time to time, Mom would give me small clues into her own personal truth. She spoke a lot in her sleep and one afternoon she spoke so eloquently about life, I wondered if she was acting as a medium for the universe. Murmuring deeply, Mom spoke to an unknown person, giving advice about living out dreams and finding the "knight in shining armor" only at the right time and place. Soul mates appear only when God thinks you are ready, Mom reasoned. I had no idea who she was talking to but I listened intently. She was saying things like "live just for love but don't give your heart away so easily. You will find everything you want." Mom always was something of a romantic and really wanted nothing more for me than to find peace and love. I couldn't stop thinking about her life with my father. Her own marriage was far from kind and romantic, so, again, I wondered what was driving her thought pattern.

After Mom's heartfelt murmurs, she started to kiss her imaginary companion good-bye. I sat there watching her pucker up her lips, stretch forward, and try to find the cheek of her "friend." Why shouldn't it be me? I leaned over the side of her bed, moving my face up to her lips. She suddenly opened her eyes, glared at me, and snapped, "Will you get out of the way!?" Her hand came up to the top of my head and she gave me a small push away. Oh, okay....I sat back down as she continued to send her kisses out into the open air. Hhhmmm...now, I was very curious who she had been talking to....and a little insulted.

But it didn't matter who she had imagined. I loved listening to her. I found her words absolutely brilliant. Unfortunately, the nurses did not. They would pull me aside and question me intently. "How long has your mother had Alzheimer's? When was she originally diagnosed? How long has she been having these hallucinations?" They didn't seem to believe me when I responded that she never had a problem until I brought her to this hospital.

Maybe I should have been more concerned. I had just assumed

that the surgery, pain, and medication just sent her on a mental trip through the universe. I told the nurses that she was fine. She was always brilliant. She never had any problems. The nurses stared at me as if I was crazy. How could I possibly blame their medications? They swore to me that the medication Mom was on could not possibly cause her to be so senile.

I noticed, though, that Mom wasn't the only patient who was suffering through hallucinations. I laid awake on the small rollaway bed, freezing, trying to wrap myself in a thin sheet as I listened to the sounds around me. Well, I tried not to listen, but I was wide awake and couldn't shut out the noise. All the patients seemed to be hallucinating. I listened as the nurses tried to convince the elderly man across the hall to stay in bed. He thought it was morning and was determined to make potato pancakes. The woman in the room next to Mom's was screaming about a baby. Her words echoed through the hallways and into Mom's room. "Jane," she would holler, "don't hurt the baby. Please, don't hurt the baby. Please, put the baby down." Her words sent chills all the way through my body and forced tears to spring to my eyes. Her voice was so vivid, I began to worry about the baby, too. I wanted to close the door but knew that was inappropriate in the hospital as patients were monitored throughout the night. Mom did tell me that she slept so much during the day because the noise kept her awake most of the night.

I was glad Mom slept during the day, but it wasn't always peaceful. Her mind swirled with troublesome thoughts. One day, Mom awoke suddenly and stared straight into my eyes. She looked away and then back at me and stated, "You are so sweet to come see me every day... but, honey...," she asked cautiously, "who are you?"

I stared at her for just a moment and answered, "I'm your daughter, Jamie."

Mom gave me the sweetest smile then and sighed, "Oh, honey." She spoke slowly, trying not to hurt my feelings. "I don't have a daughter named Jamie."

CHAPTER 13

After all of our traveling, now the only thing Mom wanted to do was go home. She would be discharged from the hospital only if she could prove that she could eat and her system was working as close to normal as possible, considering the colostomy bag.

I was at work the Thursday after the surgery when my cell phone rang. I never used my phone while in class, but while Mom was in the hospital, I never turned it off. Now, I grabbed the phone as soon as it rang at 11:15 am. Mom excitedly told me she was being discharged that day. She was coming home. It was so good to hear her happy and laughing.

Right after class ended, I ran to the hospital. Mom was sitting up in her bed. Her eyes were shining for the first time in weeks and her face lit up as soon as I walked into the room. Going home wasn't going to be easy, though.

The nurse on duty would not release Mom until I could show proof that I had purchased her medication. I left the hospital and came back about half an hour later. I had the prescribed medicine and proudly waved the bottle in front of the nurse. But it still wasn't quite enough.

The nurse asked me the name of the facility where I was taking

Mom. Several nurses now surrounded me, insisting that Mom go to an assisted living facility. I hadn't even considered it. One of the nurses then asked me who was Mom's caretaker. "I am," I answered and she stared at me as if I should be admitted to the mental ward. I didn't know how I was going to be with Mom twenty-four hours a day and work, too. But Mom wanted to go home so badly, I didn't want to disappoint her. I would just have to work it out somehow.

Seeing the disgusted looks on the nurses' faces, I had this horrible fear they were going to report me for elderly abuse when I informed them that Mom did not have an oxygen tank at home. She needed oxygen every day, they all told me at the same time. How come I wasn't allowing her access to an oxygen tank? I promised to get one if they would just let me take her home.

The nurses finally informed me that they had signed all of Mom's release papers and she was free to go. Mom couldn't wear her jeans and button down shirt. The pressure of her clothes against her abdomen had been horribly painful and uncomfortable. Instead, the nurses and I dressed her in pajama bottoms and a bathrobe. The nurses put her slippers on her tiny feet because Mom could not bend over to adjust them herself. When she was ready, I carried Mom's things, just a few clothes and toiletry items, downstairs to the car. One of the volunteers would bring Mom down and would meet me in the circular driveway.

As I pulled the car up to the front of the hospital, I saw Mom sitting in a wheelchair with the volunteer standing behind her. I parked, leaned across the passenger seat, and opened the door as the volunteer helped Mom slowly stand up. Mom's legs were very shaky, however, and the heavyset, female, senior volunteer began to scream for the valet parking attendant to help her. I stayed in the driver's seat and held on to Mom's hands, trying to help guide her into the car.

For reasons I still don't quite understand, the valet attendant and hospital volunteer decided to put Mom in the car feet first instead of bottom first. Wouldn't it have been easier to sit her into the car and then swing in her feet? The parking attendant had picked up each of Mom's small feet and placed them onto the floorboard of the car. When Mom's feet were inside the car and the volunteer was holding her underneath her arms, the attendant backed away. I was holding Mom's arms trying to pull her into the passenger seat. Her bottom was still hanging outside the car with only her feet and arms inside.

….And then she started to fall backwards. I suddenly realized that the volunteer had let go and was backing away. Mom's bottom was falling down to the pavement of the curb as she tried to cling to my arms. "She's falling!" I started screaming. "Catch her! Catch her!" Suddenly, the volunteer realized what was happening and turned quickly to catch Mom before she hit the ground. While the attendant and volunteer now tried to lift her bottom back up, I guided Mom's upper body back into the car. The driveway was getting crowded with cars trying to get through. Thankfully, no one honked at us or I would've truly become hysterical.

Finally, between the three of us, we got Mom seated into the car and fastened the belt loosely around her. I heard the volunteer comment "Well, that was frightening" just before she shut the door. Yeah, it was frightening but I pushed the thought away as I looked at Mom's face. She was beaming! She hadn't been out in the world for a solid week. She looked like she was about to go on one of our adventurous road trips for the first time in several months. As we drove away from the hospital, Mom silently sat with her hands folded in her lap. I don't know what she was thinking as she gazed out the window at downtown Palm Springs. As I drove home, though, my heart was beating very quickly. I wondered how I was going to get her up the flight of stairs to the apartment. Mom had no strength in her body at all.

I parked the car at the apartment complex, got out, and walked around to Mom's side. I opened her passenger door and reached in to grab her arms and lift her gently out. Thank goodness, she easily climbed out. She stood up slowly. I was relieved that Mom was standing by the side of the car. This was great. What a victory! She is not going to have any trouble at all being at home. We can do this! I can take care of my mother. I can help her heal. I was lost in the euphoria of false hope.

I wrapped my arm around Mom's waist and started to support her in our expedition from the asphalt of the parking lot to the concrete of the sidewalk. We began walking...one step, two steps, three... and that's where we broke down. We had just stepped up the curb onto the sidewalk when Mom told me she had to stop. "I can't walk anymore," she stated. "I need to stop."

"Mom," I whispered to her, "we didn't get far at all. We just took a few steps. We can't stop here."

"I need to sit down for a while," Mom said, "I can't walk anymore. I need to stop."

"Mom, wait just a moment." I tried to guide her around to the opposite edge of the sidewalk. "There are some steps here. Here, Mom...come over here and sit on the st..."

"No, I can't make it. I need to stop here." Before I knew what was happening, Mom was suddenly sliding down out of my arms and on to the sidewalk.

"Mom," I yelled, trying to hold her up. But it was no use. She suddenly became a heavy weight in my arms and began to slip to the ground. I held her up for a moment until she suddenly said, "I need to lie down now."

"Mom," I whispered to her, "You can't lie down here. We are on the sidewalk..."

She suddenly was out of my arms and was lying completely on her left side on the walkway. "Oh, God, Mom," I whispered. "I need to call 911."

"Don't," she screamed. "Don't call anyone. I don't want anyone to know."

"Mom," I told her, leaning down over her, "I can't get you upstairs. You're too weak."

"Let me just rest for a moment," she whispered. "I just need to rest. I will not go back to the hospital. I won't go back there! Do not call anyone!" A moment later, I tried to pick her up from the ground, but I couldn't lift her.

"Mom, I can't do this. Please, let me call for help," I begged her.

We had been on the sidewalk now for about twenty minutes. Why didn't I just pick up the phone and call 911? Because Mom's cries and her refusal to return to the hospital made me choke up so badly, I couldn't think clearly. Now, all I could think about was getting her safely inside the apartment. I had no other thought in my head.

Finally, Mom came up with an idea of her own. "Go over to the office and see if someone can help me," she demanded.

After another short argument, but realizing we had few other options, I ran off across the parking lot to the office to find help. I had left Mom's small body lying on the sidewalk with her face in the dirt! I ran as fast as I could to the management office and was relieved to find the apartment manager and one of the maintenance men inside. I explained the problem to them as best I could between my hysterical breaths. My mother had just come home from the hospital and needed assistance to get to our apartment. Could they please help?

The manager looked at me for just a moment before saying he didn't think they could...so sorry...it was a liability issue. I stared at both of the men for just a moment, wanting to plead to their sense of humanity. I asked again, but as they continued to refuse, I cringed, fought back tears, and ran out of the office and back across the parking lot. I had to hurry. I had left Mom lying on the ground, completely unable to stand or roll over. I prayed all the way back that just by some miracle, Mom would be up on her feet. No such luck. Mom was still lying face down on the ground when I got back to her side. She turned for a moment to look up at me. The left side of her face was caked with dirt as she placed her right hand against the ground and tried to push herself up.

I leaned down to her and whispered, "Mom, let me call 911,

please." I looked around to see if anyone else was close by. I prayed for help and yet felt a wave of anxiety. I couldn't take care of my mom. I wasn't strong enough to get her up to the apartment. People probably would think I was an immature, irresponsible, hateful daughter. Would they be right? Even in all of the strange places I had been before in my life, I have never felt such a moment of indecision, uncertainty...I didn't know how to respond...

I took my phone from my purse as Mom screamed at me to put it away. Her voice roared up to me as she still refused to let me call for help. "Mom, I have to do this. We need help." Mom began to cry louder with each number I hit on the keypad.

Before I could press the SEND button, though, I heard footsteps approaching. I looked up and there was the maintenance man coming to help. The manager followed close behind and carefully watched the scene playing out.

Between the two of us, the maintenance man and I were able to lift Mom from the ground. Mom looked over at the manager then and whispered to him, "I tripped." I froze as she said the words. What? She hadn't tripped. She had just been far too weak to stand on her own two feet. But I suddenly realized she didn't want anyone to know that she had just come home from the hospital. She was terrified of being sent back. She leaned on both of our shoulders as the maintenance man and I moved her towards the apartment. When we made it to the stairs, I ran up to unlock the door and turn down the blankets on her bed as the maintenance man carried her into the apartment. But as he stepped into the living room, I heard Mom say, "The couch is fine."

"Mom, shouldn't you go into the bedroom?" I encouraged her.

Instead, she said that she wanted to be on the couch. She didn't want to inconvenience the man by being carried all the way to the bedroom. That's my mom. She was so embarrassed to have to ask for help. She certainly couldn't imagine asking the man to carry her just a few more steps to the bedroom.

We were no sooner alone when Mom began to vomit. I ran to the kitchen and grabbed a vase that I had received in appreciation from my students a few months ago. I brought it in for Mom to use as bile began to run from the corners of her mouth.

A vase? I didn't know what to grab. It was just the closest thing at hand. At that point, it didn't matter. Mom was throwing up continually now. I helped her clean up but it didn't stop. She continued to vomit as I ran for additional bowls and towels.

"You were right," she whispered then. "I should have let the guy put me in the bedroom." She sat back on the couch totally deflated and then glanced up at me, "What time is it? Let's get some lunch."

Her demand for food took me by surprise. Lunch?! Now!? I told her I wasn't hungry but would be happy to make her something. Mom demanded that I go to the store to grab some tuna salad. I refused to go, but Mom did not want to hear my arguments. "Go," she whispered. "I need something to eat. I want some tuna salad. Please, go now." I stared at her completely shocked that she could think of tuna salad now after vomiting into the vase for the third time.

My hesitation made her angry and she screamed at me again to go and leave her alone. I grabbed my purse and ran out of the apartment. I tried to hurry when I walked into the store. I grabbed a few things for lunch and went running back home. I ran up the stairs to the apartment, praying all the way. It didn't help, though. I swear...I had only been gone about twenty minutes...

I opened the door to find the living room looking as if a brutal fight had broken out while I was gone! I think it had. Mom must have been fighting violently with herself. The coffee table was turned upside down, and towels, cups, and books were scattered all over the floor. I felt a shiver run through me as I stared at the position of my mother's body; she was kneeling on the floor, leaning face down against the couch, trying to pull herself up onto the cushions by her elbows. Her chest and abdomen were pressed up against the front of the sofa. Her legs were bent out to each side underneath her. She was sobbing uncontrollably.

"Mom, what happened!?!" I screamed, dropping the shopping bag I had been holding and running into the room.

"I can't get up," she whispered. "My legs. It hurts so bad. I can't feel my legs! They've gone to sleep underneath me. I can't move."

"Mom, it's okay," I whispered as I tried to pull her back to her feet. I couldn't lift her.

"I was sliding down off the cushions and I couldn't stop myself. I fell off the couch and I couldn't pull myself back up."

"I'll help you," I told her. She was so hot and sweaty. I brushed back the hair on her forehead and then slowly began to pick her up... and again I couldn't move her. She was struggling too hard for me to get a good grip. Instead, I held her against me as I tried to pull her legs out from under her. She screamed out in pain as I pulled so I backed away slowly. I then tried to elevate her upper body and she tried to help by tensing her muscles and lifting up.

Nearly an hour later, we were still on the floor. I wasn't able to move Mom back up on the couch at all. But we had at least turned her into a different position, which took pressure off her legs. At least now, Mom was sitting straight up by the side of the couch, her back against the cushions and her legs stretched out in front of her.

We took a break...just sitting on the floor, staring at each other for a moment. Mom then asked me for the food. As I went to pick it up off the floor where I had dropped it, she began to vomit violently again. I cleaned her up and then tried again to pull her up to the couch. Between the two of us, we were able to wrestle her onto the edge of the sofa, but her small body kept threatening to glide off the cushions that were now sliding away from the frame of the couch.

I finally told her, "Mom, you have to relax. *Stop* trying to help me. You're tensing up and I can't lift you."

"No," she insisted, always independent, "you can't do this by yourself."

"Mom, *don't* help me! Just take a deep breath," and with that I picked up my mother like a baby in my arms and settled her onto the couch. I didn't quite get her exactly where she needed to be for total comfort. I told her to relax again. Another deep breath and another lift and I pulled her up to a more comfortable position. Mom had been trying too hard to help me. She was tensing up her muscles to pull herself back up and only made it harder for me to move her. Once she relaxed and stopped helping, I was able to lift Mom up and set her in place on the couch. I assured Mom that I was fine, but I had lied. My back was throbbing. I had wrenched something in my muscles but refused to let her know. Mom would just feel guilty about it.... what was the point?

"When do you have to be back at work?" Mom asked me once we had her finally settled in three hours later.

"I'm not going," I responded. "I can't leave you."

"No, I'll be fine," Mom insisted. "You need to go."

After fifteen minutes of arguing and a few tears, I finally gave in to Mom's orders and got ready for work. When I came out of the bathroom, she was sleeping peacefully on the couch. I pulled the coffee table up beside her and placed everything I could think of that she might need next to her. The phone, water, pain medication, the vase...I wanted her to be able to reach anything that could possibly be a necessity.

I left for work a few minutes later, but I was a nervous wreck. I only had a two-hour class that night. I would be home by 10:15 pm. However, I cried all the way to work and didn't stop crying once I got there. I sat in my classroom before class started and sobbed. The afternoon had been harrowing and I needed time alone for a while. The class, Speech Communications, was easy and went well. I can always pull myself together in front of my students. Teaching is much like being on a stage. I was a good actress as well as teacher that night. I locked my feelings away and taught the class to the best of my abilities. Finally, it was after ten and I was headed back home.

I drove home, parked, and walked up to the apartment. I stood outside the entrance for just a moment, taking several deep breaths and wondering what I was going to find when I walked into the living room. I closed my eyes, unlocked the door, and pushed it open.

Thank God, Mom was still sleeping on the couch. I stepped over to her side and glanced down at her. She seemed to be sleeping peacefully. I brushed back her hair from her forehead, walked back into my bedroom, and got ready for bed. I still couldn't relax, though. I felt as if I couldn't breathe. I left my bedroom door open so I could listen to any sounds coming from the living room. I tried to settle down on my bed, but couldn't sleep.

Around 12:30 pm, Mom awoke, surprisingly in good spirits. She laughed and talked easily. I helped her into the bathroom and then back to her bedroom. We were able to move around the apartment smoothly...and hope began to move through me. Getting Mom into bed, though, was just as difficult and tricky as getting her on the couch. I pushed and pulled and begged her not to help me until finally she was placed securely onto the bed. Totally exhausted, I finally went into the living room where I fell into a deep sleep on the couch in front of the TV.

I awoke around seven the next morning and went in to check on Mom. She seemed to be doing better. She was wide-awake and in a surprisingly good mood as she talked about how happy she was to be back home. This joy was interrupted, however, when she began to vomit again and needed to use the bathroom. I tried to pull her up off the bed, but it was difficult to get her to stand. I had to carry her into the bathroom. I sat her inside and left her alone so she could take care of her own needs. She didn't want me in the bathroom with her. However, later, she wasn't able to get up off the toilet. I had to go in and slowly help her stand. Finally, she was cleaned up and we left the bathroom, awkwardly shuffling down the hallway one step at a time.

We moved pretty well until we got back to the bedroom. Mom could not raise herself up to get on the bed. We tried having her sit down on the edge of the mattress, but she kept sliding off the side because she could not fully get her balance. She could only hold herself up enough to lean against the side which wasn't enough to support her. I tried to help her onto the bed by lifting her up, but again her small body felt like a heavy weight as she tensed up. She wanted so much to help with her own movements. Finally, I did the only thing I could think of… I got down on all fours next to the bed and let Mom use my back like a step stool to crawl up onto the mattress. Several times that morning, I got Mom in and out of bed with this method.

Later that morning, Mom was vomiting uncontrollably again and needed to use the bathroom. Again, I got down on all fours beside the bed so she could step down. As I walked her down the hallway, I delicately mentioned to her, "Mom, I think we need to get you back to the hospital."

I could anticipate her response. She refused. She just wanted to stay home. It was finally the fact that she had to climb onto my back to get on and off the bed that ultimately convinced her that she needed more help than I could give her. The very thought that she had to use her daughter as a stepstool persuaded her that neither one of us was strong enough to handle this situation. Mom finally agreed to return to the hospital…but not just yet. "Please, don't send me back yet," she whispered. "I just want to sleep. Please, let me sleep for an hour and then we'll call for help."

While Mom slept, I did the laundry. Most of her pajamas, sheets, and towels were covered with thick, mucus-y bile. I had to wash her linens non-stop that morning. Once I got the fourth load into the dryer, I started cleaning out the bags she had brought home with her from the hospital. I reached into one bag and pulled out squishy, mushy plastic sacks. What was this? I looked inside and found handfuls of pasta and some kind of meat.

Then it dawned on me. The doctors had told Mom that she could not go home until she could prove that she was able to eat. The nurses were constantly monitoring how well she cleaned her plate after each meal. Well, when Mom was left alone, she must have hidden the food in any bag she could find. I had proof of it right here in my hand. I was holding one sack of pasta and another of a squished tuna sandwich. She had wanted to come home that badly.

I dumped the soggy sacks into the trash and walked back to Mom's bedroom and stared at her as she calmly slept. I prayed for a moment, asking for God's grace and hoping that Jesus and the angels would answer. How could we get her back down the stairs and into the car when she couldn't even stand up? There was no other way. We would have to call for an ambulance. But I would wait until Mom was ready. She had already agreed to go back. I decided to respect her wish to choose the time.

About half an hour later, Mom called out for me. I went back into the bedroom where she told me she was now ready to be taken back to the hospital. She would go without question. I went into the living room and called 911, asking for an ambulance.

After hanging up, I went back to the bedroom to check on Mom. She asked to get up to go to the bathroom. Once again, Mom stepped onto my back to get out of bed and then I walked her to the bathroom. Mom stood at the counter, picked up her hairbrush, and slowly began to pull it through her hair. My mom needed to feel clean and presentable for the EMTs. So unlike me. I wouldn't have worried about it, but it was so important to her. I tried to stop the tears burning in my eyes as I stood beside her. Her small body leaned against mine as she slowly pulled the hairbrush through her short gray hair with her long twisted fingers. After placing the hairbrush back on the counter, she picked up a worn tube of red lipstick and applied it to her dry lips as I choked back the sob building in my throat and looked away. The need to feel herself again and live her day as she normally would was overwhelming to me. These small details suddenly seemed so incredibly important and so necessary.

As soon as Mom felt respectable, I walked her back to the bedroom and, for the last time, got down on all fours so she could place her small foot in the middle of my back and pull herself up onto the bed.

I sat with her until I saw from her bedroom window the ambulance that arrived just a few short minutes later. I ran outside and lead the technicians through the courtyard, up to the small apartment, and into the back bedroom where Mom was lying on the bed.

Thankfully, the five large men now crowding into the small bedroom were kind as they prepared Mom for her journey back to the hospital. One even made the comment as he helped lift her from the bed, "Well, she's a cute little thing!" which made me smile for the first time that day. They sat Mom down in a small wheelchair that could easily be lifted and maneuvered down the apartment steps by two of the men.

I followed Mom and the EMTs out the door, down the steps, and through the courtyard. An elderly woman who lived on the ground floor several doors down from our apartment was leaning out her doorway and watching the activities. She whispered, "God bless you," and made the sign of the cross over her upper body as our troupe passed by. I wanted to thank her but couldn't find the words. I just nodded my head and kept on walking in this sad, humorless procession.

When we got to the parking lot, I sat in my car and watched while Mom was loaded into the ambulance and then followed it back to the hospital. I was not allowed to be with Mom while she was being readmitted. Finally, the nurse allowed me into the back and I found Mom lying on a gurney up against a wall in a busy hallway. She was sipping on some water and just watching everyone scurrying busily around her. I was upset at first when I realized that she had just been slapped up against a wall and left on her own. Mom was tranquil about the situation, though, and told me to be nice. We had been through worse. I just stood awkwardly by her side, holding her hand, waiting for some attention from the doctors, and trying to dodge the orderlies rushing through the hallways.

Finally, the doctor on duty approached and informed us that Mom had an infection—her white blood cell count was elevated. About an hour later, Mom was finally moved into one of the blue-curtained cubicles in the emergency room. I stayed with her while we waited for an actual hospital room to become available. Mom was exhausted and soon drifted off to sleep, oblivious to all of the bustling that was going on around her. She had been given pain medication again. I just sat in the cubicle and watched as she waved her arms around in the air as if she were dancing. I wondered what she was dreaming about now. For once, in the last few weeks, she seemed incredibly happy... even if it was just while she dozed on and off for the next few hours.

The nurses finally woke Mom up for more x-rays. Mom had to drink this fluid concentrate before her CAT scans could be done. The fluid would light up the inside of her body and make the CAT scans easier to read. The nurses refused to take Mom for the scans until she drank two cups of the lemony concoction.

That was a problem. Mom hated the taste of the thick fluid which upset her stomach. She refused to drink it which caused the hospital staff, at first, to refuse to do the CAT scan. After a small standoff, the staff finally relented and Mom had the scan after drinking only a sip or two of the concentrate.

After the scans and tests, Mom drifted back off to sleep and began to dream. This time she was hallucinating about food. I watched as her hands floated freely in the air as if she were picking up food and slowly bringing it up to her mouth. She was always so hungry, and yet refused to eat.

I stayed that night with Mom until she was finally moved into a hospital room around 2:00 in the morning. We had been in the emergency room for thirteen hours. I was exhausted by the time I finally arrived back home around three. It took me another hour before I finally fell into a deep sleep.

I awoke up around 6:00 am to get ready for the faculty workshop that was scheduled that morning. I had had only about two hours of sleep. I staggered up and slowly showered and dressed. I was so exhausted, I could barely stand up. I was half an hour late getting to campus. The meeting was already underway when I slipped into the room through the back door and took a seat next to Allison. I whispered hello to her and tried to focus my attention on the current presentation. I didn't know how much people knew about my situation but most of my coworkers were respectful of my need for solitude. Only a few people talked to me during the rest of the meeting. That was fine. I wanted to go completely unnoticed. I didn't want to explain my predicament to anyone. I was so exhausted and my mind was so preoccupied I couldn't recall anything that had been discussed when the meeting ended three hours later. I don't remember saying goodbye to anyone as I walked out of the room. I was totally unaware of anything going on around me. I walked out of the building and got into my car. I needed to get back to the hospital.

When I arrived back at Mom's hospital room, she was gone. Her whole bed...everything...just gone. I walked out of the room, and found the nurse on duty standing at her station in the hallway. The nurse explained that Mom had been taken into surgery and I needed to call the doctor. She gave me Doctor Nelson's phone number and walked away as I pulled out my cell phone and quickly dialed. I was transferred by his office to a different department. I was routed around one more time to a third and different department. I suddenly found myself speaking on the phone to the very nurse I had just personally spoken to who had given me the doctor's phone number in the first place!

Okay, wait a minute! I was on the phone for fifteen minutes just to be transferred back to the nurse I had just spoken to face-to-face! I looked at her standing at her computer as she told me again, this time on the phone, that Mom was in surgery. I suddenly was laughing at the fact that I was talking on the phone to a woman who was standing not more than five feet away from me. She did not seem to have a sense of humor about the situation and irately informed me now not to call again and just wait for information when the doctor came out of surgery.

About an hour later, I received a call from Dr. Nelson. He informed me that Mom had developed an infection from pulling the tubes out of her nose. When Mom had pulled out the tube that had been in her digestive tract, the end piece that had been attached to her colon had ripped open the tissues of her intestines and caused an infection to spread through her internal organs. Fluid had been leaking into her abdomen and lungs. The tissues were so weak and tattered that they could not be stitched back together again. There wasn't any tissue left to reconstruct. Mom would just have to heal naturally because her colon was in complete disrepair.

I fought back tears as I listened to the doctor. I didn't want to be the responsible adult. I wanted to be a child crying because she was lost from her mother. Again, I cursed myself for not being able to find the words. I couldn't speak as Dr. Nelson continued. Mom would be placed in ICU for a few days until she began to heal. I hung up the phone and hurried down to the ICU and checked in with the nurses there. It would be a little while before they could let me in to see Mom. I sat in the waiting room for about four hours. For the first time in my life, I knew I just couldn't drive away...Where would I go? I certainly couldn't run home to Momma. So I just sat and waited with random thoughts spinning in my head.

Around 4:30 pm, I was finally allowed to enter the ICU. I walked into a wide, sterile room that featured a center desk surrounded by curtained-off cubicles. A young blond nurse greeted me at the door and walked me over to Mom's compartment. Thank God, the nurse was there for me. She put her arm around me and caught me as I almost fell over backwards after walking through the curtains of Mom's cubicle. I suddenly felt the room spin and my legs began to collapse from under me. I could not believe that was my mom! She looked so tiny, so small, like a six-year-old child, in that big hospital bed. There were tubes running up into her nose and piercing both of her arms. Her lower jaw caved inward, her lower lip curving over her gums. Mom's dentures had been removed for the surgery. Mom hated for anyone to see her this way. I couldn't stop thinking how mad she was going to be when she realized she no longer had her teeth.

I couldn't stop crying. Tears began to fill my eyes and run down my cheeks. I was so tired and so sad. After a few minutes, the kind nurse left to get some tissues. She told me that Mom was sleeping peacefully and her vital signs were good.

After the nurse left the cubicle, I held Mom's hand, kissed her cheek, and tried to keep myself from sobbing too loudly. Mom opened her eyes a few times and stared straight at me. "Home," she whispered, "I want to go home now."

"I know, Momma," I would answer. "As soon as I can, I'll take you home." I sat with her for a while, brushing her hair back. I kept my thoughts to myself as Mom again asked to go home. I wondered if we would ever find our way back home again.

CHAPTER 14

$\mathcal{V}$alentine's Day arrived while Mom was still in ICU. I had no one to celebrate with. Never used to bother me before, but it was certainly different this time. I was alone on Valentine's Day watching Mom slip in and out of consciousness. I stayed with her all day. We didn't talk, of course. We were just in a state of being, of being together in a still-hearted silence.

By the end of the evening, Mom was finally moved up to a fifth floor room. I tried to stay out of the way as the nurses and the transporters moved Mom onto the gurney and prepared her for her trip up to the fifth floor and yet I was terrified of losing her. Ever since she first entered the hospital, I needed to be there. I stayed for hours every single day. I couldn't run away. But there were many times I wish I could.

One day, after Mom's first surgery, she had looked up at me with wide eyes and stated, "I looked at my scar today. It's not as big as I thought it would be. I thought it was going to be really long but it is so small." She held the thumb and index finger of her right hand only about two inches apart to demonstrate.

"Really?" I enthused, feeling encouraged. "It's that small?"

"Yes," she answered, "do you want to see it?"

I didn't answer at first. I wasn't sure I wanted to see her surgery scar even though Mom had said it was so minor. Then suddenly she said, "No, really, look. It's so tiny," and with that she raised her hospital gown. Mom had said it was a small scar so I was completely unprepared for what I saw. I fought to hold back my gasps and nausea. Mom seemed completely unprepared as well. She looked down at the red, crusting scar that ran from under her rib cage down to her pubic area. The staples holding the reddened edges together gleamed in the lamplight. A large brownish-purple bruise bloomed on her upper right side. She stared down at the gash for just a moment and then turned to look at me, her wide eyes accusatory and filled with tears.

"What did they do to me?" Mom murmured. "Jamie, what did they do to me?" She lowered her gown slowly and turned her head away. Her last comment shook my final reserve of strength, "What did you let them do to me? What did you let them do?"

Mom turned her head into her pillow and cried before berating me about how I allowed the doctors to mutilate her. Mom had endless questions about her situation and I had no answers. I struggled to find solutions and came up with nothing. I was always able to find my way around this world, travel without a design or plan, but I have never felt so lost. So lost for an explanation. So lost about our destination. I was a total idiot. I had no answers. I couldn't understand it myself. She is such a tiny woman. How could the scar be that long and that angry? How could she handle a scar running through her body, almost cutting her completely in half?

There was one question Mom always asked me in tears and I was at a complete loss for a response. "Why am I being punished? I don't know why I'm being punished," Mom would scream to me over and over again. Maybe she really wasn't looking for an answer from me; maybe it was just a hypothetical thought. But either way, every time she asked it, I could feel my heart rip a little more. I kept trying to tell her that she wasn't being punished but it was hard to convince her when a scar ran all through her abdomen and her body would curl up in pain.

I was so exhausted from her questions and from my own lack of understanding. I suddenly began to realize exactly what I know about this life. Nothing! I took on the world all by myself and now, what could I do? I had nothing left. Nothing I could say.

One afternoon, I was so exhausted, I fell asleep sitting in a chair beside Mom's bed with my head resting on her right leg. Even with all of her pain, I awoke to find Mom's hand carefully stroking back my hair. I suddenly felt forgiven for all of my inept handling of this situation. It was one of our quieter moments. At other times, we would be at odds with each other, both of us moving in opposite directions. Struggling, crying, misunderstanding...

One of the biggest problems was that Mom kept trying to get out of bed. The nurses told me I had to keep her in bed and the tubes in her nose. It wasn't an easy task. Mom was so determined to go home she would struggle against the pain and the limitations of her own body as she tried to pull herself out of bed. She would beg me to help her get dressed and go home. She was too weak to pull herself up on her own and continually asked for my help. I was tired of arguing with her, so instead, I just put minimal effort into helping her. I would pretend that I didn't have enough strength to pull her up or that she was lying at an angle where I couldn't reach her. I didn't know what else to do when she continually begged me to get her out of bed.

It was especially worse when she had to use the bathroom. Mom did not want to use the bedpan, but I would struggle to get her out of bed in time to run for the bathroom, even though it was no more than just two feet away.

One day, Mom begged to use the bathroom. I started out to the hallway to find the nurse, forgetting about the call bell again, but Mom stopped me. She wanted me to be the one to help her without any professional assistance. I couldn't get her up to the bathroom so instead I grabbed the bedpan and tried to slide it underneath her. Oh, man, I felt as if I was trying to help birth a baby! As Mom started demanding that she needed the bathroom NOW, I panicked. I just lifted Mom up the best I could and shoved the bedpan underneath her. I had no sooner completed this task when the nurse walked into the room.

"She needed to go to the bathroom," I explained weakly. "I tried...I tried to get the bedpan under her. I just don't..."

"Oh, honey, don't worry about it," the nurse responded. "I'm sure you did a good job...oh..." She abruptly stopped talking as she raised Mom's sheet and saw the bedpan. I didn't quite get it into place. That could be because I had it turned in the wrong direction and upside down. Oh, what a mess!

Mom also had some problems with her colostomy bags. The bags would constantly make a lot of weird noises, especially gas sounds. One day, Mom was asleep while I sat beside her quietly reading a book. Her colostomy bag suddenly produced a loud gas sound that shook Mom awake. She glanced over at me, snarled her upper lip, and stated, "Jamie, shame on you!" What? That wasn't me! She rolled over and fell back to sleep while I stepped outside, laughing so hard I couldn't stop. I had to take a few minutes to pull myself together before walking back into the room.

Mom would also have days when she would be in so much pain that she couldn't relax. Many of the nurses were not gentle and didn't seem to have any patience. Mom would get very upset with them. In turn, the nurses would continually pull me aside and complain that my mother was cranky, senile, and difficult. Their constant complaints would reduce me to tears. Mom was in pain; couldn't they see that? Even a simple cough would pull on her scar and cause her to scream out.

The physical therapists were the worst. Mom did not want to get up and exercise. She was too weak. But the therapists insisted. The longer Mom stayed in bed without any activity, the more likely it was that she would contract an infection. But it was difficult for Mom to work with the therapists. They would pull her up and get her to set on the edge of the bed and then, eventually, in the bedside chair. Mom would get in position but then the therapists would walk away, leaving her sitting there for two or three hours. Mom would be crying out in pain because the therapists seemed to have abandoned her once they pulled her out of bed. Many times, I had to call for the nurses to get her back in bed which only made the therapists angry. Mom didn't want to work with the therapists any longer. It was difficult for the therapists to understand, so along with the nurses, they, too, were constantly pulling me aside to discuss Mom's situation.

Their complaints made me furious. My mother was an elderly lady who was in tremendous amounts of pain and constantly sick. How could they not understand that? It was difficult to understand their constant grievances. Excuse me, she's sick! I wanted to scream. I felt that I had to calm the therapists down while my heart was racing and my head was splitting with a devastating headache while I tried to figure out what to say. My mother is not senile, or cranky, or unkind. She only has been sick for a few weeks. You should have seen her two months ago, I wanted to tell them. You should have seen her then.

I was having my own personal struggles with Mom's illness. After a rough day at work, I wanted to be hugged and feel her stroking my hair and twisting it into tiny braids. But I arrived at the hospital almost every day to find Mom completely out of it from medications. She slept most of the time and gave little indication that she even knew I was there. I just sat beside her, staring at her, tears running down my face. I had totally collapsed.

I treasure the one afternoon when Mom greeted me with a huge smile as I walked in to her room. "I missed you," she told me. "I wondered when you would be here." I was thrilled by her reaction and by her smile, something I hadn't seen in several weeks. She hugged me for a while as I felt my heart relax and my hopes soar. It wasn't long before Mom slipped, though, back into her ongoing state of confusion. We continued searching for a cake in the bed sheets and looking for the dining room table. I didn't care. Mom seemed to remember who I was now and was happy to see me.

Mom was showing unusual signs of improvement. Ever since we started traveling together, we had a ritual. No matter where we were, every time one of us saw an attractive, younger man, we would shout out "Cougar." It was a basic signal to each other, ("Hey, check him out!"), but also a playful warning that one of us was striking a claim to the young guy. We *never* acted upon our claim, of course, but it was a fun game we both very much enjoyed.

This particularly happy afternoon, a very handsome, young male physical therapist came in to the room to work with Mom. He was very gentle with her. He didn't yank her up out of bed by her arms and force her to sit in a chair for hours. Instead, he spoke to her softly and sweetly as he took her through a few simple leg and arm stretches. I was pleased that Mom cooperated fully without a single complaint or resistance.

After about thirty minutes, when Mom began to get drowsy, the therapist told her he would be back the next afternoon and walked out the door. I couldn't help myself. I followed him out with my eyes, watching him step out into the hallway….and, all of a sudden, I heard this little voice calling out from the bed behind me, "Cougar." I turned around to see Mom with a happy, big smile on her face and a gleam in her deep emerald green eyes. Was this progress? Was she recovering? I took the moment as a sign that Mom may be returning to herself again.

The next morning, however, we started to backtrack. I walked into Mom's room and, completely surprised, she jumped when she saw me. Mom told me how happy she was that I was there. I was very encouraged…and then tears filled her eyes as she looked up at me.

"Nobody likes me," she moaned.

"What?" I asked surprised.

"Nobody likes me," she said again as a tear rolled down her face.

"Mom, why are you saying that? Everyone likes you." I wiped at her tears as I held back my own. My heart was breaking for her. I didn't tell her about the conversations that the nurses had with me. I didn't tell her they complained about her crankiness and stubbornness. How could I? It would have broken her heart.

It made me think of all the times I would come home from school, crying and screaming about the bullying I had received from the other kids over the way I talked or looked. It broke my heart to stroke back my mother's hair, wipe her face, and reassure her how much she was loved.

Is this what my mother had gone through with me so many years ago? Did it break her heart the way it was breaking mine now? I understood now why Mom would be so upset when I came home from school in tears. Flashbacks of her breakdown in Atlantic City filled my mind as I again held her and told her she was loved.

I stroked back my mother's hair and wondered why people could not see her the way I did. Why did there have to be so much pain when all anyone ever really needed was love and acceptance? I held Mom until she started to shake and vomit again, forcing me to let go. Thankfully, the vomiting didn't last long this time and she settled back down to sleep. I sat by her bedside and hoped that she wouldn't have any more upsets.

Little things, though, seemed to bother Mom. One day, she had introduced me to two of the nurses as her daughter. "Your daughter?" they had responded. "Why, she looks just like you!" They continued to point out the similarities between our hair, eyes, and skin.

Once they left the room, Mom was very agitated. "We don't look *anything alike*. How can they say that?! I'm a dried up, old lady. You are young and beautiful. What the hell are they thinking? I told you these nurses don't know crap." I just let Mom talk, quietly smiling to myself. She was getting a little riled up and I loved seeing her fighting spirit, even over such a trivial matter.

I did try my to keep her calm, though. One day, as I stood by her bedside brushing her hair back, I lulled her to sleep by telling her about all of the places we would travel to once she was well again. We just had four more states to visit: Oregon, Washington, Alaska, and Hawaii. I told Mom that she had to get better so we could finish up our tour of America.

"We have to get to Washington, Mom. We have to see the Space Needle. And Oregon…we haven't been to Oregon yet, either. What's in Oregon, Mom?"

"Portland," she would whisper.

"Yeah, Portland…we have to go there, Mom. What else? What else do you want to see? We have to go to Hawaii…"

"Can't fly," Mom would suddenly fret.

"I know," I would answer. "We will find away. And Alaska…"

"Sarah Palin," Mom would cheer.

"Yeah, we'll go visit Sarah, "I promised her, hoping that talk of our travels would inspire Mom to get better.

Then I mentioned that I couldn't go without her because we were the best of friends. Mom nodded her head and whispered, "Best buds." I was excited by her response and felt more loved than I had in a very long time.

CHAPTER 15

*A*ll of my hopes that Mom was starting to get better came to a crashing halt one morning. I found out that Mom was scheduled for another CAT scan. The nurses had delivered to her room two big foam cups full of the lemony concentrate which Mom hated. She refused it even though I kept telling her how important it was to drink. I tried everything I could think of to tease and cajole her into drinking the concentrate but she caught on to all my tricks rather easily and would not even take a sip.

The nurses came back into the room several minutes later ready to take her downstairs for the CAT scan. Mom wasn't ready. The cups of concentrate were still full. Two of the nurses looked stunned as if they had no idea what they were supposed to do. A third nurse did. She looked at the amount of concentrate still left in the cups and announced, "We'll just use the tube again." Her words certainly caught my attention. Tube? Oh, God, no. Mom hated the tube.

"Mom, Mom," I tried talking to her as soon as the nurses left the room to get the supplies. "They are going to put a tube up your nose and down your throat again if you don't drink this. Please, take it, please. You don't want the tube."

Mom's eyes suddenly lit up with understanding. As I held the cup up, her lips slowly closed around the straw and she began to drink some of the fluid. But it was too late. The three nurses came marching back into the room; the last one through the door carried the plastic, long tube.

"She's drinking it. She's drinking it," I called out as the nurses approached the bed. I was still holding the cup up for Mom as the nurses pushed me aside and surrounded her. I was pushed back behind them as Mom grabbed my hands and tried to hold me beside her, but we were outnumbered. One horribly sick, elderly woman and her incompetent, overwhelmed daughter were no match for the "nurse squad." They pushed towards the bed, two of the nurses holding Mom down as the third stood in front of her and tried to force the tube up her nose, into her throat, and down into her stomach.

Mom still had a strong hold on my hands, but now I had been pushed behind the nurses and couldn't really see what was going on. The cup of concentrate had somehow been pulled from my grasp. I don't know where it went. It was just gone.

I stood there, pulled by Mom up against the backside of the nurse with the tube, unable to move away because of the grip Mom had on me. My hands were mangled in Mom's own. Struggling against the knot of nurses and trying not to cry, I listened to Mom cough and gag, and felt her twist and turn with each push the nurse gave the tube. The procedure seemed to last all afternoon.

But, in reality, after just a few minutes, the ordeal was over and the nurses marched out of the room as quickly and surely as they had entered. I sat by Mom's side, stunned, feeling manhandled and depressed as Mom fell asleep, totally worn out from the battle. I watched the tube fill with, and then empty, the yucky yellow fluid into Mom's nose. It would be a while before the full content of the bag hanging over her bed would be empty of the concentrate. The nurses had stated that they could only give Mom a small amount of the fluid at a time through the tube. There seemed to be no rush, no urgency now to get the fluid into her body. Why didn't they just let her drink it slowly then? I don't know but I was exhausted. Maybe that's why I couldn't control my tears. I was glad Mom was sleeping right now. I cried for quite a while.

I can understand death, but I can't understand suffering. Why couldn't Mom just be at peace? But instead she had to fight and cry and be punished for a crime she never committed. Why does it all have to happen this way? But I couldn't find the right words to ask God for help. I wish I could pray but the expressions failed me. When I pray, I usually thank God rather than ask Him for anything. So now, when I really needed the prayer, needed to ask God for something so important, so life-changing, prayers failed me. Was my lack of prayer the problem? The thought terrified me and yet no prayerful words would come to mind. I realized I needed help learning to request blessings from God. Unfortunately, I would never learn in time.

But, thank God, and I did, things were smoother the next day. Mom was in a blissful, happy mood when I walked into her hospital room. She looked up at me from her bed where she was sipping on some water through a straw. The tube was out of her nose and she looked at peace. She smiled up at me and stated, "I saw my daddy!"

"You did?" I answered shocked. "When? "

"Last night," she whispered. "He came to see me."

I smiled at her words. Grandpa died in December of 1962. Forty-eight years ago...and here was my mother claiming she had seen him. As I looked at her peaceful, happy expression and bright eyes, I believed her completely. I believed that she saw the kind man with the balding head and black plastic glasses. A man I only knew from photographs and Mom's memories. Mom had loved her daddy. I believed he had been here for her now, but I worried about what it could all mean. Was it a visitation? Was it a premonition? I didn't let my mind go there but felt thrilled that she was so happy and calm.

The next day, Mom was scheduled to have a thoracentesis and I needed to be there for her. I *wanted* to be there. I sat around with Mom in her room for most of the day. Finally, around five-thirty, hospital transport arrived to take Mom downstairs. I was relieved until I heard the young transporter say something about an EKG. What!? Mom was having the fluid removed from her chest, a thoracentesis. The transport aide told us that the doctors were completely backed up and that we would just have to wait for that procedure, but the EKG was taking place right now.

I walked behind the transport following Mom's bed to the elevators. I was shocked by the rudeness of the people around us. People crowded into the elevator with us, actually pushing Mom's bed aside roughly, and squeezing in on all sides. People knocked into Mom's bed from every direction as it was pushed through the hallways to the EKG lab. I was becoming increasingly frustrated and it was only looking down at Mom's face that calmed me down. I was thinking about our time on the road and how frustrated Mom would be with me when I would yell at the other drivers and honk my horn. Mom would always say to me "Be nice" when she saw my aggravation with traffic. I thought about that now and whispered in my own head "Be nice." I finally calmed down by the time we reached the EKG office.

Mom was rolled into the room and I sat on a blue hard plastic chair by the door. I watched as her gown was pushed aside gently and the pads were placed on her chest. I was pleased that the young woman performing the EKG was kind and tender with her.

Still, the procedure was uncomfortable for Mom. Lying in her bed across the room, Mom suddenly turned moist eyes on me and whispered, "Help me." My heart broke. I looked at her and shook my head gently. She stared at me and again whispered, "Help me."

I shook my head slowly and helplessly at her. "We need to do this, Mom," I whispered to her. She angrily turned her head away from me and faced the wall. I wanted her so badly to know that I would have taken her away from all of this if I could. I wrestled with my feelings until, finally, the procedure started. I heard strange soggy thumps as if Mom's heart was beating under water. I turned to look at the screen that showed a shadowy outline of her chest. It looked like I was seeing Mom's heart through tears. I could see fluid splashing around her thoracic cavity. I wanted to cry but could just watch in silence until it was mercifully over.

Mom was taken back upstairs as I followed again struggling with people in the hallways as if we were sailing against the current. We were settled back in Mom's room for about thirty minutes when the transport people came up again. They were ready now to take her for the thoracentesis. Mom's bed was rolled back downstairs, through the crazy hospital traffic, and into a small, narrow room to have the fluid removed from her chest. As she was being prepped for the procedure, a male nurse asked me if Mom could sit up.

"No," I whispered. "She can't sit up. She's too weak and in too much pain."

Mom's situation seemed to cause a minor dilemma. At first, the professionals were very confused about what to do. The male nurse tried to explain it to me. "To do a thoracentesis, we have to place the tube into her lungs through her back. We need to get to both sides. We cannot put the tube in if she is lying down and we can't get to the full thoracic cavity if she is just lying on one side. She needs to be sitting up. If she lies down, the tube will be blocked. You'll have to hold her during the procedure."

I stared at him for a moment, completely alarmed. No, I was just here for emotional support. I didn't want to be a physical part of this! I didn't say anything to the nurse but I'm sure a look of anxiety crossed over my face. I stopped panicking when Mom suddenly told the attendant no. She didn't think it was a good idea. I don't think she wanted me to see her in such a vulnerable state. So now, I finally spoke up telling Mom it wasn't a problem. I could certainly help. I assured her it would be okay. I needed to do it. I didn't want Mom to worry. I would just have to do it.

The room was so small there was barely enough space for all of us. There was the doctor, three nurses, mom, and me all squeezed together in this little area. I just closed my eyes and reminded myself of all the family vacations we used to take packed together in the family station wagon. We can make it through this.

Slowly, we sat Mom up and pulled her legs over the side of the bed. She then leaned her head on my shoulder and the nurse held her up as well with his arm around her upper back. The doctor inserted a tube with a large, thick needle into the left side of her back after swabbing the area. The tube was inserted…and the next thing I know this yellowish/greenish fluid came pissing out of my mother's back, through the tube, and into a large clear glass jar. I couldn't believe what I was seeing! I don't know what I was expecting. I thought that maybe the fluid would come out of her thoracic cavity through the tube like a drip, but I was wrong. It just came spewing out in an ugly thin yellowish green flood.

And then the nurse was calling for another jar! The first one was completely filled. Mom leaned against my shoulder and cried for a while. The doctor assured her that she would begin to breathe so much better now as he removed the tube and inserted another needle into the right side of her back.

The male nurse moved behind Mom to give her support from the back and I continued to hold her from the front. Finally, it was over but Mom kept her head on my shoulder for a few more minutes. After removing the tube, the doctor needed to do a chest X-ray. Now, I was sent to the waiting room across the hall while Mom was taking into the adjacent room.

After about twenty minutes, we were finally able to return to Mom's room. The night nurse, Janice, walked in as the transport assistants were getting Mom settled again. I commented to Janice that Mom needed some pain medication so she could sleep through the night.

Janice glared at me and stated, "I have been her nurse for the past two nights. I *think* I *know* what she needs."

I was surprise by her comment and stopped myself from saying,

"Well, I've been her daughter for forty years. I think *I* know what she needs!" I choked the words back. I didn't want to argue in front of Mom. I just nodded my head and backed away.

Janice finished her work and moved out of the room. I stepped back up to the bed and grabbed Mom's hand. "Janice yelled at you," Mom stated. Darn, she had heard. Then she continued, "She yelled at me yesterday. She told me that I was a crabby, old woman that nobody liked."

I stared at Mom for a moment. "She told you *what?*"

"She said that nobody liked me." My breath caught then as I thought about Mom's tears the other day when she had cried over being unloved. Mom could probably feel the tension in my hand as I yanked away and turned to the door. But before I could go off to find Janice, Mom's voice stopped me. "Do you love me?" she whispered.

"Yes," I told her, as I took her hand again. "I love you so much."

"I love you, too," she whispered as she squeezed my hand.

We were together that way, just holding hands, for several minutes. Then something strange suddenly happened. I began to feel this incredible warmth move through me. As I held her hand, I felt her heart rate begin to relax. I held her hand and I suddenly felt surrounded by the color blue. It was everywhere around the room and surrounded us completely. I could feel Mom's heartbeat racing through me. I could feel her spirit moving down her arm, through her hand, into my palm. Mom's spirit moved into my heart and I could feel her in my soul. The feeling lasted just a few minutes, but I had never felt so connected with Mom and God as I had at that moment. There was a oneness between us and all things that I had never felt before or since. Then, Mom was calm, quiet, and grinning softly in her sleep. I held her hand for a while and smiled down at her. I watched her peacefully sleep and I suddenly had this feeling that no matter what happened, we were held in God's best graces.

It was unfortunate that the feeling didn't last long. The next day I was in a really bad mood. Maybe that inspirational feeling had been so intense that when I arrived at the hospital the next day and Mom wasn't any better, I was angry that she was not showing any signs of improvement. What had I expected after last night? I expected a blessing, a miracle…and was angry that nothing had changed.

I was experiencing the worse case of road rage just walking down the hospital corridor. I was angry with everyone who was moving too slowly or had stepped casually in front of me. I took out my frustration on everyone around me. I was tired of the nurses yelling at me and complaining to me. It was even worse when I asked JoAnne, Mom's current day nurse, to help with Mom's bedpan. She did, but was not happy about it. She came in to help but let me know that "Bedpans are not my job. You shouldn't have asked me to do this. I am far too busy to take care of situations like this." I never asked her for help again.

There was, however, good news from Dr. Nelson that raised my spirits. He let us know that Mom could go home if she became stronger. There was no infection in her lungs and she would hopefully soon be healthy enough to leave the hospital. The news was exciting for both of us and we eagerly made plans where we would go first once Mom had regained her strength. Oregon, Washington…

But our euphoria did not last long. Mom was beginning to slip away from me again. That afternoon, she asked me if I would take Manny, her evening nurse, home and was furious when I refused. She told me she was angry with me. She told me I was selfish and she didn't raise me to be that way. I tried to explain to her that Manny was the nurse and did not need me to take him home. She didn't understand and riled against my self-centeredness. The only thing that saved me was that Mom was extremely exhausted that day and easily went back to sleep. Her tirade had worn her out.

The next day, Mom was in a better mood but wasn't sleeping so easily. She kept complaining that she was very hot and was angry that the nurses kept covering her up. She needed to have the sheets and blanket off of her sweaty body. I swept the covers off of her, held onto her hand, and brushed back her hair. I suddenly felt the need to know all of her, body and soul. I wanted to touch her and just hold her in place for a few minutes. I just wanted to hold her still for a while. I wanted to listen to her heartbeat and be reminded that she was still alive and functioning. I liked those few quiet moments of being with her and trying to stop her spirit from sliding away from me. It made me feel like I was doing something, contributing in some way to her healing. Was this prayer? Was this my way of asking God to heal? I never said any words, but just held her close and tried to stop her from leaving me.

It didn't work, though. I don't know if I lacked faith or strength. The days had been exhausting. I was running to work and then to the hospital. The bright part of one morning was when Nancy and Esmeralda, two of my students, stayed for about an hour after class speaking to me about my mother and asking what they could do to help. A sweet card from Esmeralda had me crying for hours. She gave me a beautiful handmade card that offered me comfort and sympathy. Her kindness was greatly appreciated.

Very few people actually knew that Mom was in the hospital. I wanted to keep it quiet. I needed time to assimilate the information in my own heart and mind before I shared it with a lot of other people. I would sit with Mom in quiet moments and contemplate the way the world worked. Why was this happening? What was its purpose? Even in my quietest moments, I couldn't hear an answer. But sometimes I would think about the destiny of events. Can anyone actually survive a fight with fate?

I wonder if a lot of tragedies are the result of our refusal to be still. Does our constant fight to create our own destiny create our own misery? For instance, sometimes I wonder that if Prince Charles had been allowed to marry Camilla years ago, would Lady Diana still be alive today? Was it her destiny to become Princess Diana, loved by billions of people and then to die so tragically? Was Prince Charles just the catalyst to fulfill her destiny? Do we do that for and to each other?

I thought about our own situation and wondered how much

influence I had over Mom's illness. I couldn't help but wonder what I might have done differently. What if I had worn red last Tuesday... would that have changed anything? But it's amazing how tragedy strikes and the mind clings to anything that might make sense. Is it human nature to want life to make sense? Randomness can be scary. Not the fear of the unknown, not the fear of the challenge, but the fear that there is no reason at all, the fear that events don't happen for a reason. Right now, I couldn't figure anything out.

I wondered if the same thoughts were zooming through Mom's mind as well. One morning, when Mom was fully awake and lucid, we were watching the news together on the small TV that hung in the corner of her hospital room. Every news item made her cry. Before the news had ended, Mom was sobbing and repeating over and over "Those poor people...Those poor people" as if she had known each person in every violent story personally. Her cries absolutely broke my heart. Here she was, in the hospital, colon cancer, fluid in her chest, and she was crying over the death and pain of people she didn't even know. Her compassion overwhelmed me. She may not have known exactly why I began to cry, but she reached up and wrapped me in her arms as we cried together over the impossibilities of fate.

I don't know if Mom's sobs had exhausted her and taken too much of her energy, but after we wiped our tears away, Mom claimed she was hungry and wanted some ice cream from the cafeteria. I was pleased to run down and get it for her. She cried when I wouldn't let her pay for it. I thought I was being kind by paying for everything she needed. But, now, I suddenly realized I was actually taking away her dignity. I wasn't allowing her to be her own person. So I just smiled at Mom and took her purse out of the cabinet. I stood by patiently for once while she slowly counted out her change. I struggled not to drop the coins as her hand shook them into mine. I smiled at her and accepted the money to buy her ice cream. "And get something for yourself, too," she insisted.

Mom was scheduled to have another thoracentesis that day. The thought made me cringe. We both would have to find the strength to do it again. I needed to be there. No matter how the situation upset me, I couldn't stand the thought that she would have to go through it alone.

Mom told me about a procedure she had a few days ago when I was at work. I had known nothing about it. Mom tried to explain it to me through her tears. She had been given a procedure in which a tube was inserted up into her colon. Apparently it was a technique to clean out her intestines. During the procedure though, her abdominal wound was torn open and fluid had leaked through, soaking her bandages. I don't know what actually had happened and talking to the doctor did not offer any new insights.

Now I was determined to be at all procedures. So here I was, waiting to go with Mom to her next thoracentesis. I sat quietly by her bedside while Mom slept fitfully. She kept complaining that she was incredibly hot as she kicked the blankets off. I asked the nurses several times to please check the room temperature. They told me that it was still cool and they couldn't figure out why Mom was so hot. I spent most of the morning wiping spongy mouth swabs over Mom's lips and the inside of her mouth. It was the only fluid she would get until after the procedure was completed.

Finally, a nurse came in to check Mom's oxygen level and was surprised to find it severely low. She told me that Mom was hot because of her lack of oxygen. Her heart had to beat three times as fast to push the little bit of oxygen she could get through her body. The quick beating of her heart had pushed her body temperature way up.

The nurse ordered an emergency thoracentesis. "We have to drain her lungs now," she explained, "so she can get more oxygen."

Mom was immediately wheeled downstairs, again fighting against the people on the elevator, and rolled into the small room. She was rotated to her left side, then forced up. Her legs were thrown over the side of the bed. Her head was resting on my shoulder. Mom cried as the needle was placed through her back and into her lungs. I thought I knew what to expect…and yet, I was taken by complete surprise.

Instead of the yellow-greenish fluid, bright red blood came shooting through the tube and into the glass jar. I caught my breath trying not to scream out as I held Mom against my chest just as I had done before. I turned my head away, not wanting to see the blood. After about ten minutes, it was finally over, but I couldn't tell Mom to let go of me. I'm not really sure exactly who was clinging to whom. I was holding Mom during the procedure but I needed her arms around me. I needed my momma to comfort me. We clung together until the nurse finally pulled us apart and laid Mom back down on the bed. I was sent back to the waiting room again while Mom was sent for more x-rays. Then the journey back up to her room began again.

Finally, we were settled back in but this time I did not feel connected at all. I felt lost, isolated, adrift…and the nurse, checking on Mom, certainly didn't help the situation. The nurse, JoAnne, told me that Mom was not going to survive. I sat in that room, numb and broken, listening to JoAnne talk about my mother dying. "She's already gone," she said. "You know that, don't you? The doctors will tell you all kinds of things to give you hope but I won't do that. I don't think it's fair when there really is no hope at all. Your mother is as good as dead. And you don't want to put her on life support. You know what they do for life support, don't you? They'll crack open her chest. How do you think she'll survive that? She's so small and weak. Putting her on life support is cruel. You need to ask not to resuscitate her if you care for her at all. Just let her die."

Why didn't I say something to JoAnn then? Why didn't I scream at her to shut up? I don't know why I just sat there. I was stunned and grieving and just couldn't talk or think. I was so exhausted and horrified by all I had witnessed at the hospital, I could have easily been manipulated by anyone at that point. That's the only explanation I have, and it's not a good one. It's as if life no longer existed in or around me.

I just sat there by myself in the growing darkness of the room after JoAnn left. I got up and stood over Mom's bed and told her that I was going to be okay if she needed to…and I couldn't finish, couldn't say it. I couldn't tell my mother that she could let go. The words just wouldn't come. I just didn't have the strength. If I told her it was okay for her to go, would she think that she was unloved? I was worried that she would think I was giving up the fight, and that was something my mother would never forgive me for.

About an hour later, I was leaving the hospital after a hard day of knowing my mother was so hot because she wasn't receiving oxygen into her lungs. I was finally leaving the hospital after my mother, who had been a smoker for several years, had to have her lungs cleared again, this time of blood, so she could breathe. I was finally leaving the hospital and had just stepped out the front door when a young woman stopped me. "Hey, you gotta light?" she asked me as she waved her long, unlit cigarette in front of my face. I just stared at her for a moment.

"No, no," I whispered with a shake of my head, trying to stop the convulsion of my body and the tears pushing at my eyes. I stared at her for a moment, then just shook my head, and walked away.

CHAPTER 16

The next day, March 13, 2010, my nerves were shattered. I wasn't at the hospital for very long before the first upset started. I had stepped inside Mom's room when I saw that the nurses were bathing her. I stepped back outside the doorway. While I waited for the nurses to finish, I checked my messages. I had a message to call Dr. Nelson. I began to dial his number when JoAnne walked up behind me.

"Excuse me, excuse me," she started calling and waving her arms at me.

Oh, now what? I hung up my phone before the doctor's office had actually picked up. Once JoAnne had my full attention, she told me what was so important. "You need to call the doctor," she informed me.

"Thank you," I answered through clenched teeth, biting back the fact that I was actually on the phone to the doctor's office when she interrupted me. She calmly walked away and I dialed the number again.

I listened to the office phone ring once, twice, and then was distracted again by JoAnne's fingers in my face. I waved her away once but when she wouldn't leave, I hung up the phone again. JoAnne then informed me, "I have the doctor's number right here for you." She held a piece of paper in front of my face.

I stared at her in complete disbelieve for a moment before I could find my voice. Once I found it, I couldn't stop the words pouring out of my mouth. "I have the doctor's office on the phone, but you keep interrupting me!" The tone of my voice was sharper than I had intended and I was a little embarrassed when it echoed for a few seconds against the concrete walls and tiled floors of the hallway.

"Well, I'm sorry," JoAnne sarcastically apologized before she turned around and huffed back down the hallway to the nurses' station. I'm sure I could hear her making comments that I was just as rude as my mother. I wanted to run down the hallway, grab her shoulders, force her to turn and look at me. "We are dying here," I wanted to scream in her face. "We are dying here, and I don't know what to do. We are good people. We are kind people. We were people who were used to living and moving. We were people who traveled and appreciated this world. We don't know how to handle this. We don't know what to do with this. Haven't you ever seen a family die before? This is a hospital, and you all act as if you have never seen anyone dying before!"

But I didn't do it. I couldn't breathe. I wanted to drop down to the floor and cry until the hurt was all gone again. I think there was a part of me that was concerned how the nurses would treat Mom if I had any kind of outburst. They had already proven to me time and again that sick people baffled them. What kind of treatment would my outburst create? I pulled myself together and went into Mom's room where she spent the afternoon asking me once again to take her home. She was frustrated when I didn't help her out of bed.

"Mom, I can't now," I tried to explain to her, trying to keep the frustration out of my voice. "I can't take you away from here. We have to stay."

Mom flopped herself back down on the bed, turning her head away from me.

"Mom, I'm sorry. I'm so sorry," I whispered to her but she didn't answer me. "Mom," I asked then, "do you love me?"

No answer. She wasn't asleep this time because my question caused her to kick at the covers and jerk closer to the side of the bed away from me. Her reaction suddenly caused a memory to float up to my conscious brain. When I was twelve years old, for some reason, my mother stopped loving me. I don't know if she was frustrated or just needed time away from me. I remember, though, that during my twelfth year, every time I told my mother I loved her she wouldn't respond. My mother could not tell me she loved me and I never knew why. Something about me had upset her. I never knew what it was. I was too young to realize that maybe it was her own bitterness, depression, and anger at herself and her own life that took away her love. Maybe she saw herself as unlovable. I don't know what it was then. My mother now had turned away from me and again couldn't tell me she loved me. Only this time I knew why.

The next day, however, I was extremely encouraged. The doctor had informed us that Mom might be able to leave the hospital if she would continue to eat. Dr. Nelson needed to make sure her system was working as well as possible before they could release her.

That morning, I had brought a package of doughnuts with me to Mom's hospital room. She used to love doughnuts so much. I was hoping that the glazed treats would tempt her to eat. I opened the box slowly and placed one of the pastries into her shaky, excited hands. She bit into it and slowly began to chew. Yes, she was eating! But there was a problem. Mom was never able to get her dentures back into place after they had been removed for the surgeries. I tried to help her and I asked the nursing assistants to please help, too. But Mom refused, shaking her head violently and slapping away anyone's hands that came near her mouth. She was afraid we were trying to take away her dentures again. She fought to keep them. I tried to explain to Mom what was happening, but it didn't help. This morning, she still fought against me and I backed away. Thank God, at least, she was eating

…And then the worst thing at that moment happened.

Two of the nurses came into the room and saw Mom trying to chew the chunk of doughnut that was in her mouth. "What did you do?" They suddenly spun on me. "What did you give her?" One of them began to squeeze the sides of Mom's face together to force her mouth open. The nurse was reaching inside of Mom's mouth to pull out the doughnut as Mom twisted her head from side to side and tried to slap her hands away. The one nurse not involved in this combat turned around to glare at me. "Why did you give that to her?"

I started screaming back. "You wanted her to eat! She's eating! Why are you taking it away from her?" I don't know what it was about a darn doughnut that suddenly forced me into this verbal clash with the nurses now.

The nurses easily shoved me aside. "She has to go for a CAT scan this morning. She can't have food right now!" One nurse stomped out completely exasperated with me. The other stayed by Mom's bedside, hanging over the rail of the bed, trying to pull the doughnut from her mouth.

"Just let her swallow that one piece," I interjected. "I won't give her any more. Don't pull that out of her mouth!" After all Mom had been through, having food pulled from her mouth seemed absolutely humiliating.

The nurse pulled her hands away from Mom's face then but did not back away. Instead she leaned over the bed, hovering over Mom, and stared directly in her face as she repeated over and over, "Swallow it. Just swallow it now."

Though her voice was soft and gentle, her repeated phrase wore on my nerves and I finally shouted, "Well, she can't swallow with you in her face like that!"

The nurse glared at me for a moment and then, with an exasperated sigh and roll of her eyes, walked out of the room. I looked at Mom and stood holding her hand while she chewed for several more seconds before finally swallowing. Victory!

I talked to Doctor Nelson later that afternoon about Mom's

discharge. I already knew the answer; however, I wouldn't have said it as harshly as he did. He answered, "If she leaves, she dies." I never asked him again. I never told Mom his response either. With all of the talk the nurses and doctors did about death, Mom was showing stubborn defiance by hanging on. I hoped that she was oblivious to their attitudes.

I sat by her bedside all afternoon. My thoughts kept turning to my journey through her body, knowing I had come from her. I wanted to be back with her. I wanted to start over again. I wanted to begin the journey again from the very beginning. I wish that was possible. I should be pleased that I had my mother for over forty years, but now I was tired and sad. Suddenly for some reason I had it in my head that this moment, being with my mother at this time of our lives, was never going to come again. Learn from it. Hold on to it. It's all a lesson. That's all life is. Just a series of lessons to bring us closer to God. I can never experience everything in this world, but I can learn from the lives of other people. If I listened, if I paid attention to those around me, I can learn so much from other people's journeys....And Mom was proving to be an amazing teacher.

CHAPTER 17

*M*arch 15, 2010, was a day when I learned more lessons than my head and heart could actually comprehend. My resolve had finally broken down completely and there was no turning around now. No U-turns in sight. I cried in front of everybody that day. I couldn't seem to stop. My emotional outburst started at work that morning and continued at the hospital that afternoon. It was unconsciously egged on by Manny, Mom's nurse. He pulled me aside as soon as I arrived at the hospital and asked me if I wanted to put Mom on life support. When I was undecided, he explained the procedure to me.

Mom had a feeding tube going up her nose for the first few weeks that she had been in the hospital. It was later shifted to a catheter in her left arm. Now, Manny explained to me that an incision would be made into her abdomen and the tube would be placed directly into her intestines. But that wasn't all. In the next few days, the tube would be placed in a hole that would be cut into her thin, smooth throat. Manny explained that the tube would have to be moved around her body. If it was left in one place for too long, an infection could start.

I listened to his words. I understood in my mind. I knew what had to be done. But my knees shook so hard, I could feel myself beginning to fall. I leaned against the wall and started to cry while Manny went to call one of the Hospital Social Workers who help families through tragedies. I sat with Mom for a few minutes until the social worker, JR, arrived. I didn't want to talk in Mom's room. I still wasn't sure how much she could hear and comprehend of conversations held around her. JR and I moved down the hallway to an empty hospital room. We no sooner sat down across from each other and I began to cry. Huge sobs wracked my body and I couldn't breathe.

JR was so kind. He just sat holding my hand until I could finally catch my breath. We had only been talking for a few minutes when Dr. Nelson arrived and asked me about putting Mom on life support ...and I was at a loss for words. I didn't want to be the one making the decisions. What if I choose wrong? I was the idiot. How could I be trusted with this decision? This was my mother's life. Did she want to suffer just to live? Did she want to go peacefully, quietly, and with dignity? Would I cling to her selfishly when she needed to leave? If I was holding onto her spirit after her first thoracentesis, how could I let go now? Dr. Nelson noticed my confusion and asked, "Well, is she awake now?"

"She was," I answered, "when I left the room."

"Well, let's go ask her then," the doctor responded.

I trailed behind him as he led the way back to Mom's room. Dr. Nelson and I each took a position on either side of Mom's bed. JR positioned himself behind me. Manny stood just inside the doorway. I leaned over Mom as Dr. Nelson very matter-of-factly asked her the question that I couldn't answer. "Mrs. Zunick, do you want to be resuscitated if anything should happen?"

Mom's eyes sparked bright and sharp as she looked at the doctor and said in a steady voice, "No." Just that one simple word, but it spoke volumes.

"Mrs. Zunick," he spoke again, "do you want to be put on life support?"

This time she not only stared him in the eyes, but her bony

crooked arthritic index finger pointed up and shook from left to right just under his nose as she stated again, "No."

"Momma," I whispered to her from the other side of the bed like the little devil now sitting on her opposite shoulder. "Momma, is this what you want?"

"Yes," she whispered to me...and tears began to pour down my face.

"Momma," I whispered again as I started to choke up. My voice had become raspy. I suddenly felt a hand on my back. JR? I didn't know. I didn't turn around. I just took comfort in the touch. "Momma," I whispered again. "Are you sure? Please, I just need you to be sure."

And then she smiled at me and whispered, "No life support."

"Well, that's it," Dr. Nelson stated. "She's decided. She will not be resuscitated."

That was it?!? That was all there was to it?!? That summed up her whole life, and it was done now? I looked at the doctor. "Well, do I need to sign anything or..."

"No," he answered. "We all heard her say no resuscitation. It's good."

And I wanted to leap across the bed and throw my arms around him in a gigantic hug. I wanted to kiss his hands and thank him for what he had just done. After weeks of hearing that my mother was hallucinating because she was senile and demented, her request not to have life support had been accepted! She had been able to make a decision and it had been held up with dignity. Dr. Nelson had suddenly become my hero. He could no longer save my mother but he had not treated her like a senile old woman, a pet, a person without dignity.

As Dr. Nelson, JR, and Manny left the room, I held my mother's hand as she started to drift off to sleep. I wondered if she had actually known what could happen now that she had refused the life support. She probably did and she had made her choice with quiet acceptance.

It made me think about the situations in my own life. I had always fought and ran and knocked down walls when the doors closed and the windows wouldn't open. I suddenly realized as I held my mother's hand that afternoon that no matter what had happened to me in the past or what my future held, tragedy does not give me license to behave badly, to injure other people, to wallow in my own self-pity.

I kissed Mom goodbye about an hour later and headed back out to work with my head held high. It was time I began to behave like the woman my mother taught me to be.

CHAPTER 18

Tuesday, March 16, 2010, just twelve hours after Mom had refused life support, the phone rang at 3:30 in the morning…and I knew.

I had arrived back home from work at around eleven pm. I got cleaned up and went to bed, finally settling down around midnight. I was restless even after I went to bed. I didn't drift off to sleep until one in the morning. I came jumping out of bed when the phone rang at 3:30 am. I grabbed the receiver and whispered a hello. A voice on the phone whispered back. I couldn't make out everything the man said. I just heard "Your mother…agonal breaths…come now."

Agonal breaths…I got stuck there. I recognized the term from teaching CPR for the last several years. Agonal breathing is not real breathing. It's a gagging sound of air escaping from the lungs. I didn't ponder what this meant any further once I hung up the phone. I threw on my jeans, jumped in my car, and took off for the hospital. It had only been twenty minutes since I had received the phone call. Twenty minutes….

The doors of the elevator opened on the fifth floor. I stepped out, started down the hallway…and was intercepted by the nurse before I could make it to Mom's room.

I didn't recognize this nurse. I had never seen her before, but I was relieved that she had been the one on duty that night. She was young, gentle, sweet, beautiful…and her eyes were filled with tears. She grabbed my shoulders and forced me to look at her. "Are you Jamie?" she asked. "Are you Mrs. Zunick's daughter?"

I could only nod my head. Tears began to pour down her face. I knew. I just knew then. But I wondered for a moment if this was the young nurse's first lost patient, if this was the first death to have occurred on her shift…and my heart broke for her. She stared into my eyes for just a moment before saying, "She's gone. She passed on about five minutes ago."

Five minutes. I missed saying good-bye by just five minutes! It had only taking me twenty minutes to dress and drive to the hospital and I was still too late. I hadn't been staying at the hospital since the nurses had removed the cot after realizing that they had placed it in the wrong room. It had never been meant for me to use. The nurses had started chasing me out every night when visitors' hours ended. I hadn't argued. I had just gone home…and I hadn't been there.

While thoughts and questions spun in my head, Jolene, the nurse, wrapped an arm around me and walked me down the hallway to Mom's room. I took a deep breath, and Jolene and I entered together. After whispering that she would be back in a few minutes, Jolene stepped out and I finished the long journey across the room to Mom's bed by myself. I stood beside her and looked down at her still, quiet body. Her eyes were closed and her small, dainty hands were resting together on her chest.

I still told her hello, still kissed her forehead, still brushed back her hair. I had the strangest sensation that time had suddenly stood still. I had never had that awareness before, not even when I had been at Bandelier or the Grand Canyon. I had never felt before that time and space did not exist, not even when I was staring into the Pacific Ocean or walking across a Civil War battlefield. But now, I suddenly found myself lost in some unusual, vast, unknown continuum even while everything still looked so familiar. I had been lost so many times in America, but I had never felt the world stand still as it did at this time. After a few moments, I suddenly realized all of the machines— the machines that had been feeding her, cleaning her, keeping track of her heartbeats, giving her oxygen—all of the machines that had surrounded my mother for the past several weeks, had been turned off. The machines had been silenced. It was deafening and intense not to hear them. The sudden quiet made me dizzy and sick. I had to stop listening to the silence or it would have completely overwhelmed me.

I did the only thing I could think of at that time. I called my sisters and brother in Kansas to give them the news. They needed to know but I called mainly to hear their voices and fill the quiet. Our conversations were very short and to the point. There really was nothing more to say. I just gave them the news, "Mom passed away this morning." They answered with, "Oh, oh, God, I love you." And then we hung up. That was it. What more was there to say? The calls lasted just a few minutes.

I finished the last call when Jolene reappeared and asked me to sign a few papers. She explained them to me but I don't remember what they were. Jolene then helped me pack up Mom's belongings. There really wasn't much. We just needed to pack a few personal items like her clothes, hairbrush, and makeup. All the small things that had given Mom hope that she would be going home soon.

I gathered up Mom's things and headed for the door. Jolene walked me to the elevator. She gave me a hug and asked me to call her as soon as I got back home. She didn't want me to be alone. She worried about me driving around on the highways by myself, not knowing that that's where I would feel the most at peace. I told her I would be okay but agreed to call her.

I kept my promise, sort of. I called Jolene about fifteen minutes later, but I wasn't at home. I was on my way to work. What was I supposed to do? Sit at home by myself? Walk around in circles in the apartment? Cry on my own shoulder? I needed a distraction. So, four-thirty in the morning, I entered the school alone and prepared for my classes. I needed to keep doing normal things. This was just the first week of a new term. Brand new students. I felt that I couldn't desert them right now, not at the beginning.

I walked through the day in a daze. I didn't want to speak to anyone. No one knew. I wasn't ready to talk yet. I needed to keep it mine for a while. I needed to hold it close. The only person I spoke to that day at any length was my sister, Theresa. Over the phone, her comfort was so appreciated and I had never felt closer to her. This sister proved to repeatedly be my greatest source of strength and comfort. My relationships with both of my sisters and brother have grown stronger since Mom's passing, which was something I had always feared. Mom had always been the centerpiece of all family affairs. I had deep concerns that I would lose contact with my family if something happened to Mom. But that wasn't the case. My sisters, Theresa and Carol, and brother, Anthony, are my true heroes. They have loved me and stood by me like I could have never imagined when we were younger and being ripped apart by my father's anger and my mother's depression. We have all matured in graciousness, gratitude, and unconditional love.

I also called Aunt Nancy, my mother's sister, to let her know what had happened. I hadn't called her before when Mom first became ill. I think I was hoping that Mom would be fine in a few weeks and I shouldn't bother and upset everybody. Now here I was, calling my Aunt Nancy to let her know that her little sister was gone. I could finally feel the tears pushing their way into my eyes and I struggled. I didn't feel that I could let them flow and feel my own pain when Aunt Nancy mentioned that she was now the last of her immediate family. I wondered what that would be like as a shiver run through me and I hoped for the longevity of my own brother and sisters. I have been alone on the road so much, but always by my own choice. I could not stand the thought of loneliness being forced upon me by the suffering of my family. I tried to hold myself under control as Aunt Nancy reminisced and laughed about all of our trips to Colorado when I was a child.

My sister, Carol, flew to California and helped me with a few of the arrangements but I had most of it already taken care of by the time she arrived. Mom had wanted to be cremated and the process had already started. There wasn't a lot for Carol to do except help me clean out Mom's room. I was probably doing it too quickly but I preferred taking care of the situation while Carol was here. I didn't really want to do everything by myself. Mom's room didn't take us too long to clean out. She didn't have a lot of items since her move to California. Her clothes, furniture, and a few personal items were donated to a local charity. I was happy to be able to give the items to an organization that could really use them. I'm not going to say it's what Mom would have wanted. I really didn't know what Mom would have wanted and I'm surprised when people always say that about their loved ones.

Given the choice, I think Mom would have wanted to live. I think she would have loved to go back to the mountains and see the Pacific Ocean again. I think she would have loved to be back on the road again, traveling aimlessly around in circles with me. I think she would have wanted to finish our goal to travel through America by driving to Washington and Oregon. She would have wanted to find a way to get to Alaska and Hawaii, too. That's what she would have wanted. What to do with her things....I don't think she really would have cared.

It really wasn't hard to donate her clothing, actually. She didn't have anything that was fashionable. All of her clothes were just functional. Clothes just served the function of covering her tiny body. She didn't really care about the styles or colors. Cleaning out Mom's closet wasn't too overwhelming.

It wasn't until I saw her crossword dictionary that I started to break down. Mom loved crossword puzzles. I could feel tears sting my eyes as I looked at the dictionary that was still resting on the table next to her reading glasses. The dictionary was a small paperback book that was literally split in two. Mom had used it so much that the thing was seriously falling apart. She held the pages together with a rubber band. I held on to her dictionary as if it were her personal bible. I finally had to throw it away when I could no longer keep it together. The pages fell out like autumn leaves. One by one, they pulled away from the spine of the book and floated gently down to the ground around my feet.

My early stoicism returned. I kept everything buried deep inside of me. I retreated to my early methods of responding to life. I wanted to feel and I wanted to respond to everything that was happening around me, but I didn't know how. Everything was locked inside of me.

I began having many dreams about Mom. In one dream, I came home from work and Mom was waiting for me inside the apartment. She was walking around asking me what I did with her clothes and furniture. I didn't know how to tell her that I had given away all of her things.

Everything seemed lost now. I used to think that it was fun to be lost. I remember driving on lonely highways and feeling so free to think that no one in this world knew exactly where I was. I loved the feeling of being lost to the rest of this world. Mom used to be upset with me about this. She always wanted me to call to notify her of my exact location wherever I stopped for the night. I didn't care. I wanted the freedom of just drifting away.

Now, after Mom's death, I suddenly realized how she must have felt. I wanted to know exactly where Mom was. I wanted to know her location. I knew Mom believed in heaven. I wanted to know that the passage was clear and bright for her. I wanted to know she arrived safely. I wanted to see her there. I wanted to know what she was experiencing. I didn't want her lost somewhere in the universe like I was lost on earth, not knowing where to land. Mom was a navigator here on earth with me; I had to believe she would find her way around heaven.

I wasn't sure if I would find my way, though. I didn't know if the pain and confusion would ever end. But, honestly, I didn't want it to.

For a while, I didn't want to feel better. I didn't want to forget what it felt like to lose someone I love. I wanted to feel this hurt until my brain could record and remember everything that had happened over the last few years. I didn't want to let go of the pain until I knew I would never forget the woman Mom was.

But several months later, I was driving down highway 111 passed the San Jacinto Mountains and I suddenly crashed…not literally, but emotionally. I couldn't stop crying. My heart just hurt so badly. I suddenly found myself letting go. I pulled over onto the side of the road. With no one to talk to, I finally started to pray. I was making a request to God.

"Oh, God, please," I began to beg. "Please, I need your help. I need to be somewhere. I need to go some place. I don't know where I should go. I don't know where I should be. I don't care if you want me to get married or move back to Kansas…or if you want me back on the road. But I've been so stuck. I feel like I'm in a huge traffic jam and I can't get to the exits. I've been so stuck here in this place for so long. I have no home. I have no place to go on the road, no place to travel to. Please, God, I don't care where you take me but please don't leave me stuck in the middle. Please don't leave me here. I've been here for so long, so trapped with no direction. I don't know where to land. I'm floating between earth and sky, heaven and hell….please, don't leave me here…stuck in the middle of nowhere…God, don't let me break down here."

I must have cried for over an hour until all of the agony seemed to leave my heart. I cried until I ran out of tears and couldn't express myself any longer. I wiped off my face, brushed back my hair… and then I drove. I just drove my car around the streets of Palm Springs endlessly with no destination while I struggled with my deep thoughts.

I have learned from all my experiences that life doesn't end. The body is nothing more than a vehicle to carry the soul. The body just moves the spirit from one situation and experience to the next, like a car. The body breaks down...but the spirit inside lives on. Life is never over. It is continuous and doesn't even pause. Death is not an ending. It is a continuance of our life process. It is a passageway to our next reality. Every death, not just our own, carries us through to the next phase of our lives, the next way of being if we are willing to go. I was willing. I wanted to go. I was ready to travel again. I did not want to feel this inertia, this uncertainty, this cruel uselessness...

A few months later, Carol called to tell me my nephew, David, had just enlisted in the army. He would be going to Afghanistan soon. Her words sent chills through my body. I wanted so badly to tell him not to do it, not to go. It's not because I don't love my country or the men and women who serve with such honor. Instead, it was a selfish need to hold on. A fear of the challenges David had set for himself. But Carol understands life so much better than I do.

My sister, Theresa, is the same. Her son, Andy, will be spending several weeks in India on an externship for his business degree from the University of Kansas. And my cousin, Jo, a woman with a purpose, has true meaning in her life and lives it fully. She lovingly cares for her sons even though she knows the unusual challenges they will face. She is beautiful and strong, a woman of class and style even in the most difficult circumstances. Jo is an amazing woman capable of loving her two sons enough to allow them to be who they are with their own dreams and challenges.

I thought of my sisters and cousin. Strong women who understand the process of opening their arms and allowing their children to move through their lives; of opening up their hearts and allowing their children to move on while knowing they will never truly be gone. My family does an excellent job raising children. My three nieces and three nephews are all happy, beautiful, unique, pure products of their loving homes. Just purely good kids. All of them raised to face life's challenges with strength and grace.

Strange, mothers not only know the most about love, but about letting go. The ultimate understanding of life's process; it is more than I have ever known. But I understand now...I now understand letting go...

And little by little, I, too, began to accept life's basic offerings. A few months after Mom passed, a silly little song, "Rolling Through the Sunshine" by Trailer Choir, came on the radio as I was driving to work. I smiled first, and then I laughed. I began to realize that this was the first time I had felt good in a long while. That song became my anthem for moving into the next phase of my life.

I began to appreciate simple and sweet pleasures, like laughing out loud. I felt ready to laugh again, so I would spend evenings just watching comedy shows and movies. Why did that feel so good?

I started noticing strange occurrences in nature. Before going into the hospital, Mom really wanted a hummingbird feeder to hang on our balcony. She loved the little birds and felt a connection to them. Most afternoons, after Mom's passing, hummingbirds would appear on my balcony and spend part of the afternoon with me, even though we had never put up a feeder. I could sit on my front porch and spend minutes face to face with hummingbirds.

I danced with butterflies, too. For one full summer when I was a little girl, Mom would seat on our back patio in Kansas every evening for about half an hour quietly reading. And every evening, a beautiful yellow butterfly would seat on her head and not leave until the day grew dark. Every butterfly reminded me of this situation and I laughed and felt loved every time I saw one after Mom was gone.

One day, I was driving home and as I turned along the curve of the Dinah Shore Bridge in Palm Springs, there was a large squirrel standing in the curb of the road. He was standing straight up on his hind legs and waving his little arms to all of the cars as they zoomed by. I laughed all the way home.

I usually get home from work around 10:45 pm. On most nights, a large bullfrog usually sits out by the swimming pool at my apartment complex, soaking up the moonlight. One particular night, I saw the frog sitting by the pool as I walked towards my apartment. But this time, instead of jumping in the opposite direction when I approached, he sat on the sidewalk waiting for me. As I walked by, he jumped along, keeping pace right by my side until we got to the stairs of my apartment building. As I climbed up, he maneuvered himself to sit right in the middle of the bottom step. When I reached the top, I turned to see him sitting on that step staring up at me, right into my eyes. He didn't leave even after I had entered my apartment. For the next two hours, every time I looked over my balcony, he was still there, gazing up and gently serenading me. Could it be my prince, my knight in shining armor that Mom had mentioned that day in the hospital? I don't know. I didn't take the chance. I didn't kiss him to find out. But for the rest of the night, I felt protected and loved.

"For a while," a friend told me, "you'll see significance in everything." And I did. Everything I saw, held, tasted, smelled, and heard was sharper and clearer than ever before. Sad, that it takes a death to realize the importance of everyday life. I want to forever live a life of endless surprise, awe, and wonder.

One day at work, I was teaching an ethics class. I gave my students this scenario to work through. A plane crashed into the Pacific Ocean and only nine people survived. There was just one lifeboat that could only hold four people. The students were given the challenge of deciding which four of the nine survivors they would place in the lifeboat to be saved. The other five would perish. The students gasped in shock at the scenario before them. How could they possibly decide? "You expect us to play God?" a few demanded, completely outraged. One student read through the short bios of the nine survivors. "Wow!" he stated with a shake of his head. "God has a difficult job."

Yes, He certainly does….I cried…and then I laughed…and then I prayed…and then I began to realize the simple sweetness of life.

EPILOGUE

*S*o when I die, and I'm facing God, and He asks me what I liked best about my life, how would I answer? What if I said, "Well, God, I was really depressed. Life was hard. I had a lot of unfair tragedies. I had pain and sadness." God would look at me then and answer, "But I made mountains for you...and the ocean. I made a blue sky and trees and flowers... And you didn't like anything? You enjoyed none of it?" How insulted would God feel? He must have the most unappreciated job in the universe.

But He keeps on trying, I realized as I gazed out of the van window at the glorious world around me. Happiness is a choice every single day. I laugh now, and I'm happy now, all in the honor of God.

"We'll be leaving in a few minutes, folks," the driver, Barry, announced to the twelve of us sitting in the tour van. "We are just waiting for two more people to join us. They should be here any minute." I huddled down in my seat looking for warmth but feeling inside myself cozy and restful. I had now been on the island of Maui for two days. I had decided to spend Christmas, the first without Mom, in Hawaii. It was a celebration of so many blessings and an accumulation of so many adventures. I knew that I didn't want to spend the first Christmas without Mom at home alone. I knew that my life would continue on and yet it would be somehow different.

I spent the first few days in Hawaii, just roaming the island, completely lost. On the first day, I made a turn into a coffee plantation thinking it would be interesting. I was there for an hour. Actually, I was ready to leave after the first fifteen minutes but took another forty-five to find my way back out again. Every field looked the same with no landmarks to guide me back to where I had come from. But that describes my life lately. Maybe I was looking for a way back home but all of my familiar landmarks had faded away. I was slowly feeling my way back to my life again. I was hoping Hawaii would enrich my spirit, reunite me with myself again. I hoped it would stop me from being so lost in the middle of life again.

I have learned to enjoy my own form of meditation. I have never been able to sit quietly. My mind is always too busy for that. Instead, whenever I am overwhelmed by the beauty of mountains, flowers, and the ocean, I allow myself the time to just relax and enjoy it. I find myself becoming peaceful and light in these moments and God opens up to me. God has given me the greatest gift of all. Faith. Though it may have been unusual, I'm so blessed that God gave me the ability to look for miracles and a belief in angels at an early age. As I gazed out at the lush world around me, I realized that God didn't make a single mistake. Everything happened exactly the way it was meant to. Even through the hard times, I realize now that I had always been protected. There had always been a plan. A plan that now led me here to this very moment.

Now, I sat in the van in Maui waiting for everyone to settle in so we could start on our journey to Hana. I felt a calm sense of peace come over me as I waited for the van to leave. It was a mixture of fear and joy; I was alive again. Fear and sadness and depression and excitement and happiness and so many other emotions and I knew…I was alive again! Finally, the driver climbed abroad with two young women who ran to the back of the van.

"Well, it looks like we are all here now," Barry announced. "We are going to be on this van together for about six hours. Let's begin by introducing ourselves before we get going. Please state your name, where you are from, and one interesting fact about yourself."

When it was my turn, I announced, "My name is Jamie. I'm recently from California. My interesting fact is that I have this goal to drive through all of the states in America and I just have three left."

"Wow," Barry responded. "You are very adventurous."

"Thank you,' I smiled. "I get that from my mother."

And I knew that she was there beside me as we started on the road to Hana. On the tour, Barry would park the van and let us out to see beautiful waterfalls, black sand beaches, volcanoes, and eucalyptus gum trees. Barry was thoroughly enjoying his job, pointing out all of the sights to us. He then told us, "People are always told to go to Hana when they visit Maui and they get really upset that they make the drive there...and see nothing. The village of Hana is so small, it only has three buildings! But it's not Hana that's amazing; it's the journey there. Most people don't know what to stop and see on the way. That's why people should always have a guide, someone who is familiar with the area and can show them all of the gorgeous scenery. They have to appreciate the journey."

And now I understood. I have had many guides in my life: Mom, Dad, angels, my sisters and brother, friends, and teachers. And they have shown me so much on this amazing journey. I've realized that my real life isn't financial worries, exhausting jobs, or relationship conflicts. My real life is traveling through America, living in England, exploring Europe and Malaysia, dancing in city streets, dreaming of Canada, hummingbirds that bring messages from Momma, visions of angels, pennies from heaven, visiting spirits, waving squirrels, serenading bullfrogs, floating butterflies, waterfalls and gum trees, writing, music, books, photography, prayer, meditation--that is my real life. If it wasn't, why are those the miraculous moments when I am the most fully alive? That is the sweetness of life.

ACKNOWLEDGEMENTS

I would like to extend a very special thank you and loving thoughts to all those who have joined me on this amazing voyage. And thank you for sharing your journeys with me. I've learned so much from all of you.

Mom, you'll always be my favorite traveling companion. Even today, I know you still explore life with me. I love you.

My sister, Theresa Smith, thank you for your support and guidance. You were the first to read my travel journeys and encourage me on this path. Thank you to you and John for your thoughts and prayers.

My sister, Carol Zunick, your strength continues to inspire me. Thank you for your endless love and kindness.

My brother, Anthony, thank you for your humor. Have you ever noticed that you are the only person who never lets me whine or complain? You always just toss off my concerns with a joke and a smile. It is so appreciated. I love you.

My nieces, Jennifer, Diana, and Jessica, and my nephews, Andy, David, and Logan. I am so proud of all of you. You are all so talented, intelligent, and beautiful. All of you are a great testament to the strength of family and rock-solid, pure living. I love you.

Aunt Nancy Jenkins, my Wal-Mart buddy. Thank you for your

love and enthusiasm. You can now tell your lunch ladies the book is available. Thank you for being so proud of me even before the fact. Love You.

Cousin Jo Jenkins. Thank you for your encouragement. Love to you and your boys!

Connie Ryan. So happy I got to know you. Thank you for all the love you sent to my mother over the years.

Olga De Leon—Thank you for being such a kind friend. You not only listen to all of my unusual stories but have the courage and strength to share your own. Blessings to you, Jolie, Val, Lucy, and the rest of your amazing family.

Carmen Lujan. You have been such a source of support. I can't believe how long you have endured my flakiness with kind words and a constant smile on your beautiful face. You are the very definition of friend.

Allison Fedrick. Thank you for your encouragement. Love our philosophical and inspirational lunches. When are you free next?

Rob Ritchie. Thank you for your support. Now, it's time to tell your story.

The staff and faculty of Santa Barbara Business College. Thank you for your support and guidance.

All of my students, past, present, and future. Thank you for everything you have taught me. Dreams do come true. Hey, I wrote a book. Now it's your turn. Let's go.

Amy Osmond Cook, thank you for your advice and guidance. You were the first outside of my family to tell me I was a good writer. This book developed out of your kindness and consideration.

The staff of Balboa Press, especially Fatima, Rick, Elizabeth, Amanda, and Adrian. Thank you for your kindness and your help in shaping this manuscript.

And to my Lord and Savior, Jesus Christ. Though I may be lost to this world, I am forever found in you. You always had a plan. I just needed to learn to trust and follow. Thank you for sending your many angels to guide and protect me.

—

CPSIA information can be obtained at www.ICGtesting.com
Printed in the USA
BVOW05s0911100414

350211BV00003B/4/P